TRACKING
WORLD WAR II
RAILROAD OPERATIONS ACROSS NEW MEXICO

TRACKING
WORLD WAR II
RAILROAD OPERATIONS ACROSS NEW MEXICO

MIKE BUTLER

AMERICA
THROUGH
TIME

A note on the photographs: unattributed photographs were taken by the author or are from his collection. The source of all other photographs is noted in their captions.

America Through Time
An imprint of Sutton Publishing inc
www.through-time.com

First published 2025
Copyright © Mike Butler 2025

ISBN 978-1-63499-511-5

All rights reserved. No part of this publication may be reproduced, stored in a retrieval system or transmitted in any form or by any means, electronic, mechanical, photocopying, recording or otherwise, without prior permission in writing from Sutton Publishing Inc.

Typeset in Minion Pro 10pt on 13pt
Printed and bound in England

CONTENTS

1	Jack Delano: OWI Photographer	7
2	Prelude to War: An Unprepared Railroad Industry	12
3	Preparing for War: Constructing and Maintaining the Line Across New Mexico	15
4	Diversity: A Wartime Necessity	21
5	Along the Rails: Texico to Fort Sumner	27
6	Along the Rails: Fort Sumner to Vaughn	44
7	Along the Rails: Vaughn to Belen	55
8	Along the Rails: A Detour to Albuquerque	69
9	Along the Rails: Belen to Gallup	90

Endnotes	107
Bibliography	111

1

JACK DELANO: OWI PHOTOGRAPHER

When photographer Jack Delano hopped aboard an Atchison, Topeka, and Santa Fe Railway (AT&SF) freight train in Chicago for a cross-country journey to Los Angeles in 1943, his mission for the Office of War Information (OWI) was to record the efficiency of the rail system in delivering troops and materiel across the country. Delano rode the train across New Mexico in March 1943 when "heavy rail traffic, essential freight loads, the endless changing of engines, and ongoing maintenance made the rail facilities in New Mexico fundamental to the war effort."[1]

Jack Delano's photographs of the AT&SF Railway across New Mexico in 1943 form the bulk of the historic photographs in this book. Delano was a newcomer to New Mexico and some of his photo captions are erroneous as to names of places and people. The author has tried to correct those errors in this book where possible. Delano's work was immensely important though, and it is equally important to understand the story of his life.

President Franklin D. Roosevelt inaugurated his "New Deal" in 1933 to help America pull out of the Great Depression. It was an effort that lasted until 1941 when the U.S. entered World War II and ramped up war production which finally pulled the economy out of depression. The New Deal spawned an alphabet soup of government agencies (WPA; RSA; CCC; FSA; OWI) to deal with the depression. The Resettlement Administration (RSA) was created by Executive Order 7027 in 1935 to provide cash loans to struggling farmers. Rex Tugwell, head of the agency, hired photographers to document the struggles of those farmers. In 1937, the RSA became the FSA (Farm Security Administration). Roy Stryker was hired as the director of the photographic division of the FSA. As director, Stryker hired photographers and sent them across the south and west to document the lives of agricultural workers.

In 1942, the FSA became part of the OWI. Stryker lost one of his main photographers, Arthur Rothstein, when Rothstein was hired by *Look* magazine. Stryker wrote to Vernon Pope (managing editor at *Look*): "I hate like Hell to lose the boy [Rothstein], but you take him with my blessing. It is going to be an excellent experience for him, and I am certain that he is going to serve you people very well."[2]

Thus, Stryker had a position to fill at the OWI, and he hired promising young photographer Jack Delano. Delano had sent Stryker a portfolio of his photographs of miners in the coal mines in Schuylkill County, Pennsylvania. Stryker was impressed, and with Rothstein's resignation, Delano was immediately hired on May 6, 1940.

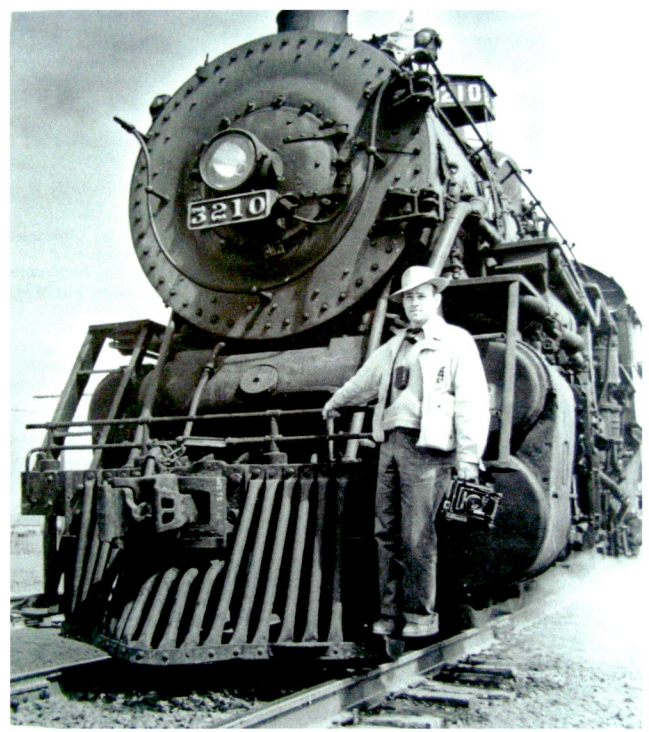

Left: Photographer Jack Delano posed with his camera on a steam locomotive as he traveled across the country from 1942–1943 taking railroad photographs for the Office of War Information. (*Library of Congress, LC-USZ62-120966*)

Below: Farm Security Administration photographers, 1937. From left to right are photographers John Vachon, Arthur Rothstein, and Russell Lee meeting with their boss Roy E. Stryker. (*Photo by Beaumont Newhall, Library of Congress, LC-DIG-ds-01154*)

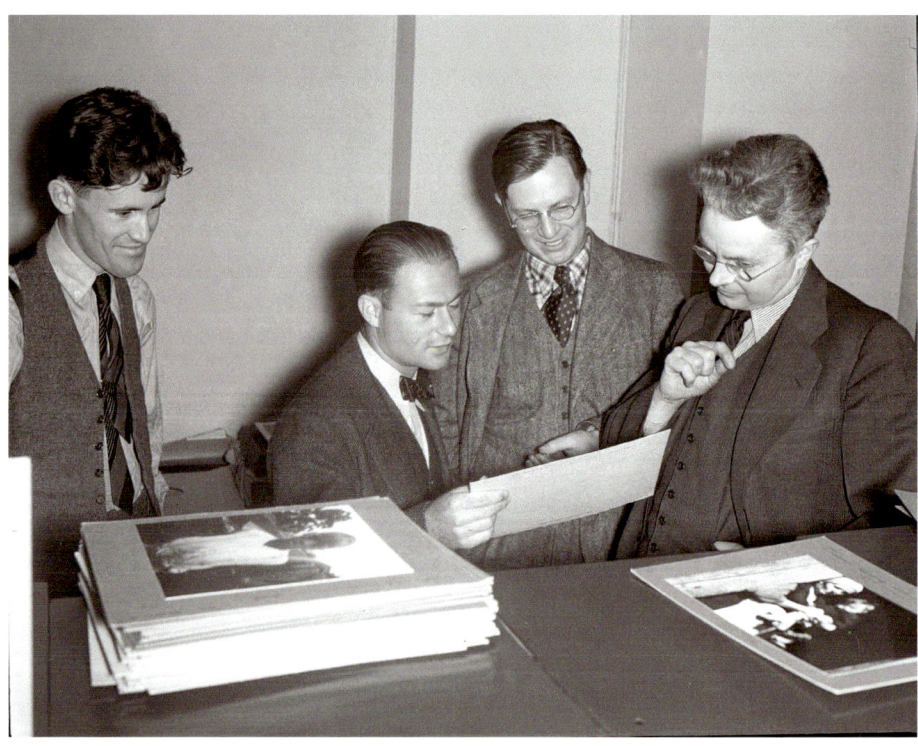

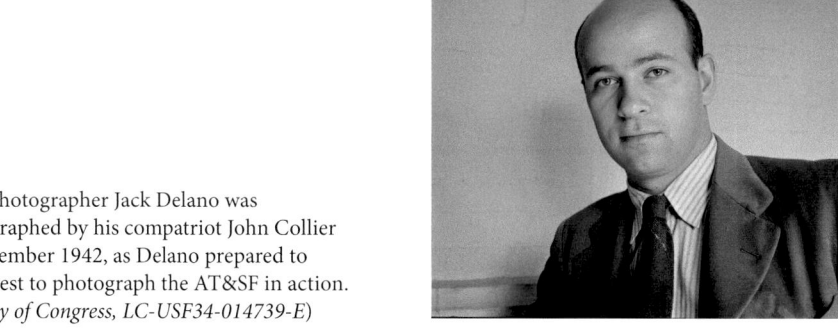

OWI photographer Jack Delano was photographed by his compatriot John Collier in September 1942, as Delano prepared to head west to photograph the AT&SF in action. (*Library of Congress, LC-USF34-014739-E*)

Delano was born as Jacob Ovcharov on August 1, 1914, in Kiev, Ukraine. His family emigrated to Philadelphia in 1923, where they lived in the home of his mother's cousin. Jacob graduated from high school in 1932, and then attended the Pennsylvania Academy of Fine Arts where he majored in illustration. He went to Europe for four months on a scholarship. There he bought a camera and "began to think that perhaps in photographs I could show the same concern and understanding of ordinary people that I found so compelling in the works of the [European] artists I admired so much."[3] Back at the academy in 1937, his friends urged him to "Americanize" his name, which he did, taking the name of "Jack" from boxer Jack Dempsey whom he admired and "Delano" from the last name of a female friend at the academy. He had his name legally changed to Jack Delano in 1940.

While at the academy, Delano became aware of the work of the FSA photographers. "Delano found the images by Walker Evans to be 'extraordinary,' as he did those by Dorothea Lange, Arthur Rothstein, and Ben Shahn."[4]

After graduation from the academy, Delano got a job with the Federal Art Project of the Works Progress Administration (WPA) taking photographs of coal miners in Pennsylvania. It was those photographs which Roy Stryker saw and became impressed with Delano's work. After he was hired by the FSA, Stryker had Delano photograph migrant workers in the South as a training assignment. In 1942, Delano was assigned to photograph railroads for the OWI. Delano had married Irene Esser, whom he had met at the academy, on July 5, 1940. She accompanied him on his photographic journeys, and Delano stated that "it was very helpful to have Irene along. Irene kept the conversation going and kept people interested while I was working away furiously [taking their photographs]."[5]

In 1942, Delano moved to Chicago and "with the cooperation of the Association of American Railroads, shot a vast portfolio of images focusing on the US railroad industry's contribution to the war effort."[6] In November, Delano received instructions from Stryker to document the wartime freight rail system. He spent several months photographing rail activities in Chicago, and then in 1943 began his journey west on the Atchison, Topeka, and Santa Fe Railway to Los Angeles.

As an OWI photographer, Delano was paid $35 per week plus $5 per day for expenses and 3 cents a mile for travel. "He was also supplied with plenty of 35mm film, chemicals to develop the film [generally in hotel bathrooms], and three government-issue cameras."[7] Delano's work became known as "The Railroad Photography Project," and it was "an essential part of the government record about the vital role of domestic wartime transportation. Delano's photographs

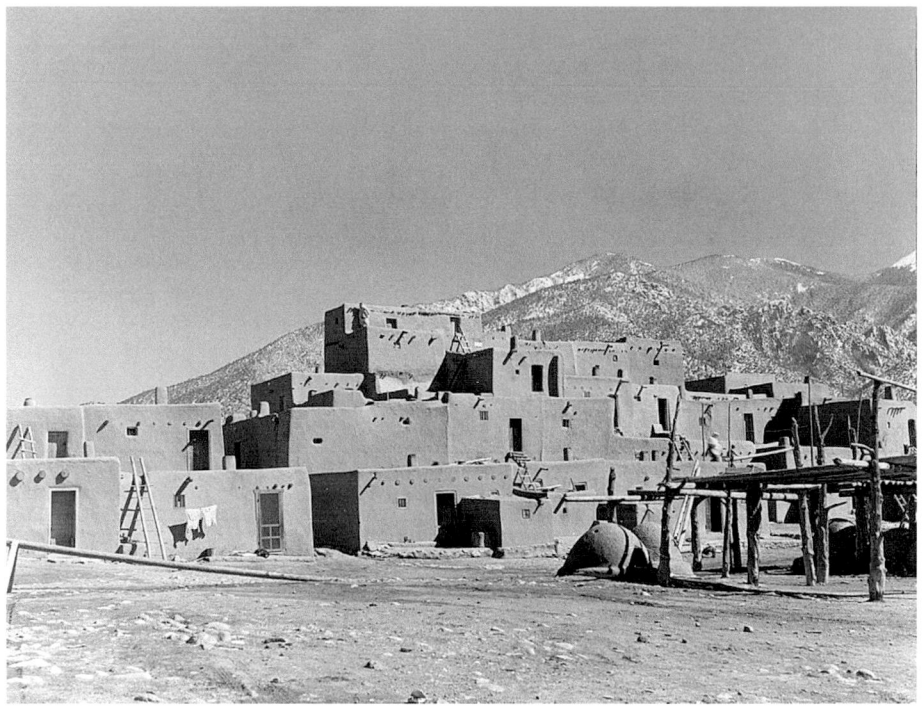

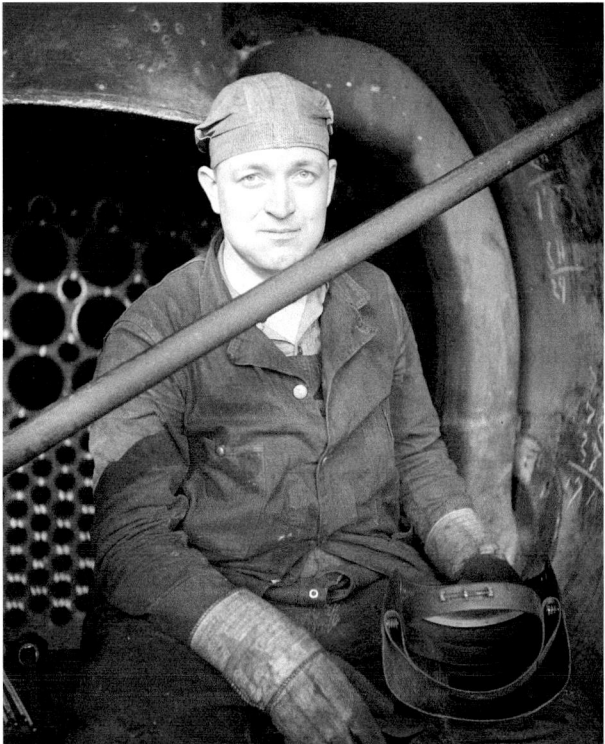

Above: This photograph of Taos Pueblo by Arthur Rothstein in 1936 impressed young Jack Delano and whetted his desire to work for the FSA/OWI. (*Library of Congress, LC-USF34-002937-D*)

Left: In late 1942 and early 1943, Jack Delano photographed the workers and railyards around Chicago, including this welder at the Chicago & Northwestern Railroad Repair Shop in December 1942. (*Library of Congress, LC-USW3-012631-E*)

documented the steady commitment of the experienced and inexperienced men and women who worked to keep the freight trains moving in America."[8]

Jack Delano traveled on an AT&SF freight train across New Mexico in March 1943. His photographs from Clovis west to Gallup capture the war effort of New Mexico's diverse population to keep the trains running across the state. In late 1943, Delano was drafted and served as a wartime photographer until 1946. After the war, he and Irene moved to Puerto Rico where he took thousands of photos of the island and its transportation network. Irene passed away in 1987, but Jack lived on until 1997. Delano is best remembered for his photographs "depicting working people with dignity."[9]

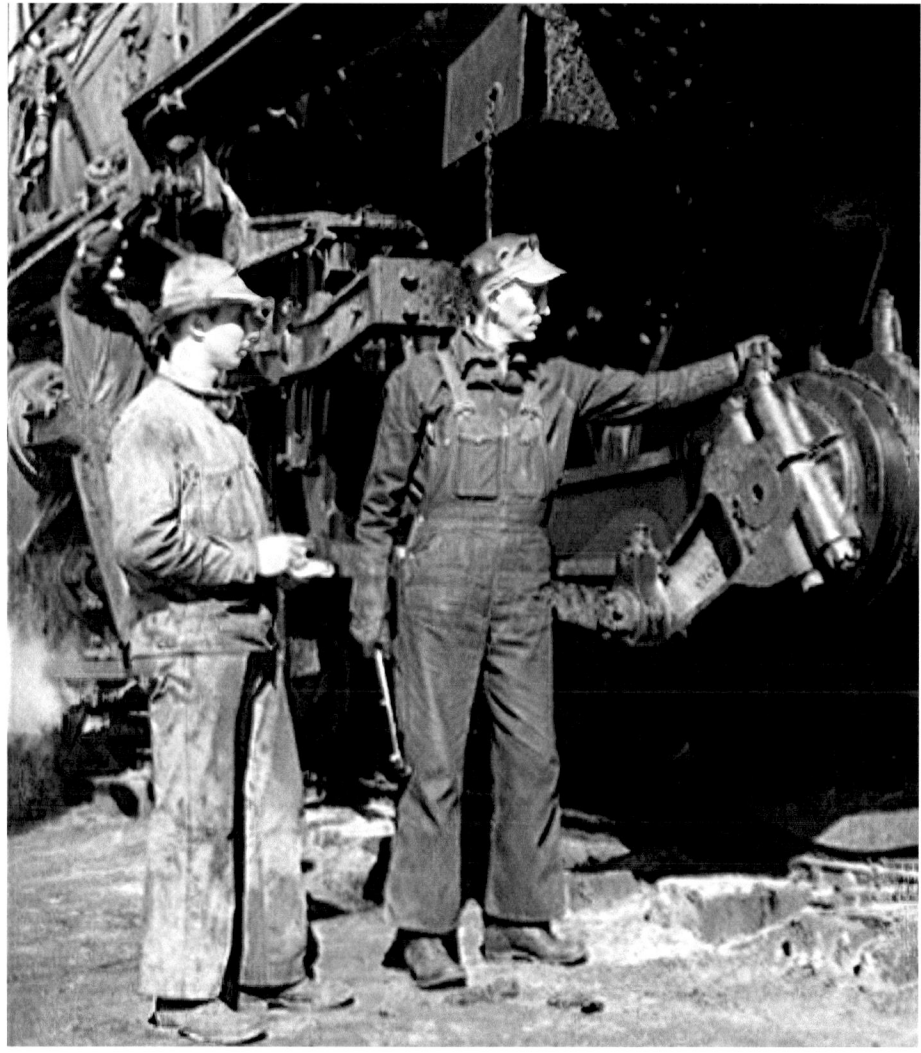

Delano's portraits of the workers were as important as his photographs of the trains. Inspecting a locomotive in Clovis, NM, in 1943 were Private Clarence Stephens (left) of Streeter, Illinois, and locomotive inspector Sidney Mack. (*Library of Congress, LC-USW3-020428-D*)

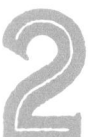

PRELUDE TO WAR: AN UNPREPARED RAILROAD INDUSTRY

In 1939, as war raged in Europe and America's entry into the war was still in question, the state of readiness of U.S. railways for war was highly doubtful. The Great Depression of the 1930s had seen a large decline in U.S. rail shipping, with a consequent decline in rail and steam locomotive repair. In 1940, "the railroads had so much less equipment than a decade before that it seemed improbable they would be able to meet all the demands [of war] for both freight and passenger service."[1] With the Japanese bombing of Pearl Harbor on December 7, 1941, the U.S. was drawn into the war, and "there was widespread doubt that the railway industry of the United States was in a fit state to take on the huge extra weight imposed upon it that … day in 1941."[2]

> After long years of Depression-bred neglect and stagnation, the railroad industry was suddenly confronted with a task of heroic proportions. A vast flood of traffic, raw materials, fuels, munitions, weapons, and an enormous quantity of foodstuffs and manufactured items of every size and description had to be moved quickly and efficiently so that a global war effort could be nourished and sustained. In addition to the crushing volume of freight there was also an enormous increase in passenger traffic.[3]

The demand for railroad services was certainly there, but the infrastructure was not. "As of January 1, 1939, 18.6 percent of all the railroads' steam locomotives were unserviceable."[4] Yet "the most powerful weapon the railways of the United States had at the ready to bring to bear in the Second World War was the steam locomotive."[5] The steam locomotive had to be the war-horse, since diesel engine production during the war was allocated to submarines and landing craft. "Consequently, diesel locomotives for the railroads were a small part of diesel production."[6] However, AT&SF had gained a head start on diesel locomotives:

> By 1938, AT&SF operated ten new streamliner passenger trains powered by yellow and red diesels. The sleek "warbonnet" paint scheme, first introduced on those diesel engines, became an integral part of the railroad's image. The railroad also ordered the first freight diesels in the United States, painting these blue and yellow in the same style.[7]

With 32 percent fewer steam locomotives in U.S. railroad inventory than in World War I, how were steam engines expected to meet the war's demand? Thankfully, technology had advanced greatly since the first war: "The power of the average locomotive had been increased more than 50 percent and the speed of freight trains increased more than 30 percent."[8]

PRELUDE TO WAR: AN UNPREPARED RAILROAD INDUSTRY

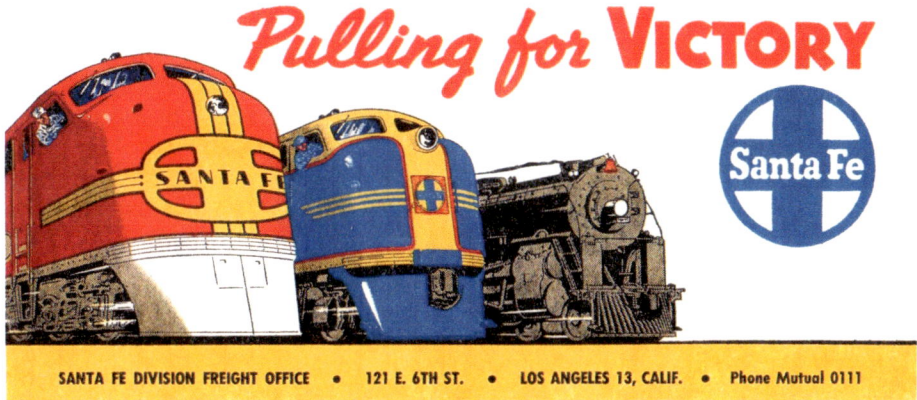

This 1942 AT&SF Railway ad illustrated the three types of locomotives in service during World War II: the red and yellow "warbonnet" scheme for diesel passenger locomotives, the blue and yellow scheme for diesel freight locomotives, and the steam locomotive.

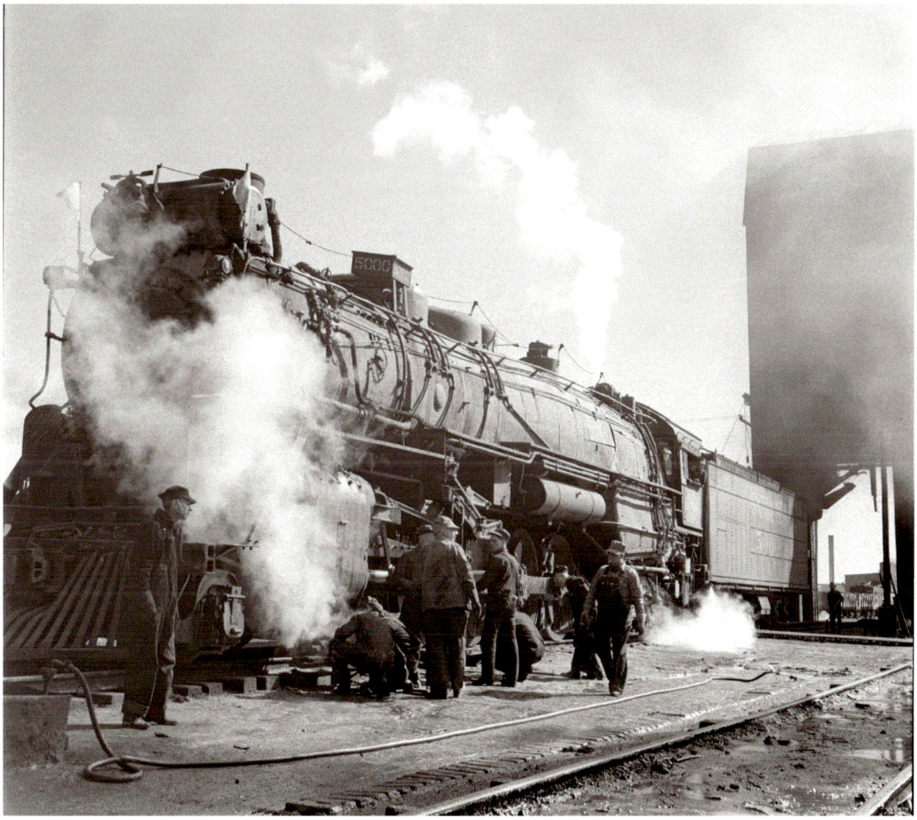

The massive size of a powerful AT&SF steam locomotive is illustrated here as eight employees check over the loco coming out of the repair shop in Clovis, NM, in 1943. (*Jack Delano photograph, Library of Congress, LC-USW3-020626-E*)

American railroads faced a great challenge when World War II was thrust upon them. News commentator Lowell Thomas stated that "We Americans needed a miracle in railroad transportation during early 1942, we expected that miracle, and by George, we got that miracle!"[9] And railroad historian Don Ball noted that "The railroads went to war with undaunted spirit."[10] The Atchison, Topeka, and Santa Fe Railway exemplified that undaunted spirit as "during 1942, with 26% fewer locomotives, the Santa Fe moved 122% more freight ton-miles and 79% more military and civilian passenger miles than in 1918, during the First World War."[11]

Nationwide during World War II, the railroads handled more than 278 million tons of freight for the army "and they did it with 600,000 fewer freight cars and 22,000 fewer locomotives than during World War I."[12] A miracle indeed! "The time period from 1941 to 1945 has been regarded as the pinnacle of American railroading. Everyone acknowledged the railroads' outstanding work of moving troops and supplies during the biggest transportation job in history."[13]

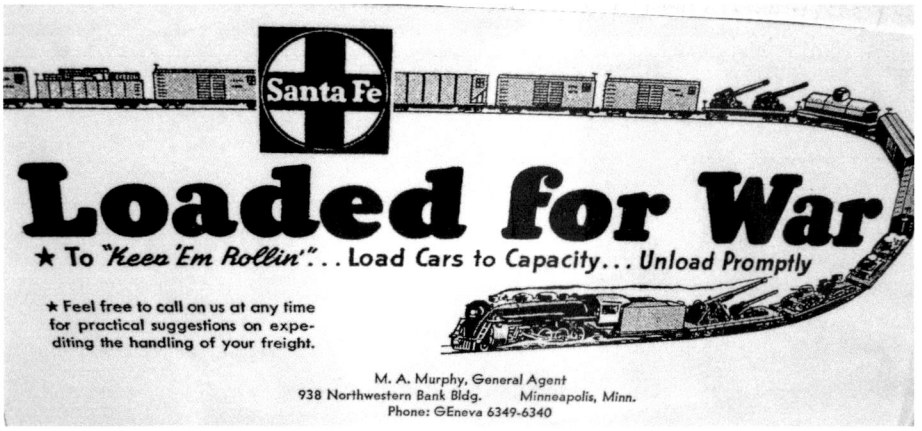

AT&SF flatcars hauled tanks and cannons across the country in the "biggest transportation job in history," during World War II. (*Albuquerque Wheels Museum*)

3

PREPARING FOR WAR: CONSTRUCTING AND MAINTAINING THE LINE ACROSS NEW MEXICO

"The (AT&SF) contribution to the war effort was fully in keeping with its massive locomotives and far-flung trackage. Revenue train miles, which had stood at 40.9 million in 1938 spiraled to 70.7 million by 1945."[1] The "far-flung" trackage of the AT&SF in New Mexico began with the construction of the rail line over Raton Pass from Colorado in 1879. Rail construction then proceeded quickly southwest to Albuquerque, bypassing the steep climb to Santa Fe from Lamy. West of Albuquerque, construction workers encountered difficulties with the local Native American tribes. "The tracks soon passed through the Laguna Pueblo and the Indians there … found it entertaining to pull up Louis Kingman's survey stakes."[2] Farther west "troublesome Navajos sent advance grading forces scurrying to seek cover."[3] Eventually, the Indian difficulties were overcome, and in March 1881, the Continental Divide was crossed at an elevation of 7,248 feet. After that obstacle was crossed, track layers proceeded quickly downgrade in the late spring of 1881 to Gallup and the New Mexico–Arizona border. Map 1 illustrates the AT&SF line across New Mexico as of 1900.

The AT&SF Railway could never have handled the huge amount of freight and troop trains required during World War II using the Raton Pass route.

> The Santa Fe needed a low-grade, all-weather route between Albuquerque and Kansas, and plans for such a cutoff developed slowly between 1878 and 1902. The 3 percent grades [of Raton Pass] limited the size of freight trains even with newer, larger power plus helper locomotives. The pass created exorbitant operating costs and limited efficiency.[4]

In anticipation of a cutoff route eliminating Raton Pass, a connection from Texico, New Mexico, to Amarillo, Texas, was constructed in April 1899. In 1902, AT&SF route surveyors concluded "a new cutoff should be built from Amarillo west to Belen [New Mexico] via Texico, Fort Sumner and Abo Pass.… Abo Pass crossed the Continental Divide at a much lower height than Raton with a maximum elevation of 6,508 feet at Mountainair … an answer to the operating department's dreams."[5]

Work began on the Belen Cutoff in 1903 and was completed on June 30, 1908. The five-year delay in construction was due to the financial difficulties of the AT&SF during those years. Map 2 illustrates the completed Belen Cutoff.

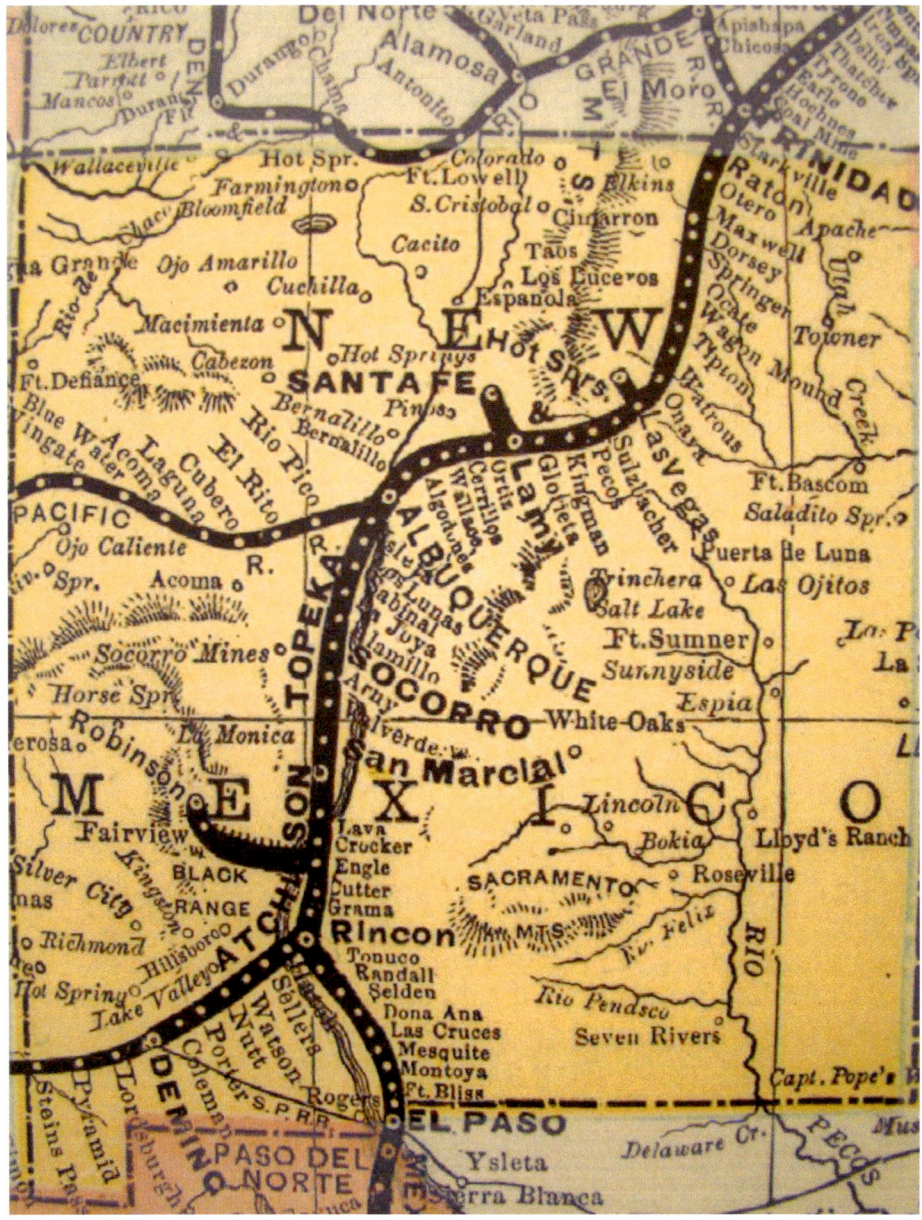

Map 1: This *circa* 1900 map shows the AT&SF main line across New Mexico from Raton Pass in the northeast, southwest to Albuquerque, and west across the state to Gallup. Towns such as Clovis, Vaughn, and Mountainair did not exist in 1900 in eastern New Mexico until the AT&SF established them in conjunction with the building of the Belen Cutoff completed in 1908.

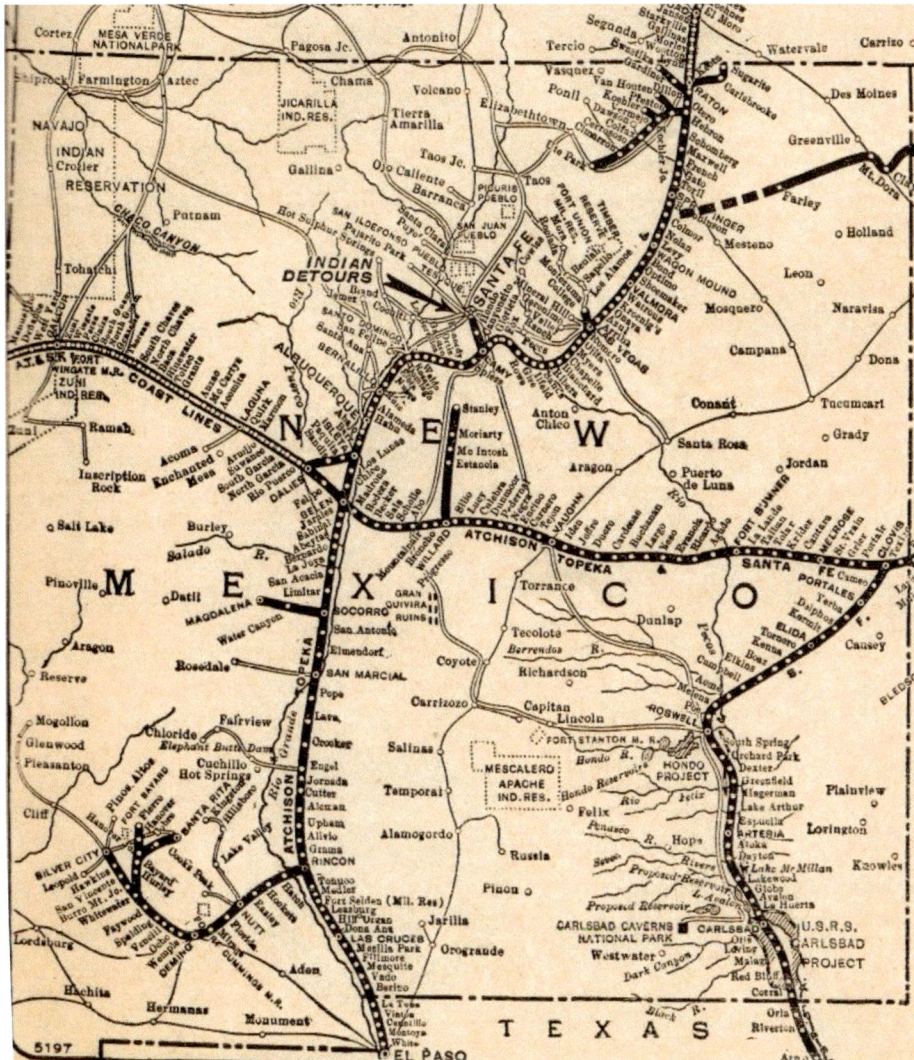

Map 2: This *circa* 1910 map shows quite a bit of construction completed on the AT&SF in New Mexico, with the completion of the Belen Cutoff from Clovis west to Belen. This eliminated the need to send freight over Raton Pass, thus greatly aiding World War II rail efficiency.

All the dots along the line on the map are not towns—many were sidings where eastbound and westbound trains could pass each other since the Belen Cutoff was originally a single-track line. Sidings were often named after local geographic features or local businessmen. The sidings had to be long enough to accommodate the length of freight trains which was generally about 110 cars, although by World War II, more powerful locomotives could pull a load of 120–140 cars, which necessitated the construction of longer sidings.

The Belen Cutoff soon became the main freight route for the AT&SF, and it was essential for the success of World War II railroad operations across New Mexico. The Cutoff "reduced the distance from California to Chicago by only six miles, but the steepest grade was reduced from 158 feet per mile [at Raton Pass] to 66 feet per mile [at Abo Pass]."[6]

The impact of the Belen Cutoff upon New Mexico was profound:

> For New Mexico, the Belen Cutoff ... transformed the eastern plains in the first half of the twentieth century. The railroad aided and accelerated the expansion of Hispano families into new areas and created the jobs and conditions that led to so many homesteaders coming into the region. Significantly, New Mexico grew more from 1900 to 1910 than in any other 10-year period; its population increased by 67 percent overall and the area along the Cutoff experienced an astounding 140 percent growth.[7]

Most of the towns and villages along the Belen Cutoff in World War II simply did not exist before the coming of the railroad. From east to west, new towns such as Clovis, Melrose, Tolar, Yeso, Vaughn, Encino, Willard, and Mountainair sprang up. The Belen Cutoff soon became a boon to AT&SF freight business, significantly benefiting the small towns along the line.

When World War II began, track supervisor B. M. Naylor, living in Belen at the time of the Pearl Harbor attack in December 1941, described "track conditions as they were at the

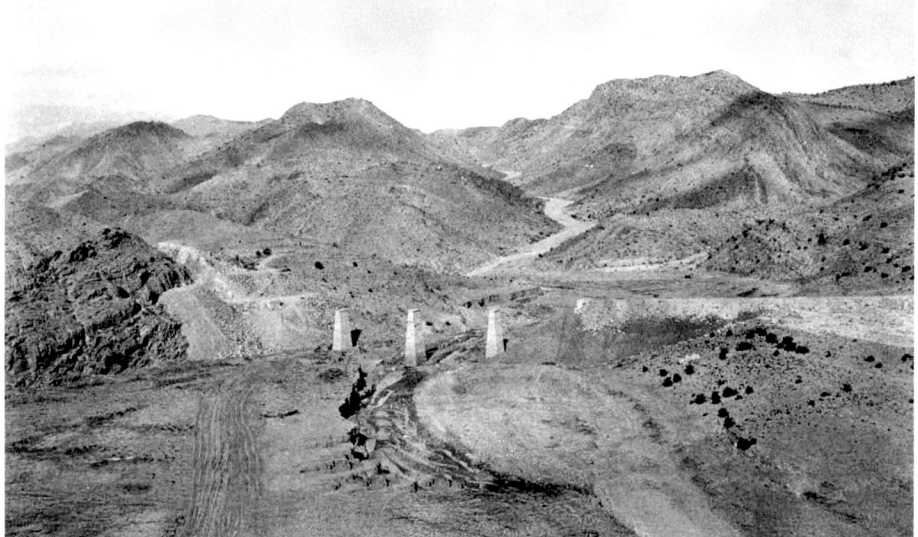

Construction is ongoing at Abo Pass in 1906 with the erection of these concrete bridge pillars. (*Photo: Creative Commons*)

PREPARING FOR WAR: CONSTRUCTING AND MAINTAINING THE LINE ACROSS NEW MEXICO 19

beginning of World War II. A good word to describe them would be 'bad.'"⁸ Naylor went on to say that "all during the Depression years track work of all kinds had been cut to a minimum, with a minimum number of men to each section.... With track already in very bad condition and extra mileage, a lot of 'slow' orders were placed on the track as the only safe means of getting our trains over them."⁹

Freight business on the AT&SF began to increase just before America's entry into World War II. But with the "bad" track conditions, Naylor noted that "By now, every day it was necessary to spend on mainline repairs and then we got further and further behind.... By the time Pearl Harbor took place we were up to our necks in work."¹⁰ Finally, the AT&SF realized the critical nature of the track situation:

> In the latter part of April 1941, the second district, Vaughn to Belen, New Mexico, was allowed several extra gangs with from 60 to 75 men in each gang. Work started in earnest, going into all phases of track work.... I had six extra gangs and sometimes two work trains under my jurisdiction ... from April of 1941 practically all through Worl War II.¹¹

Tracks could not be repaired fast enough at the start of the war, and several calamities resulted. Naylor noted two such calamities:

> One very cold night a main train [troop train] stopped at Vaughn where it was snowing and blowing violently. It was discovered that half of a wheel was missing from under the back end of a Pullman car. The car stayed on the track like that for 26 miles when every time the wheel turned it could have been disastrous ... causing a bad derailment. On another occasion, just west of Clovis, a main train, loaded with Red Cross Nurses, derailed the entire coach section. Some of the coaches went out into the right-of-way fence, but no one was seriously hurt. Many things happened in such a way that it surely made me think more strongly than ever that, by the grace of God, our railroads helped to save our country even more than it might appear on the surface of things.¹²

Another calamity occurred in the fall of 1942 when Naylor, traveling on his motor track car, witnessed a westbound freight derail west of Culebra (which was east of Willard). Naylor described the situation:

> By this time in 1942 we had a big war going on in Europe and also in the Pacific. Uncle Sam was moving thousands of troops each way across the United States every day. By 2:00 p.m. following this derailment we had four eastbound troop trains stopped just west of where we were working. These trains were already out of the Belen terminal when the accident occurred, so they were allowed to come on and, when the track was safe for train movement, they would be first over it.¹³

Naylor and his crews worked furiously to repair track, and by 10:00 p.m., they allowed the first of the troop trains to pass slowly through. Despite all these difficulties with track, Naylor was proud to state that "at the peak of the war movement, we had anywhere from 50 to 60 trains each 24 hours across this territory and still we managed to build and to maintain our tracks and still keep war materials moving across the Pecos Division without any serious delay."¹⁴

Naylor continued his commentary about the enormous amount of traffic on the rails across New Mexico during World War II with the following story:

I was headed west on a routine trip in the winter of 1945 and was between the Lucy and Silio stations when I had to set my [motor track] car off and let a westbound freight go by. This train was almost a complete train load of jeeps, large type artillery guns, and tanks. Most of this war material was loaded on flat cars and as the train went past me, I gave it a close inspection and saw nothing unusual. When the rear end of the train came by me, I waved an "all clear" signal to the crew.... Railroading continued to be a fulltime job until the close of the war in the Pacific. There were many different activities going on all the time, and monotony was something I seldom had to contend with.[15]

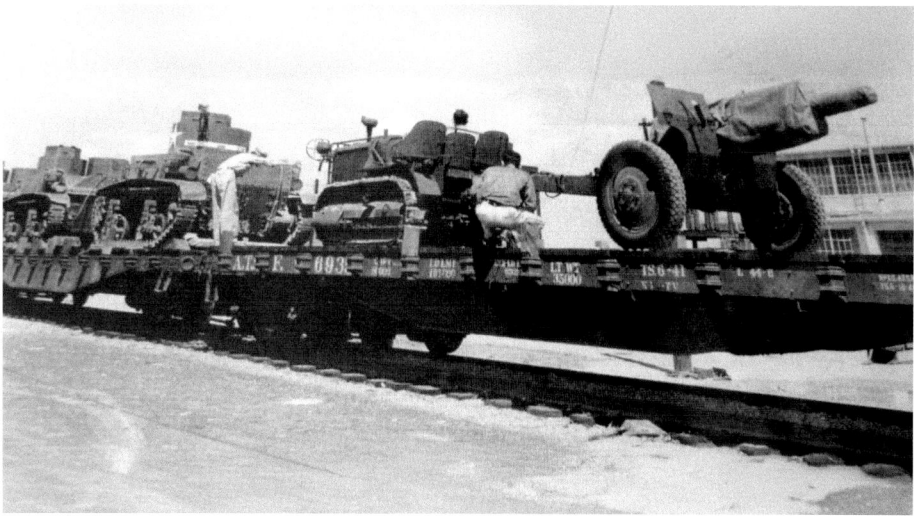

AT&SF flat cars hauled tanks and cannons across New Mexico during World War II.

4

DIVERSITY: A WARTIME NECESSITY

One of the greatest challenges facing track supervisor B. M. Naylor and the Atchison, Topeka, and Santa Fe Railway in 1942 was an extreme shortage of workers, yet the railway was one of the busiest in the nation, expected to deliver troops and materiel quickly and efficiently between Chicago and Los Angeles. Naylor noted:

> … each passing day we would see train after train west-bound, loaded with guns, boats, barges, jeeps, tanks and any and all kinds of fighting equipment…. As the war progressed the [track] work became more and more demanding, so much so that we worked seven-days-a-week and ten-hours-per-day for a long time.[1]

The AT&SF lost 12,000 skilled workers to the U.S. Army Military Railway Service. This service provided railway-operating battalions to the European and Asian theatres of war. These battalions provided essential rail freight service in occupied territories by constructing track and bridges and operating and servicing locomotives. "After the United States entered World War II in December 1941, the Army activated additional railway operating battalions under the Affiliation Plan."[2] The major U.S. railroad companies became "affiliated" with a particular railway operating battalion—in the case of the AT&SF, it was the 713th battalion which trained on the rail line at Clovis, New Mexico.

> Most of the officers and many of the enlisted men were experienced railroaders, but the new battalions included men drawn from Army training centers who needed to be trained. The newly organized battalions also had to learn how to operate efficiently as units, so the War Department contracted with commercial railroads to provide on-the-job training. An Army train crew would accompany a train manned by civilians to learn operating rules and railroad techniques.[3]

With the loss of experienced railroaders to the army, the AT&SF was desperate for workers. Where to find help? The unthinkable happened. Prior to the war, the sentiment was as follows:

> The railroad has never been a place for a woman. During the war and the manpower shortage, few railroad departments remained uninvaded by women. In 1942, 320,000 railroad jobs needed immediate filling as the War Department continued skimming the cream of rail labor for its Military Railway Service…. Clearly women were the answer.[4]

When photographer Jack Delano began his trek on AT&SF freight trains west from Chicago in 1943, he noted:

> Increasing use was also being made of women workers as freight handlers, car cleaners, locomotive shop sweepers, car inspectors, and roundhouse helpers. Women were likewise beginning to take over some of the clerical jobs traditionally held by men.[5]

Women also filled positions as ticket agents, passenger representatives, coach-sleeping car cleaners, and baggage handlers, and some even worked on track section crews.[6] "As part of his work for the war effort, Jack Delano made a special point of documenting women who had entered the railroad workforce due to the lack of male railroad workers during World War II."[7] "This expansion included African American women, even in jobs requiring heavy manual labor.… This expansion included Hispanic women as well."[8]

Women were not the only element in a diverse workforce required to keep the AT&SF running during the war: "Heavy track repairs were handled by gangs of Mexican nationals and Indians drawn from the many reservations located in the Santa Fe's bailiwick."[9] "The labor shortage led the AT&SF to request permission to hire Mexican nationals and the federal government agreed."[10] In 1943, out of a total AT&SF workforce of 58,767, there were 4,250 Mexicans employed in what was known as the "Braceros" program. These workers were returned to Mexico after the war. B. M. Naylor, based in Belen, NM, noted the arrival of these men in his crews:

> We continued to lose men to the armed services.… As a result of this, the railroads had to look elsewhere for laborers. Old Mexico was the answer. I do not remember exactly just when we received the first of the Mexican nationals, but I believe that it was in the latter part of 1943 or early 1944.… These people, most of them completely ignorant about track work, were willing to work. We would have a few that were experienced in this kind of work. We managed to get them spread out so that we continued to keep the trains running.[11]

The Indian Reservations in New Mexico supplied many laborers to the AT&SF, particularly Laguna Pueblo Indians and Navajos in western New Mexico. Near Gallup, Jack Delano found twenty Laguna Indians maintaining the tracks. His notes stated that the AT&SF "has agreement with Laguna reservation to hire Indians preferentially in exchange for rights to get water at Laguna reservation."[12] Obtaining water for the steam locomotives was a continual problem for the AT&SF all across the dry lands of New Mexico, and led to some interesting solutions, as noted in the next chapter.

Last, but certainly not least of the diverse workforce required to keep the AT&SF running across New Mexico, was the native Hispanic population. Since the late 1500s, Spanish people from Mexico had settled in the province of New Mexico. New Mexico Territory's application for statehood in the U.S. was largely delayed until 1912 because of prejudice that the region consisted predominantly of people of Hispanic origin. It is not surprising that half of the men who worked in the Albuquerque repair shops of the AT&SF were Spanish Americans. During World War II, it required the entirety of New Mexico's diverse population—Hispanic, Native American, Anglo, and African American—to keep the railroad operating. In a 1993 interview, Jack Delano stated: "I was very pleased to find that not only New Mexicans, but Indians, women and black people were also being employed on the railroad."[13] It required all this diverse population for a successful war effort, and Jack Delano's photographs aptly capture this diversity at work on the railroad in New Mexico.

DIVERSITY: A WARTIME NECESSITY

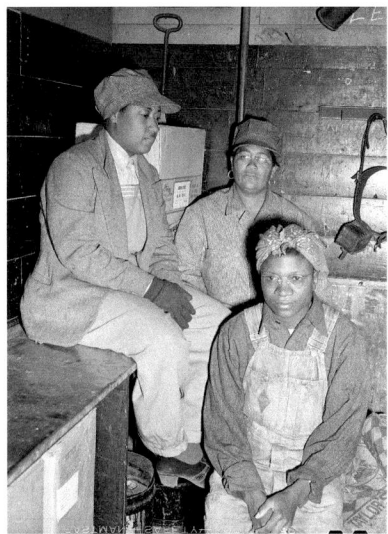 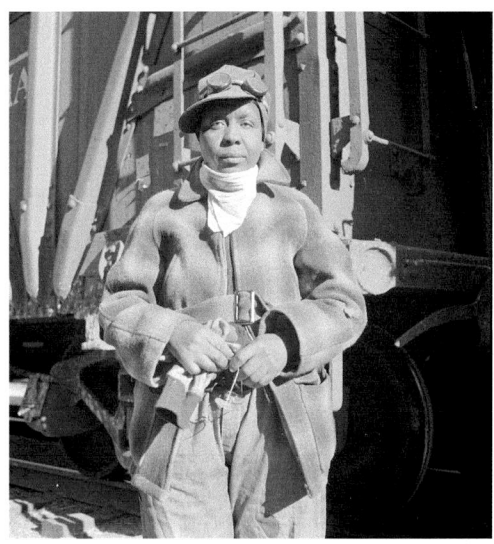

Above left: These black women were employed by the AT&SF as freight car cleaners at Clovis, NM, in 1943. From left to right are Lorraine Panol, Felicia Jones, and Vera Erdmore. (*Jack Delano photograph, Library of Congress, LC-USW3- 020466-D*)

Above right: Almeta Williams was employed by the AT&SF in 1943 in Clovis, NM, as a potash car cleaner. This difficult job was necessary as potash was used in the making of explosives. Ms. Williams was well-equipped with a hat, protective goggles, neckerchief, overcoat, overalls, and gloves. (*Jack Delano photograph, Library of Congress, LC-USW3-020607-E*)

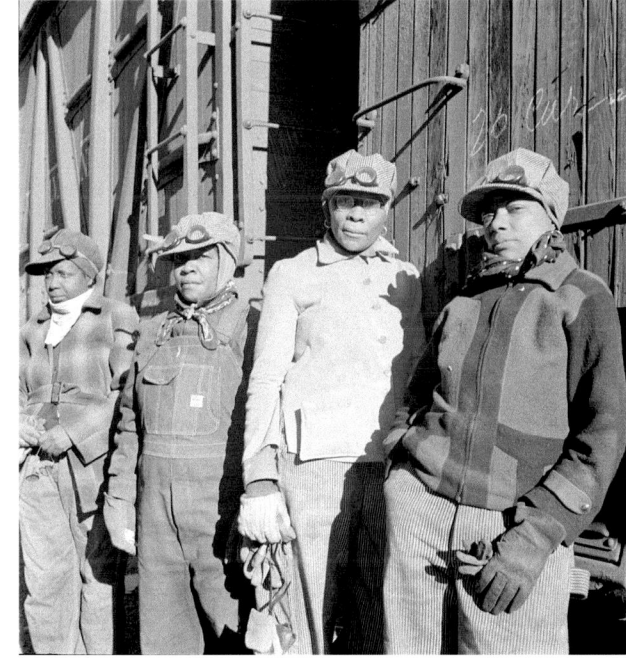

These black women potash car cleaners posed in Clovis, NM, in 1943 for Jack Delano's camera. From left to right are Almeta Williams, Beatrice Davis, Liza Goss, and Abbie Caldwell, whose husband worked in the roundhouse in Clovis, and whose son served in the U.S. Army. (*Library of Congress, LC- USW3-020602-E*)

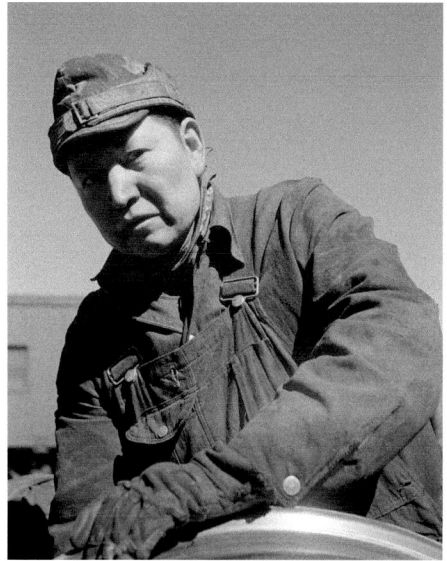 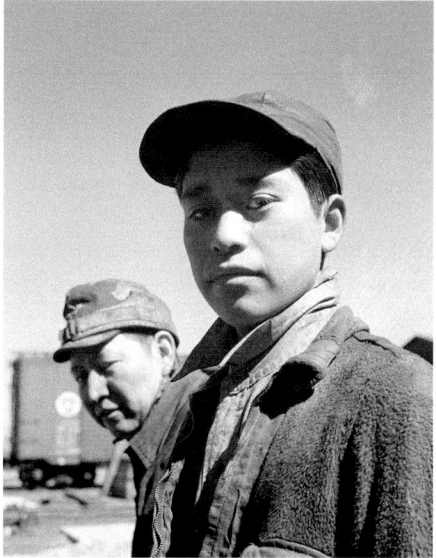

Above left: Ben Acory, a native of Laguna Pueblo, is seen working on a wheel in Gallup, NM, in this March 1943 Jack Delano photograph. (*Library of Congress, LC- USW3-021204-E*)

Above right: Ben Acory and Clyde Trujillo, Laguna Pueblo natives, pose in the AT&SF rail yard in Gallup, NM, in March 1943. (*Jack Delano photograph, Library of Congress, LC-USW3-021201-E*)

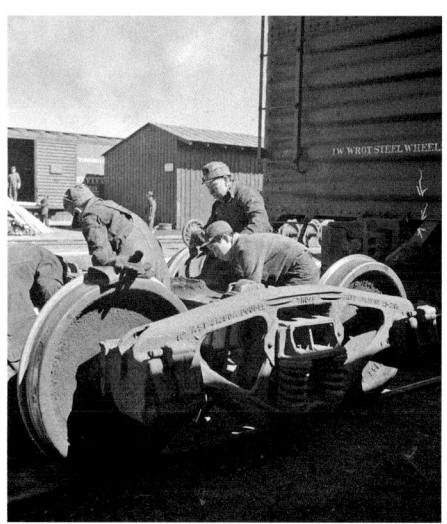 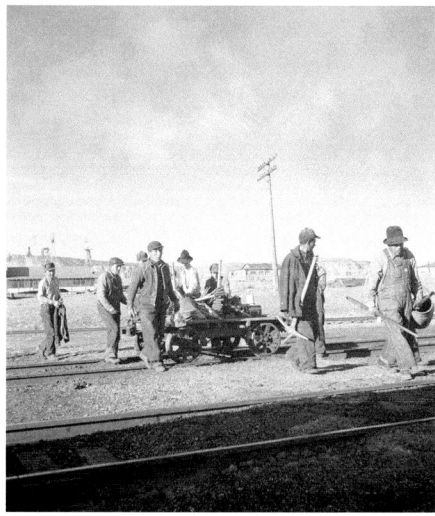

Above left: Jack Delano captured this Laguna Pueblo native crew working on a wheel set in the Gallup, NM, rail yard in March 1943. Facing the camera are Ben Acory (left) and Clyde Trujillo (right). (*Library of Congress, LC-USW3-021200-E*)

Above right: A Native American crew prepares for work on the AT&SF rails at Thoreau, NM, in March 1943. (*Jack Delano photograph, Library of Congress, LC- USW3-021188-E*)

DIVERSITY: A WARTIME NECESSITY

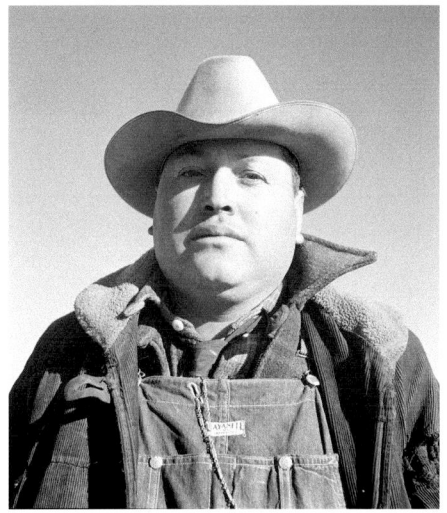

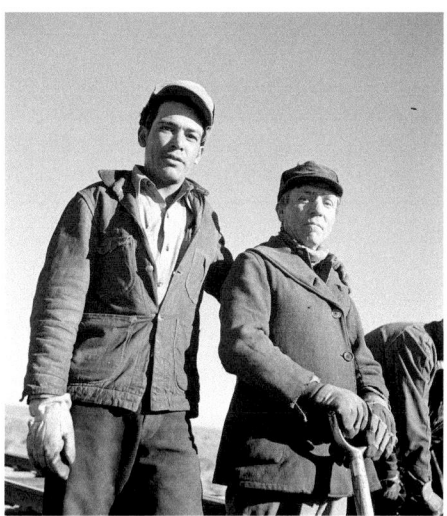

Above left: In Iden, NM, AT&SF assistant foreman George Zamora posed for Jack Delano's camera in March 1943. The work of Native Americans and Hispanics was essential in keeping the railroad running across New Mexico in World War II. (*Library of Congress, LC-USW-3-020686-E*)

Above right: Near Iden, NM, AT&SF Railway section workers Joe Melendez (left) and E. Argonne (right), Hispanics from Mountainair, NM, stopped work briefly for Jack Delano's camera in March 1943. (*Library of Congress, LC-USW3-020685-E*)

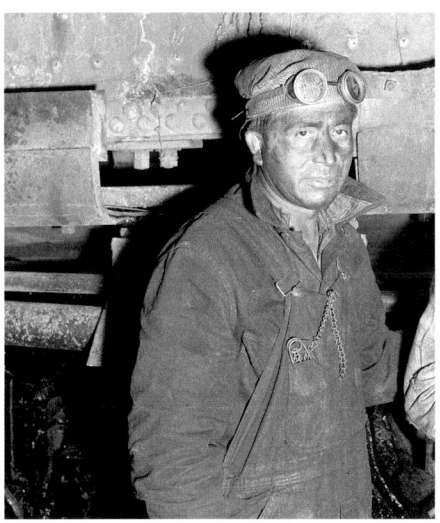

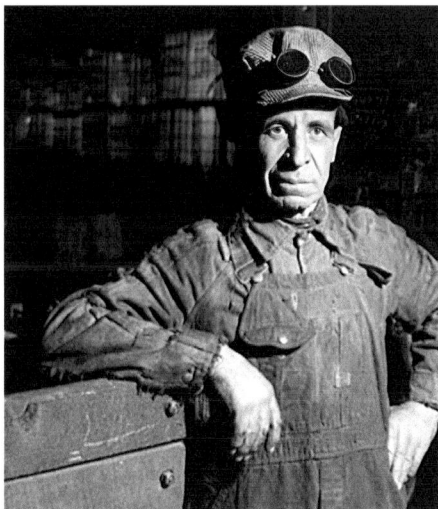

Above left: Fully half of the workers in the Albuquerque AT&SF repair shops were Hispanic, such as boilermaker Andrew Santiago, photographed here by Jack Delano in March 1943. (*Library of Congress, LC-USW-3-020439-D*)

Above right: Another Hispanic boilermaker in the Albuquerque shops was Joseph Pina. The work was hard and sometimes dangerous, but these men carried on heroically for the war effort. (*Jack Delano photograph, Library of Congress, LC- USW-3-020526-D*)

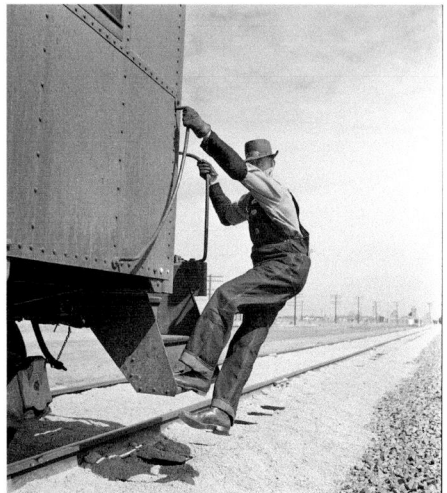 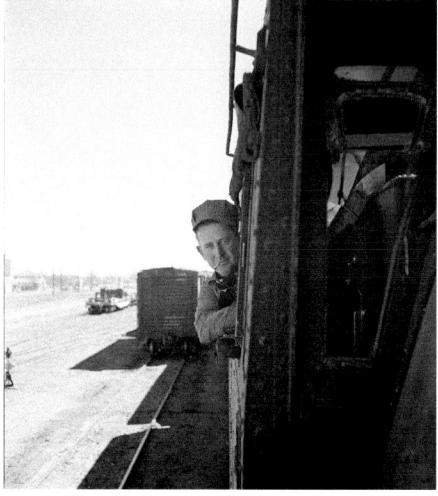

Above left: Anglo men often performed jobs on the AT&SF trains across New Mexico, while Hispanic men worked in the repair shops, and Native American men worked on track repair. The coordinated work of all was required for a successful USA war effort. Here we see E. K. Hill, train conductor, hopping off a caboose at Texico, NM, in March 1943. (*Jack Delano photograph, Library of Congress, LC-USW-3-035239-E*)

Above right: In Clovis, NM, B. L. Clark was the train engineer rolling through the AT&SF yards in March 1943. (*Jack Delano photograph, Library of Congress, LC-USW-3-020627-E*)

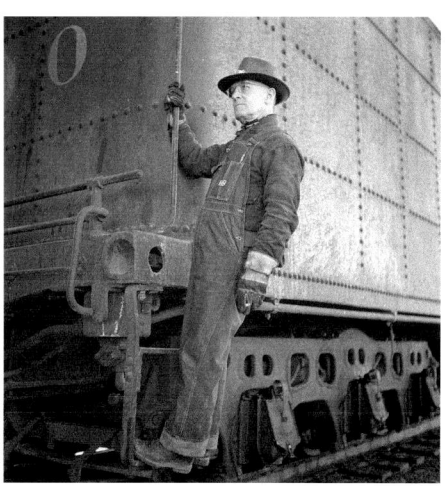 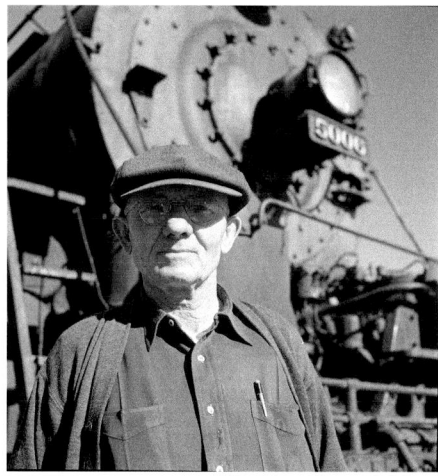

Above left: In Ricardo, NM, Thomas Knight was the brakeman on this AT&SF freight in March 1943. (*Jack Delano photograph, Library of Congress, LC-USW-3-020655-E*)

Above right: In Vaughn, NM, Ennis O'Neill, train conductor, posed for this Jack Delano photograph with AT&SF steam locomotive 5006 in March 1943. (*Library of Congress, LC-USW-3-020707-E*)

5

ALONG THE RAILS: TEXICO TO FORT SUMNER

When the AT&SF began contemplating a "Belen Cutoff," the first step was connecting Texico, New Mexico with Amarillo, Texas. Texico was a small ranching village on the Texas–New Mexico border, whose name was derived from combining some syllables from the words Texas and Mexico.

Texico was soon eclipsed by Clovis, 10 miles farther west, where the AT&SF established a division point. The Belen Cutoff was originally a one-track line between Texico and Belen with sidings established for trains passing in opposite directions. Eventually the line became double-tracked; however, double-track in Abo Canyon was not completed until 2011. This caused innumerable delays for trains during World War II as double-track became single-track through Abo Canyon.

> West of Clovis, things became a little more hectic. The sawtooth profile between Clovis, Abo and Belen was a difficult section to operate and tended to create bottlenecks as trains fought their way to the summit [at Abo] from either direction.… All trains required helpers.… The enormous volume of traffic [from Clovis] often totaled more than thirty separate train movements every 24 hours and included four passenger runs.[1]

"Clovis" seems an odd name for a town built on the high plains of eastern New Mexico. One might expect a Hispanic or Native American name, but this was not the case. Clovis was the name of a medieval French king admired by two people connected with the AT&SF. One was the "wife of Santa Fe Railway president Edward Payson Ripley, whose family had recently toured France … [the other] was the daughter of chief engineer James Dunn who was studying French history in school."[2] Which one actually suggested the name is not known.

The AT&SF established Clovis as a division point. In the age of steam engines in the nineteenth and twentieth centuries, a train crew "traveled 100 to 150 miles along the line [per day]. For this reason, railroads are divided into 100-mile operating segments called divisions."[3] The division points across New Mexico during World War II were Clovis, Vaughn, Albuquerque, and Gallup. Division points had a roundhouse for servicing locomotives, a coal tower, water tower, railyards for classifying freight cars, and a depot for serving passengers, freight agents, and railroad crews.

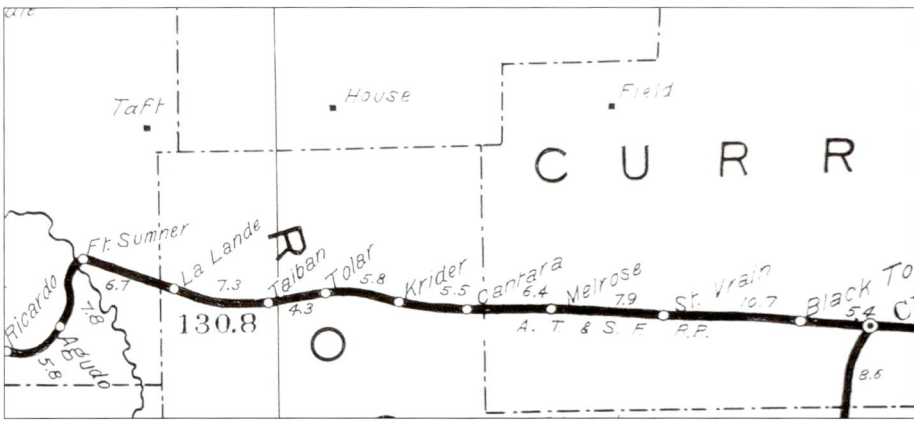

This 1913 map shows the villages between Clovis and Fort Sumner along the route of the AT&SF Railway. Clovis is just off the map to the right and Texico is another 8 miles east of Clovis. (*New Mexico History Museum display*)

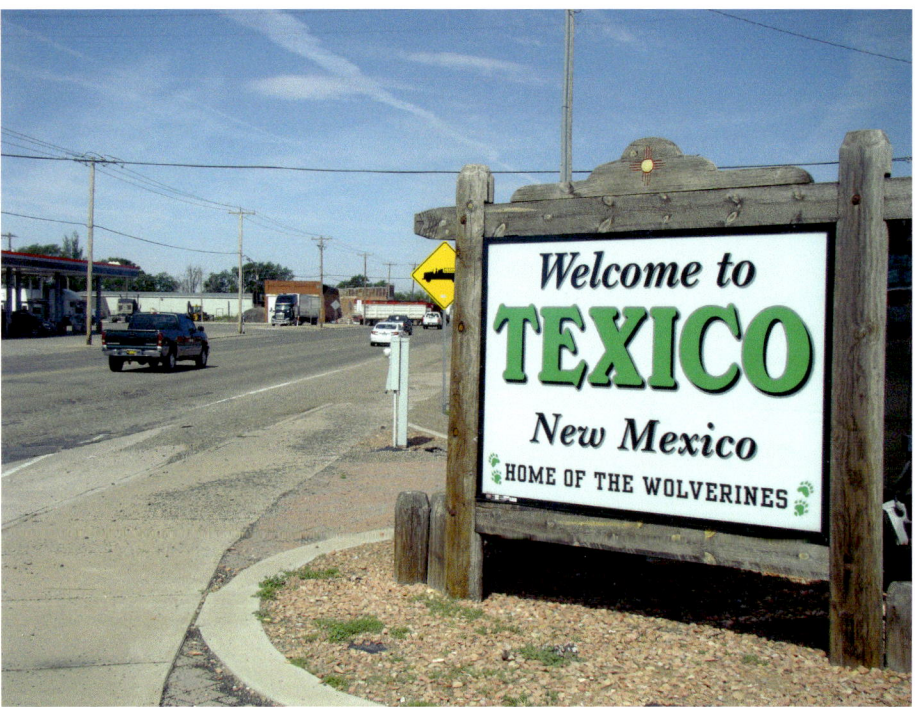

Texico, NM, is on the Texas border and is where we begin following Jack Delano along the AT&SF Belen Cutoff.

ALONG THE RAILS: TEXICO TO FORT SUMNER

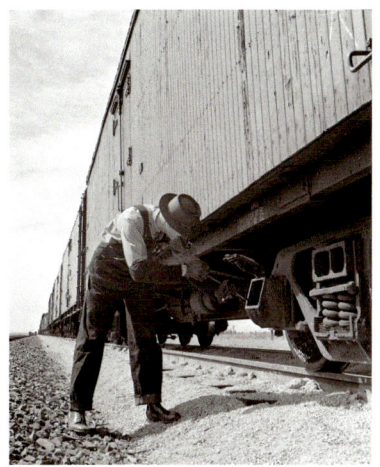
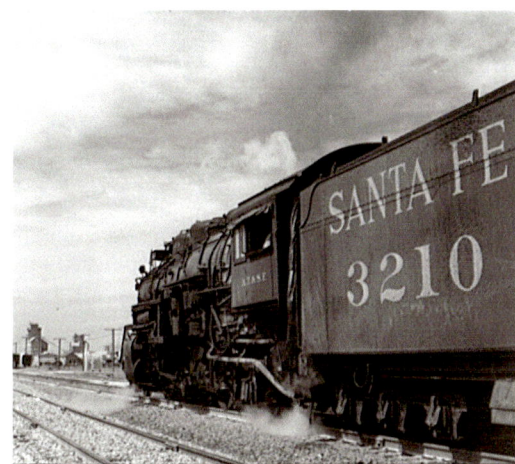

Above left: On March 19, 1943, conductor E. K. Hill was inspecting a journal box on a freight car in Texico. A journal box contains a round journal plate which secures a wheel axle. The journal box contains oil-soaked packing which lubricates the journal. If a journal breaks, the axle slips and the train derails. (*Jack Delano photograph, Library of Congress, LC-USW3-035238-E*)

Above right: Locomotive 3210 was passing through Texico headed to Clovis on March 19, 1943. Notice the grain elevators in the distance. This was cattle and wheat country. (*Jack Delano photograph, Library of Congress, LC-USW3-020457-D*)

Right: Grain elevators of the Golden West Flour Company standing tall in Texico today.

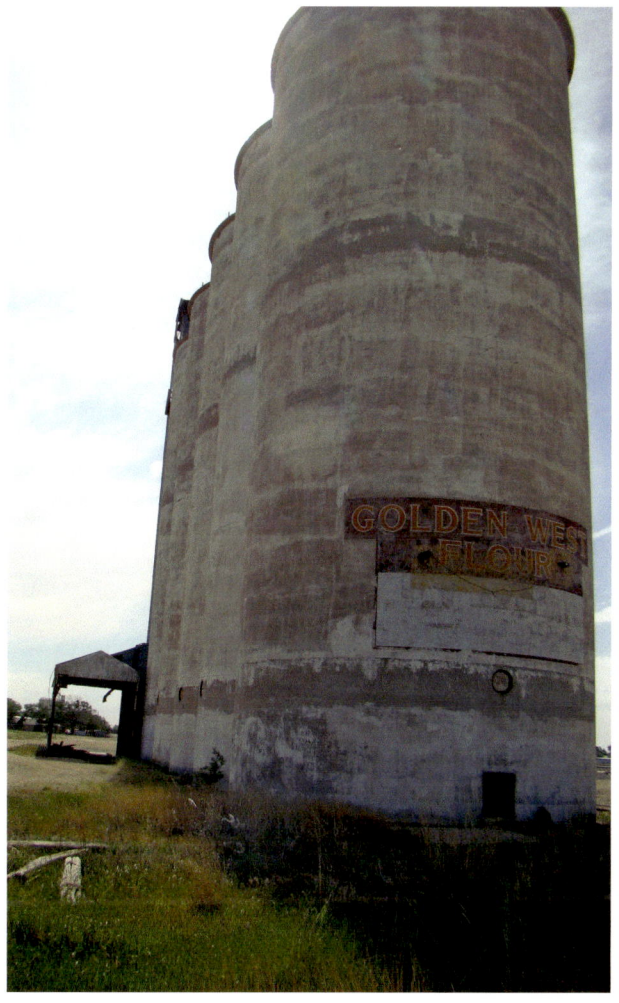

The Santa Fe built … elaborate masonry depots in key locations on the Cutoff.… The reinforced concrete and stucco depots were designed by architect Myron Church. Their simplified Mission Revival style was well suited to the hot, dry climate of eastern New Mexico, with thick walls, wide overhangs to shade walls and windows, and covered, open-air waiting rooms. All were 24 feet wide, with three standard lengths: 81 feet, 93 feet [built only in Texico], and 135 feet. The basic plan consisted of a single waiting room, agent's office and freight room on the first level, and second level living quarters, consisting of either a dormitory for railroad workers or an agent's apartment.[4]

The remaining Mission-style depots on the Belen Cutoff as of 2024 are located in Clovis, Fort Sumner, Vaughn, Mountainair, and Belen. The Melrose depot was torn down in about 2019. The Burlington Northen Santa Fe Railway (successor to the AT&SF) uses these remaining buildings as offices for their personnel. Most are now surrounded by fencing and visitors are not welcome. There appears to be little maintenance to these historic buildings today. Likewise, Fred Harvey's Gran Quivira Hotel in Clovis, owned by the BNSF next to the depot, is fenced off and falling into ruin. BNSF does not seem to be in the business of historic preservation.

During World War II, the Clovis railyard was a hive of activity. In addition to the roundhouse where simple maintenance on the steam locomotives was performed, there was a large machine shop where complex repairs, sometimes taking days, were performed. Today in Clovis, the roundhouse is gone but its turntable remains in the railyard. The machine shop is also gone, no longer needed once diesel engines replaced steam engines and required much less maintenance. The Division Point administration building still stands just east of the Gran Quivira Hotel. It is a two-story Mission Revival-style masonry/stucco building with a noticeable red tile mansard roof. It was constructed in 1920 to provide offices for division personnel including telegrapher, dispatcher, trainmaster, roadmaster, superintendent and clerks. The historic "Santa Fe–Be Safe" sign now sits at the end of Main Street where it once perched atop the freight building which was later demolished. Clovis citizens insisted that the iconic sign be reinstalled after the freight building was gone. Perhaps more influential Clovis citizens today could persuade BNSF not to

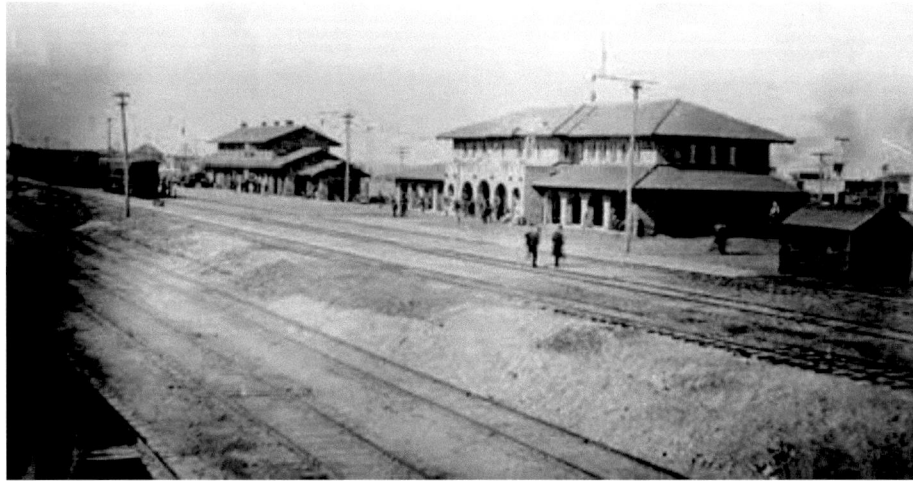

An early 1900s photograph of the Gran Quivira Hotel (right), built in 1900, and train station (left) in Clovis, with an AT&SF train standing by.

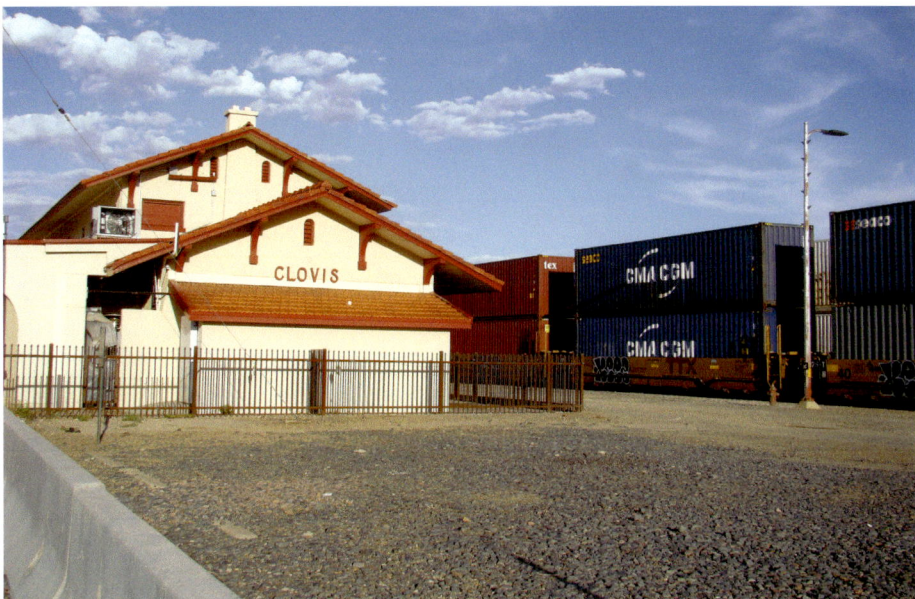

The train station in Clovis today has been restored and is now a popular restaurant known as "The Rails." Notice the double-stacked intermodal containers on the BNSF train. These types of trains form most of the traffic on the Belen Cutoff today.

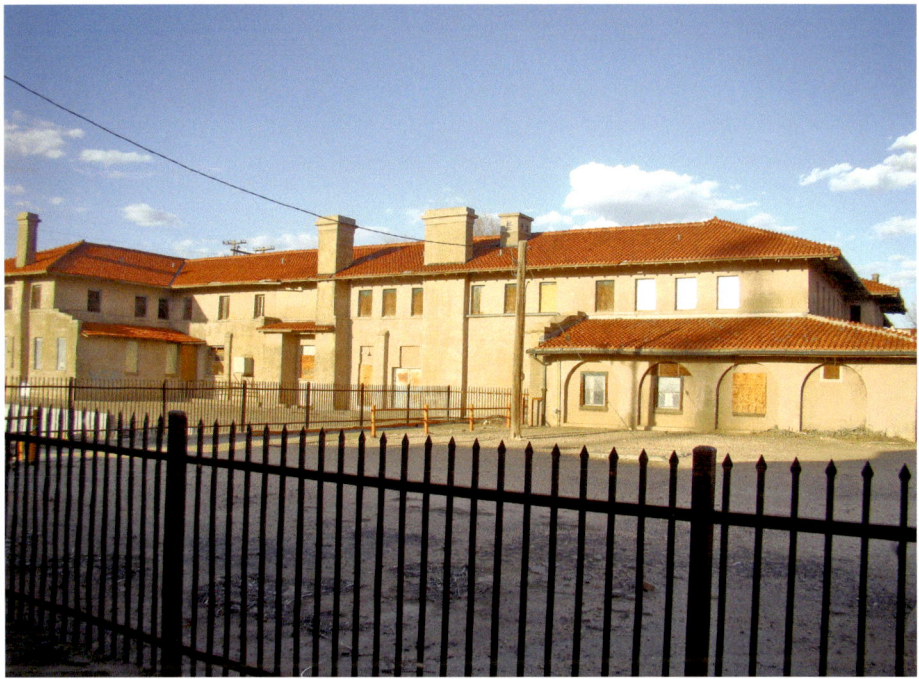

Fred Harvey's Gran Quivira Hotel in Clovis, on BNSF property, has been closed since 1948 and is in a state of decay. This is the west end of the hotel today.

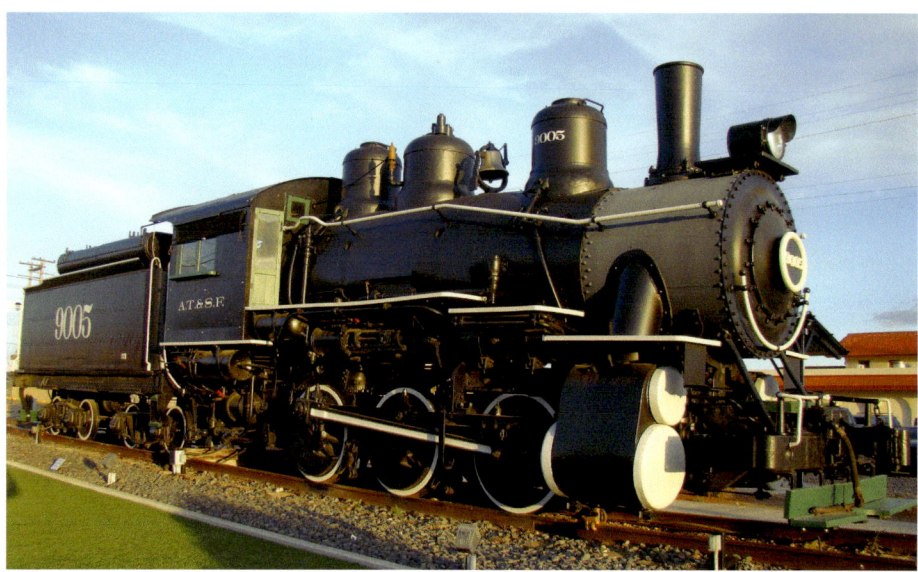

AT&SF locomotive 9005 has been restored and sits in a small park next to The Rails restaurant in Clovis. No. 9005 was used for switching purposes in the Clovis railyard for many years including the World War II era.

tear down the Gran Quivira Hotel. The depot was saved in 1995, though, when BNSF sold it to a private citizen who used it as a model train museum. Then in 2016 it was sold to new owners who have renovated it and turned it into The Rails restaurant, featuring trackside dining on the south side and patio dining on the north.

Clovis played a very important role for the U.S. Army during World War II. Its machine shop, roundhouse, and locomotives provided training for members of the 713th Army Railway Operating Battalion. The young recruits learned welding, track repair, and locomotive operation in preparation for their departure to their army railway battalion overseas. An article entitled "Railroaders in Olive Drab: The Military Railway Service in World War II" published by the Army Historical Foundation described:

> The mission of a railway operating battalion was to manage and maintain a designated section of a military railway in a theater of operations. The railway operating battalions were designed to operate 90–150 miles of line…After the United States entered World War II in December 1941, the Army activated additional railway operating battalions under the Affiliation Plan. In March 1942, the 727th Railway Operating Battalion sponsored by the Southern Railway Company, became the first battalion to be activated after the war began, followed in April by the 713th, affiliated with the Atchison, Topeka and Santa Fe Railway Company … the 713th trained on the Santa Fe line near Clovis, New Mexico.… The newly organized battalions had to learn how to operate efficiently as units, so the War Department contracted with commercial railroads to provide on-the-job-training.… The soldiers work[ed] alongside their civilian counterparts to learn the basics of railroading.[5]

In Clovis, the 713th was accommodated by "barracks hastily thrown up in the newly designated Camp William C. Reid."

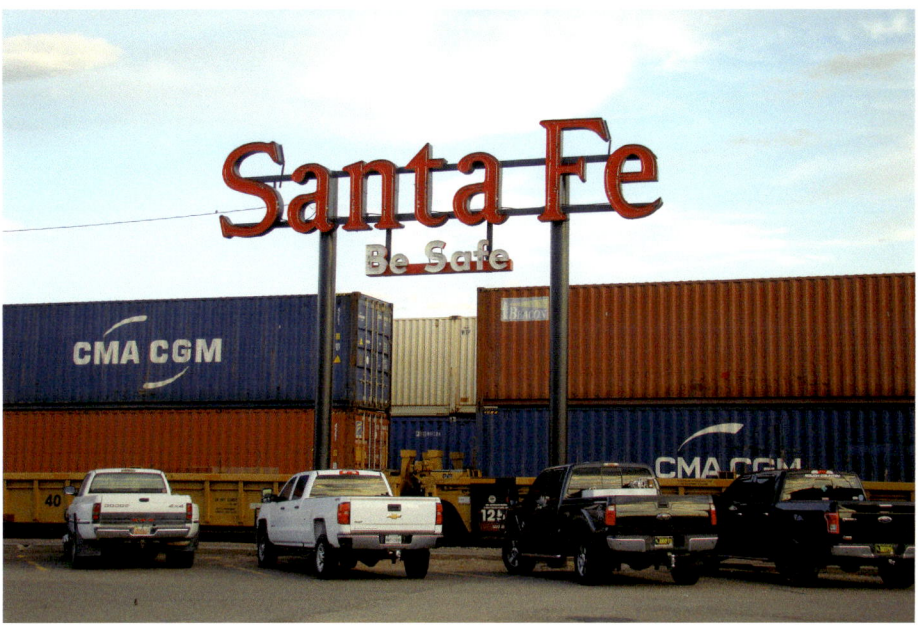

This sign sat atop the freight house in Clovis. When the freight house was demolished, Clovis citizens insisted that the sign be reinstalled in the railyard.

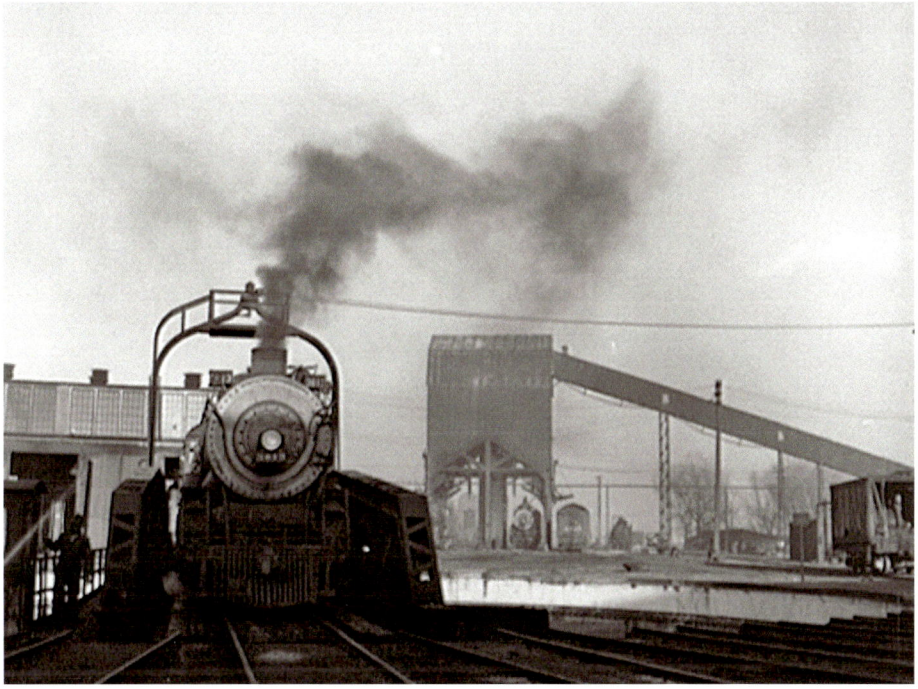

Jack Delano photographed this engine on the turntable in Clovis with the roundhouse in the background on the left and the coaling tower on the right. (*Library of Congress, LC-USW3-020467-D*)

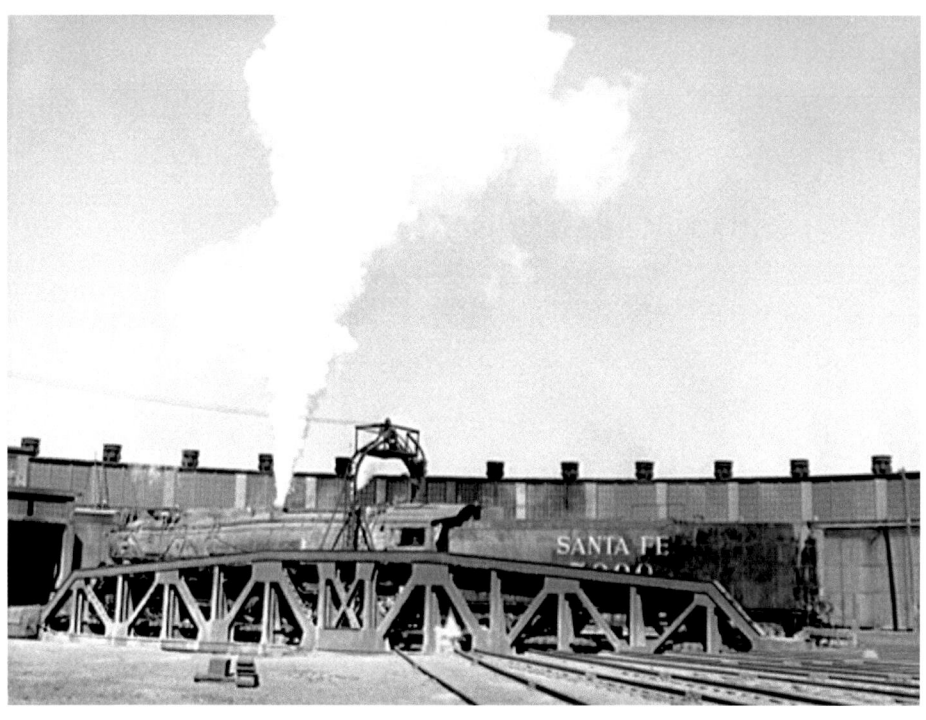

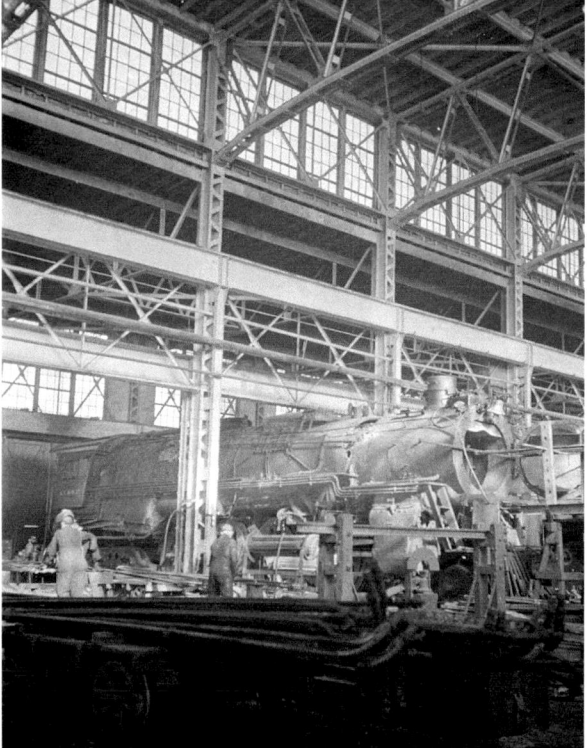

Above: A 5000-class locomotive and tender on the Clovis turntable with the roundhouse in the background, March 19, 1943. (*Jack Delano photograph, Library of Congress, LC-USW3-020608-E*)

Left: Inside the Clovis machine shop. Minor repairs on locomotives could be accomplished overnight in the roundhouse, while major repairs, such as replacing the boiler on the locomotive shown here, took place in the larger machine shop. (*Jack Delano photograph, Library of Congress, LC-USW3-020608-E*)

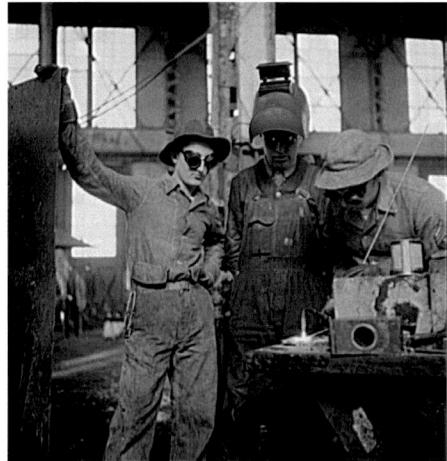 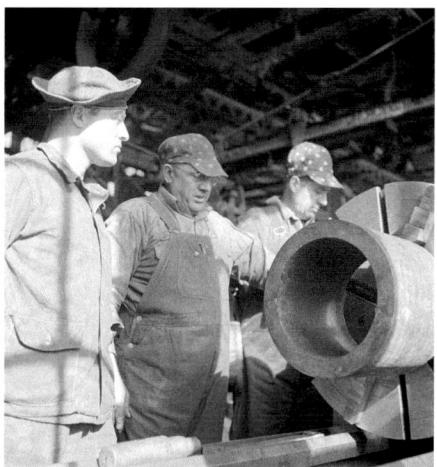

Above left: Members of the 713th U.S. Army Railway Battalion studying welding in the Clovis machine shop. From left to right are Private Edward Davis of Minnesota, Earl Weidinger AT&SF instructor, and Sergeant Arthur Cannon of Indiana. (*Jack Delano photograph, Library of Congress, LC-USW3-020609-E*)

Above right: In the Clovis machine shop, machinist John Corey (center) was teaching Sergeant Bowman (left) of the 713th U.S. Army Railway Battalion how to use an engine lathe to make steel bushings. The other person is unidentified. (*Jack Delano photograph, Library of Congress, LC-USW3-020614-E*)

> The battalion was organized into three companies: "A Company's function was to build and maintain bridges, tracks, water facilities, signal systems and whatever facilities are needed for train operations. "B" Company's function was to repair and service the cars and locomotives. "C" company was the operating company and was responsible for the movement of trains.[6]

The training paid off with the successful operations of railway operating battalions in Europe, the Pacific, and Asia:

> [In Europe] Two of the most experienced operating battalions, the 713th and 727th deployed to Marseilles and began operations at the end of August [1944] … the ports were not heavily damaged by Allied bombing or German demolitions. In October the MRS [Military Railway Service] operated 1.897 trains hauling 640,561 tons of freight in support of the Sixth Army Group. General Jacob Devers, commanding the Army group, commended MRS troops when he wrote "I want to send my congratulations to you and your splendid achievement in opening and maintaining the railroad system in southern France since the invasion of our forces."[7]

Clovis, New Mexico, and the 713th Army Railway Operating Battalion were essential partners in winning the war in Europe.

A ranching community 25 miles west of Clovis called Brownhorn was established in 1882. The AT&SF intended to establish a division point here in 1906 for the Belen Cutoff and renamed the town Melrose after their Melrose, Ohio, administrative offices.[8] However, Melrose had so little water that it could not service steam engines, so the division point was established at the new town of Clovis which had an adequate water supply. In the single-track district between Clovis and Belen, Jack Delano noted:

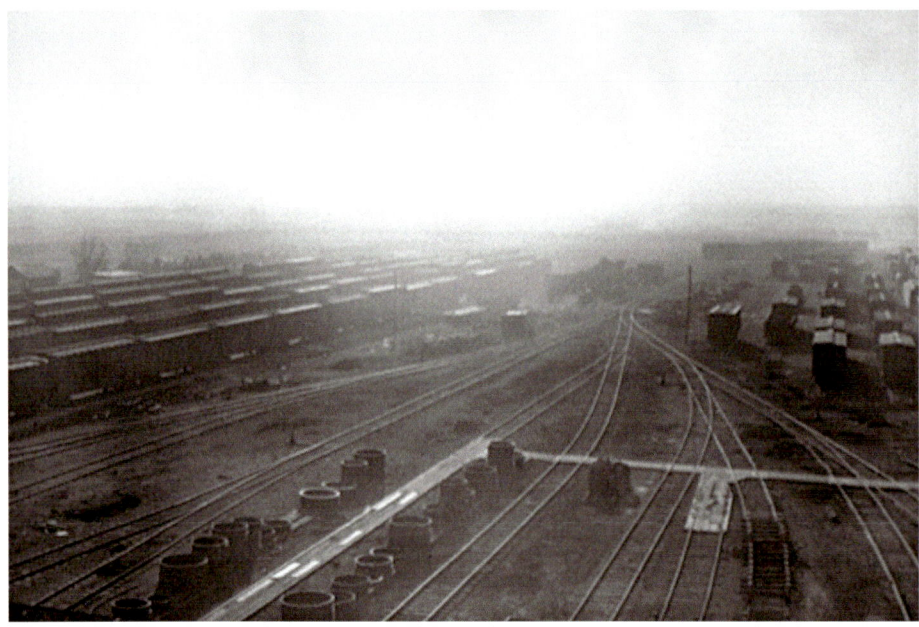

The extensive Clovis railyard was photographed by Jack Delano during a sandstorm on March 19, 1943. Winds were often destructive on the eastern New Mexico plains. (*Library of Congress, USW3-020468-D*)

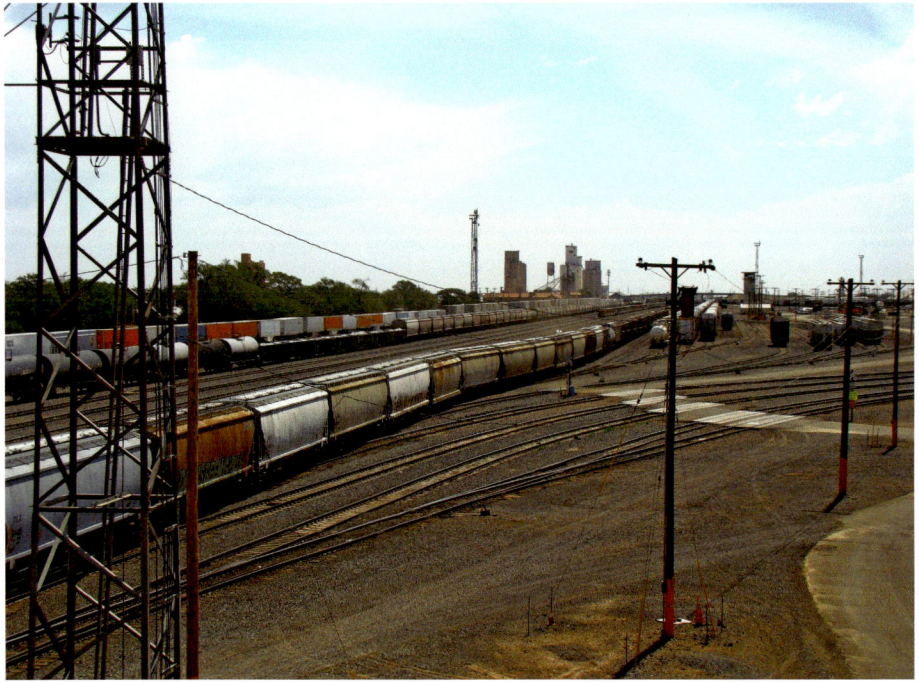

The Clovis railyard was much clearer on this day in May 2024, seen by the author.

This area is so dry that water must come from wells over 2,000 feet deep. Between Vaughn and Agudo [about 62 miles] there are no wells at all. A 200-mile pipeline owned by the Southern Pacific brings water to Vaughn where it is purchased by the Santa Fe and carried in tank cars to watering stations along the line. This water train makes a round trip each day.[9]

Many of Delano's photographs show a large number of water tank cars as seen from his viewpoint in the caboose at the rear of the train. Railroad historian Don Ball also commented on the Santa Fe's water problem:

The Santa Fe was burdened with a war of its own: it had to haul in millions of gallons of water to quench the thirst of its hardworking steam locomotives on desert and mountain divisions where local water was unavailable. This called for hundreds of tank cars…. And the more freight the locomotives hauled, the more water they needed![10]

About 16 miles west of Melrose was the little town with the strange name of Tolar. Tolar was born with the construction of the Belen Cutoff, providing a water stop for steam locomotives. The first postmaster of the town named it for his hometown of Tolar, Texas. On November 30, 1944, Tolar made the ultimate sacrifice for the war effort—the entire town was blown to bits when a freight train derailed, and a carload of bombs exploded. B. M. Naylor was called to the scene from Vaughn where he had just parked his track car for the evening. He was met in Vaughn by the yard foreman:

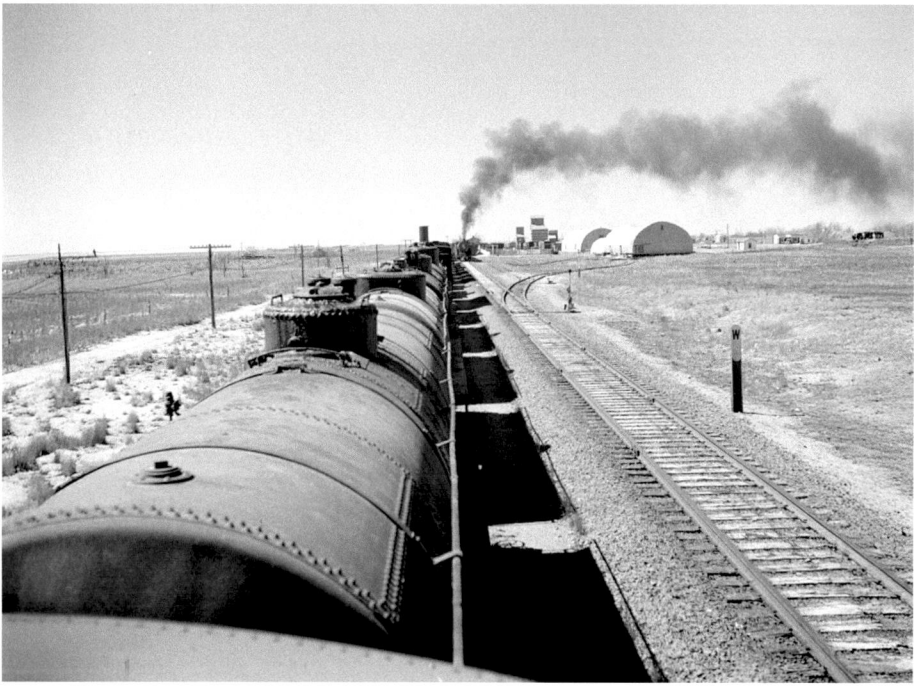

Jack Delano's train was stopped for water in Melrose on March 20, 1943, as an eastbound train approached. Notice the grain elevators in the background. (*Library of Congress, LC-USW3- 020637-E*)

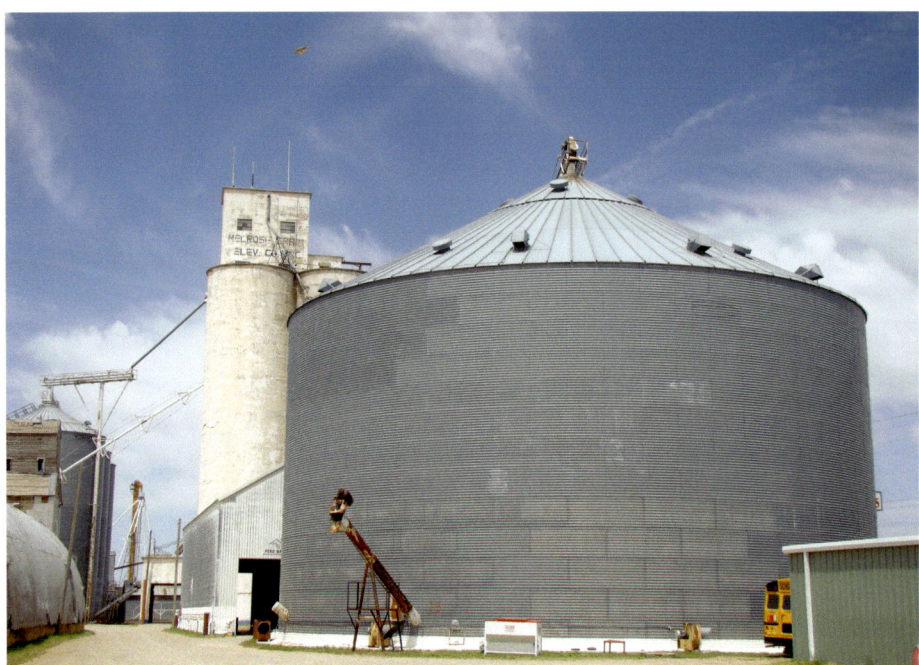

The Melrose Grain Elevator Company buildings are still standing in 2024; however, the train station was torn down in 2019. It was located to the left of the buildings shown in the photograph.

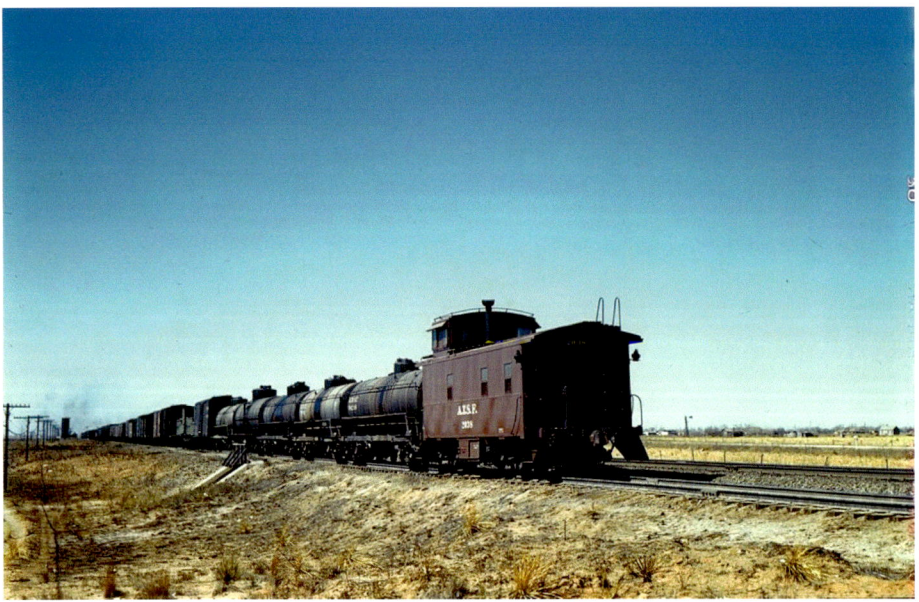

This Jack Delano color photograph shows caboose 2038 at the end of his westbound train with four water cars ahead of it as the train stopped at Melrose. Delano preferred riding in the caboose for his photos rather than the locomotive cab because it allowed much more expansive views of the train. (*Library of Congress, LC-USW361-709*)

His first remark to me was, "Did you hear about the freight train blowing up at Tolar?" I answered with a "no." Then he told me that about noon that day a freight train had stopped at Tolar with a hot box and about 35 or 36 cars had derailed and that a carload of bombs had exploded.… A few of the cars on the head end of the train were empty but about 65 to 70 cars were loaded—mostly with military supplies destined for the West Coast and eventually our armed forces in the Pacific.… Among the loaded cars was one loaded with about 40 tons of bombs. The explosion of these bombs almost wiped Tolar village off the map. Flying debris from the explosion killed one of the male residents of the village.… Among the loaded cars of the train was a tank car of gasoline. It burst into flames immediately after the pileup and this set fire to the other cars. Very soon after this the boxcar load of bombs exploded.[11]

Tolar never recovered. Virtually every house was damaged or destroyed. Today, there is nothing there except a road sign and the remains of homes.

Fort Sumner is approximately 18 miles west of Tolar. The town is named after the military fort which was about 4 miles to the south. Fort Sumner, named after Colonel Edmond Vose Sumner, operated from 1862 to 1868. Its purpose was to house 8,000 Navajos and 600 Mescalero Apache driven off their native lands and relocated here on the Pecos River to learn farming and become "civilized." It was a total failure, and the tribes, which had made the "long walk" to the fort, then began the long walk back home—the Navajos to Canyon de Chelly in Arizona, and the Mescalero to south central New Mexico.

When the Belen Cutoff was constructed in 1905, the railroad faced the daunting task of crossing the Pecos River. The river was not deep, and sometimes not even flowing, but it had

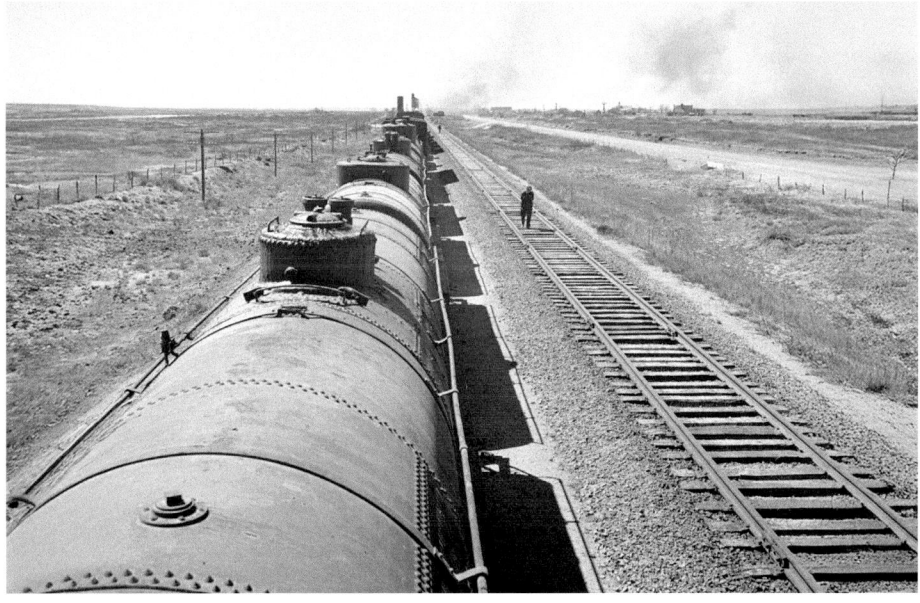

From his perch in the caboose, Jack Delano took this photograph of his train stopped at Tolar to take on water. Two brakemen are inspecting the train for hot (journal) boxes. A smoking journal box meant trouble and needed to be inspected right away to see if the journal had broken or if more grease was needed in the box. (*Library of Congress, LC-USW3-020643-E*)

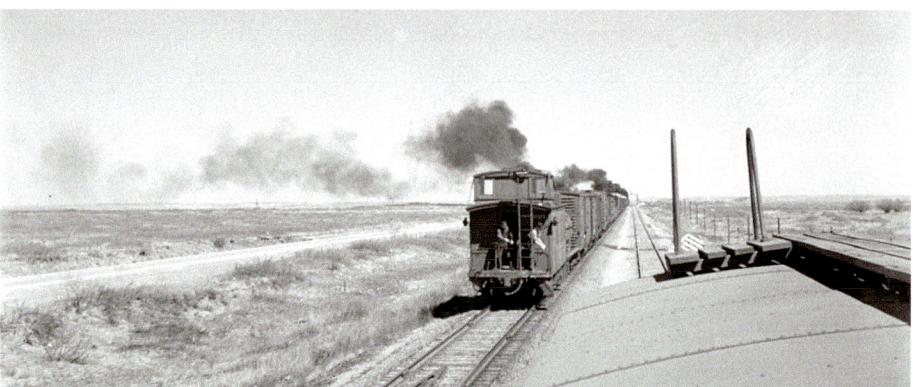

Jack Delano's view of an eastbound train as his westbound train stops at Tolar. (*Library of Congress, LC-USW3-020644-E*)

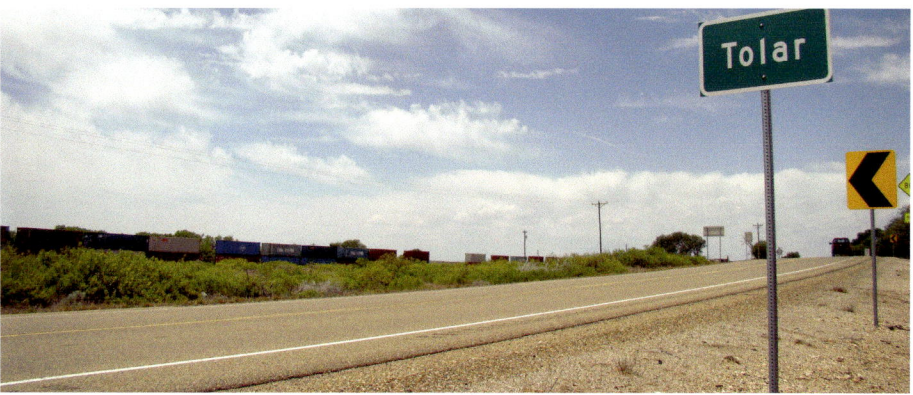

A BNSF double-stack intermodal train passes through Tolar in May 2024.

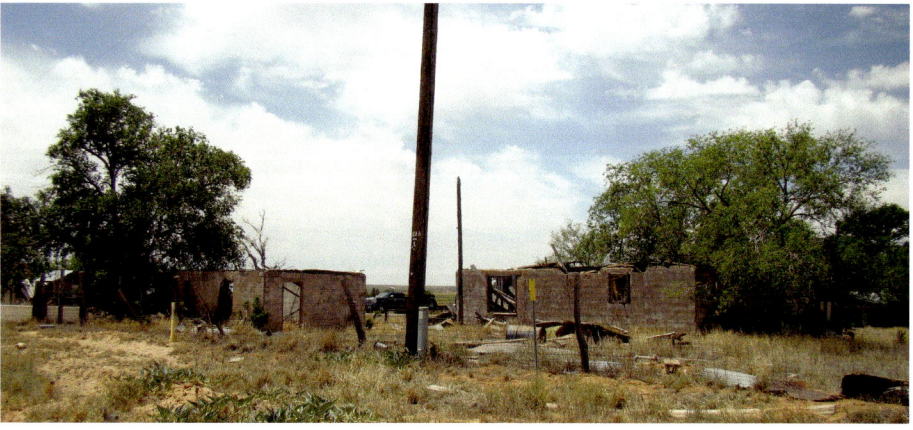

The explosion of the AT&SF train in Tolar in November 1944 destroyed most of the buildings in town. Today, little is left but shells.

carved a wide channel across the plains. A steel bridge was constructed across the river and "it was a huge undertaking. The bridge has fifteen spans of 100 feet, with a foundation of piles driven down to solid rock, 31 feet beneath the river's surface."[12] The railroad station was built over a mile east of the bridge in 1908.

Jack Delano's photographs at Fort Sumner on March 19, 1943, show trains on a broad sweeping curve of track from the station west to the bridge. James Valle provided this description of one of Delano's photographs there:

> This is the view from the cupola of a caboose tied to the marker's end of train No. 4–43 [with] 86 loads and 6 empties, powered by 2-10-4 [engine] No. 5004.… The freight in these cars is a random sampling of the diverse categories of goods needed to sustain global war. Mattresses, nails, hospital supplies, airplane parts, trucks, pipe, gasoline, steel, glass, soap, hogs, soybeans and more for a total of 4,293 tons. This was 293 tons over the normal rating … a serious matter insofar as the roadbed is already gaining altitude at the rate of 32 feet per mile.[13]

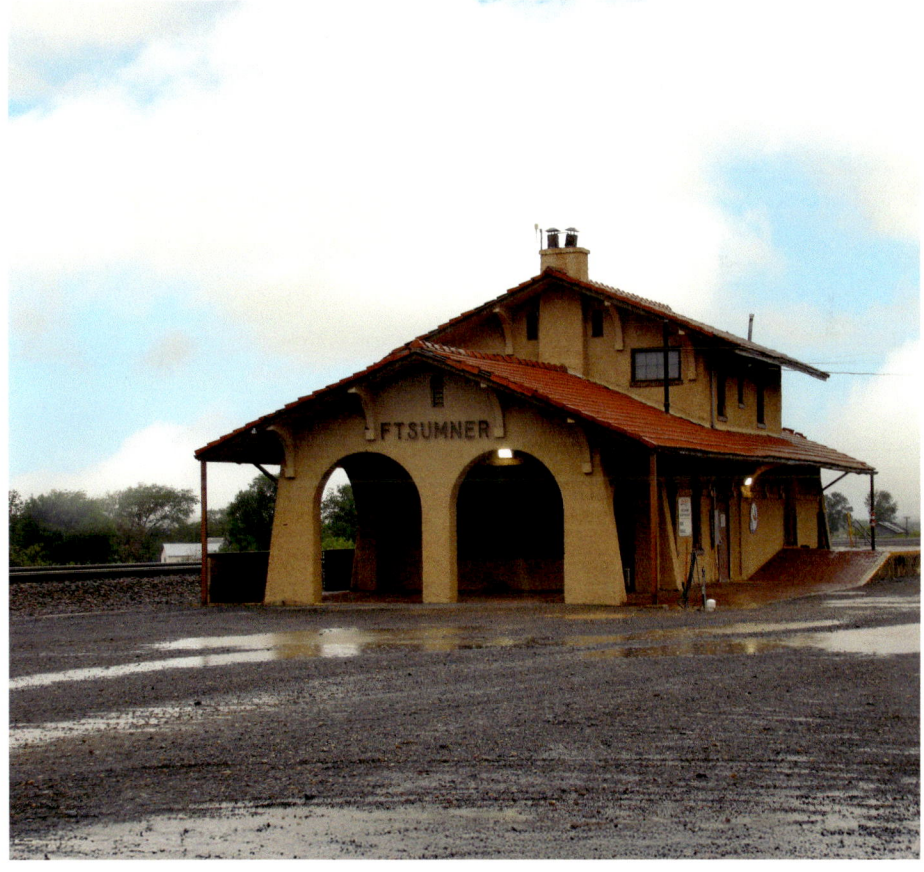

The Fort Sumner AT&SF train station is seen on a rainy day in May 2024. It is a typical Myron Church design constructed of concrete and stucco in Mission Revival style.

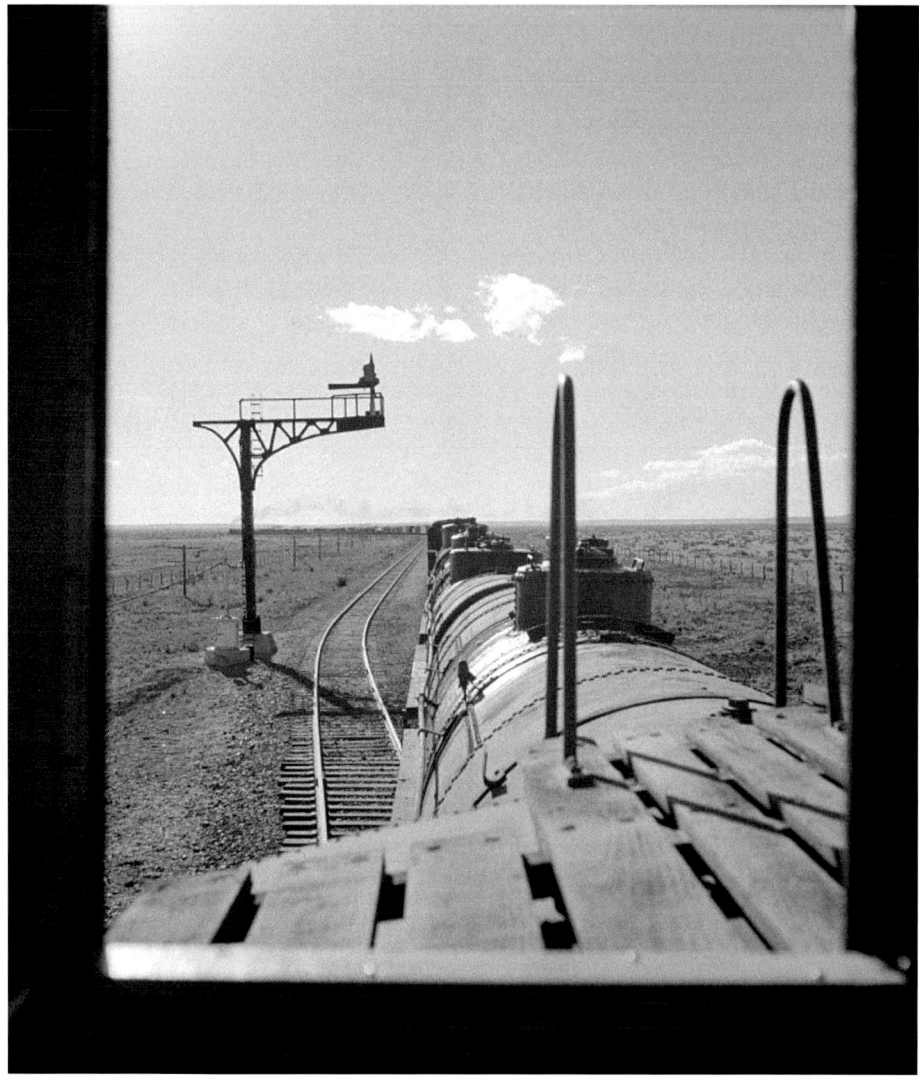

This is Jack Delano's view from the caboose at Fort Sumner. In the far distance the head of the train enters a curve to the bridge over the Pecos River. His train was powered by Engine 5004, a 2-10-4 (locomotive wheel alignment), with ninety-two cars and a total weight of 4,293 tons. (*Library of Congress, LC-USW3-020657-E*)

Opposite above: The train continued west at Fort Sumner with the engine starting to cross the bridge over the Pecos River. (*Library of Congress, LC-USW3-020649-E*)

Opposite below: A BNSF intermodal train heads east over the Pecos River bridge in May 2024.

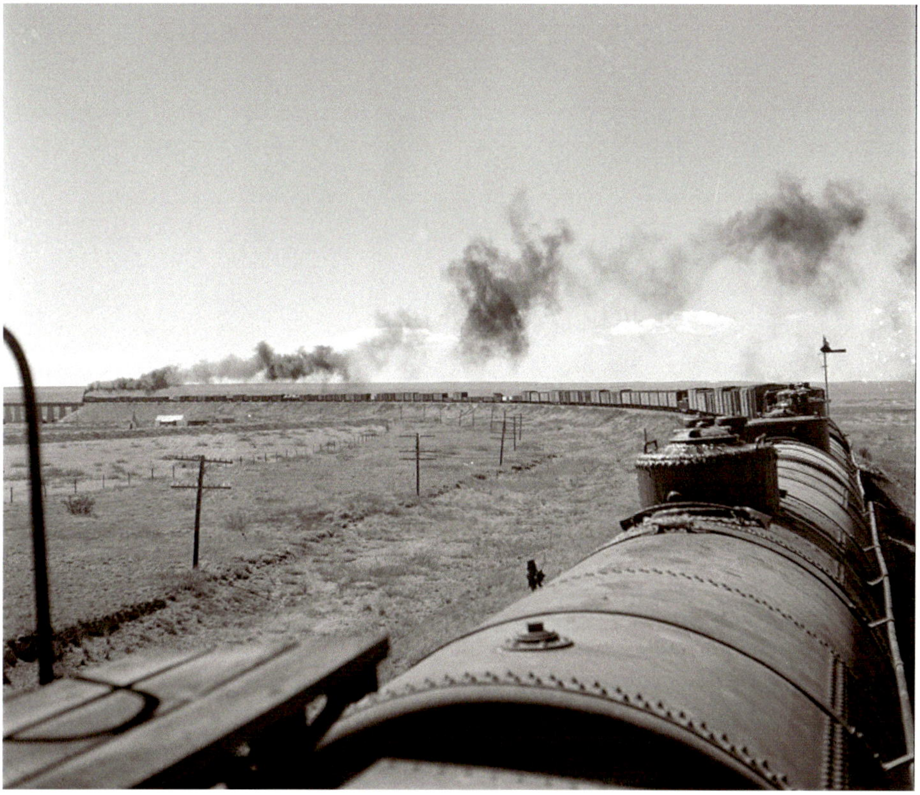

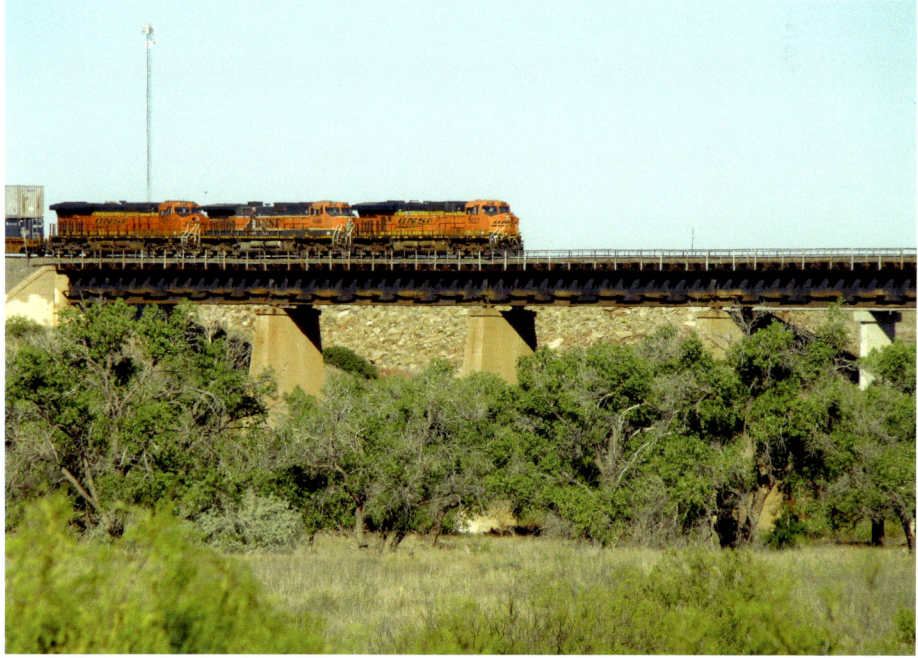

ALONG THE RAILS: FORT SUMNER TO VAUGHN

Heading west from Fort Sumner the next steam locomotive water stop was Ricardo, 14 miles away. "Ricardo was a railroad water station and section house that also had a hotel and post office. Nothing remains here now."[1] It was said to have been named after an AT&SF official. Jack Delano took two photographs at Ricardo on March 20, 1943.

Next on the Belen Cutoff heading west was the small town of Yeso, 14 miles from Ricardo. This was another water stop as illustrated by Jack Delano's photograph. Yeso was established in 1906 with the coming of the railroad. "Yeso" is the Spanish word for gypsum, and the town was named for the gypsum deposits on Mesa del Yeso which is 2 miles south of the village. Not much remains in Yeso today except for a modern post office across the street from the old, abandoned post office.

Some 12 miles west of Yeso, Jack Delano encountered the village of Buchanan established by the AT&SF in 1907. It was named for President James Buchanan (1857–1861).[2] Unfortunately, the town declined rapidly after its founding, probably due to its isolated location and scarcity of water.

Jack Delano photographed a passing water train at Duoro 13 miles west of Buchanan. These water trains were a necessity for the steam locomotives as there was no natural water between Vaughn and Agudo. The water tank cars were filled in Vaughn and then pumped out at these little villages into holding tanks where passing locomotives could fill up if necessary. Duoro had a train station and a post office until 1944 and is abandoned today. The source of its name is unknown.

Iden was a few miles southeast of Vaughn. It probably served as a siding for work trains, keeping the busy main line open for passage to Vaughn. Jack Delano took several photographs of a work train and track gang at Iden. These photographs help viewers today understand the nomadic life and hard work of a railroad track gang.

Just west of Iden, the site of Vaughn was selected as a division point for the AT&SF. The Belen Cutoff was built both from the west and from the east. Construction from the west reached Vaughn in 1905 and from the east in 1907. A turntable was built in 1907, followed in 1908 by a roundhouse, depot, and reading room. Vaughn was named for a civil engineer of the AT&SF, Major G. W. Vaughn. A Harvey House, "Las Chavez," was built in Vaughn in 1908. While the dining room served an eager public, the few hotel rooms in Las Chavez mainly were occupied by Harvey Girls and schoolteachers, as lodging was very limited in town. Las Chavez was closed in 1936 and eventually torn down, so it was not there to serve the troop trains of World War II.

ALONG THE RAILS: FORT SUMNER TO VAUGHN

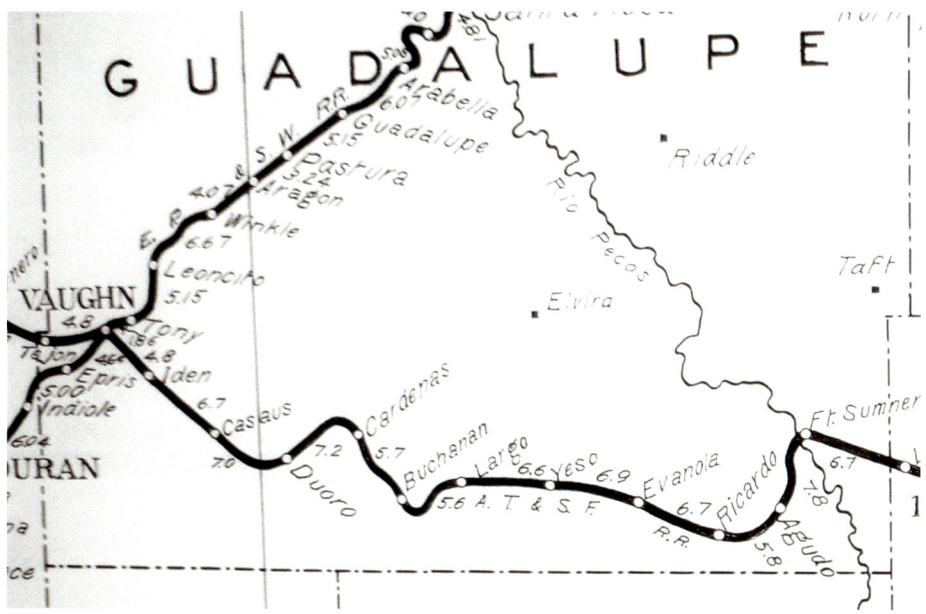

The route of Jack Delano's journey along the Belen Cutoff on the AT&SF from Fort Sumner to Vaughn is shown. (*New Mexico History Museum display*)

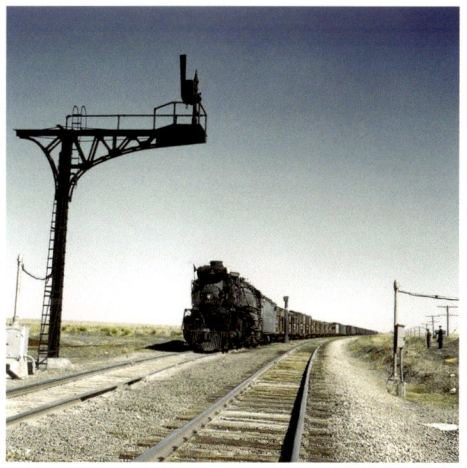
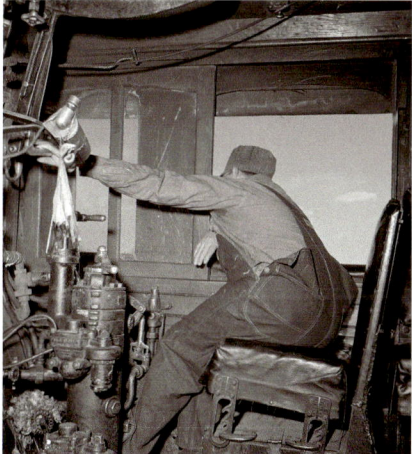

Above left: Jack Delano's color photograph of his westbound freight stopped on the siding at Ricardo waiting for an eastbound freight to pass. Delano had been riding in the locomotive cab as the next photo illustrates. (*Library of Congress, LC-USW361-685*)

Above right: Engineer B. L. Clark is starting the train after a stop at Ricardo, 14 miles west of Fort Sumner. (*Jack Delano photograph, Library of Congress, LC-USW3-020653-E*)

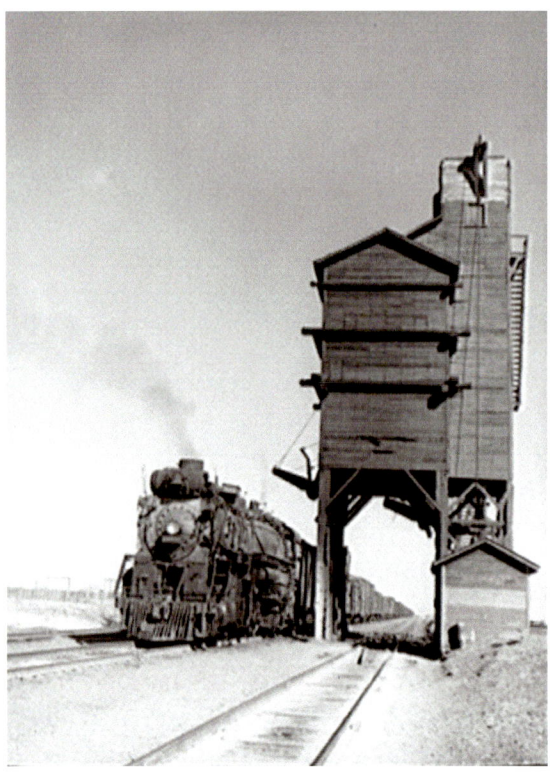

Left: Once again Jack Delano hopped out of the locomotive cab and photographed the train stopped for water at Yeso, 14 miles west of Ricardo. (*Library of Congress, LC-USW3-020427-D*)

Below: Yeso today is mainly a ghost town, but there is a new post office across the highway from this old abandoned one.

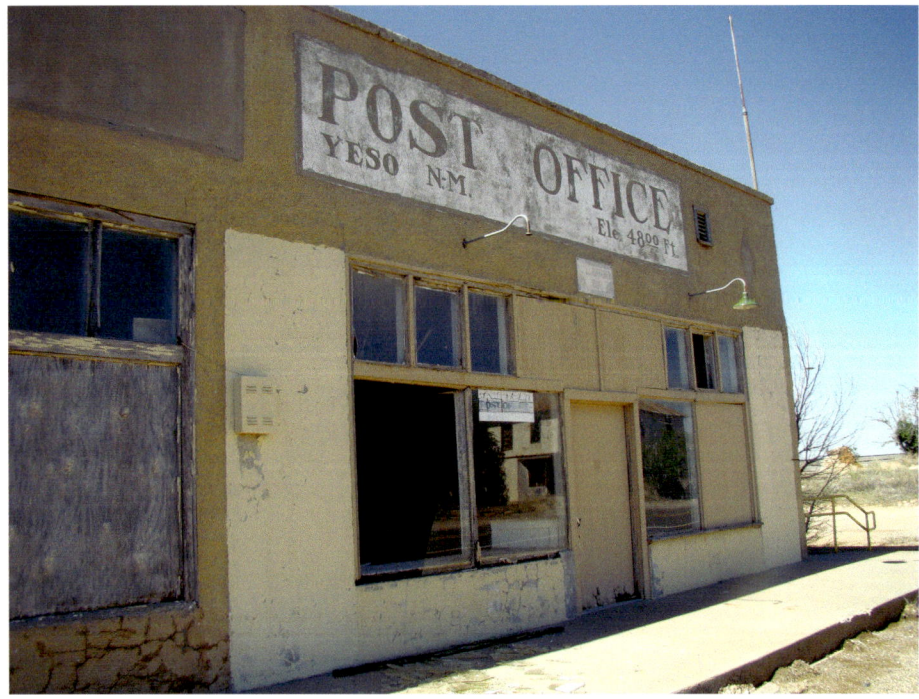

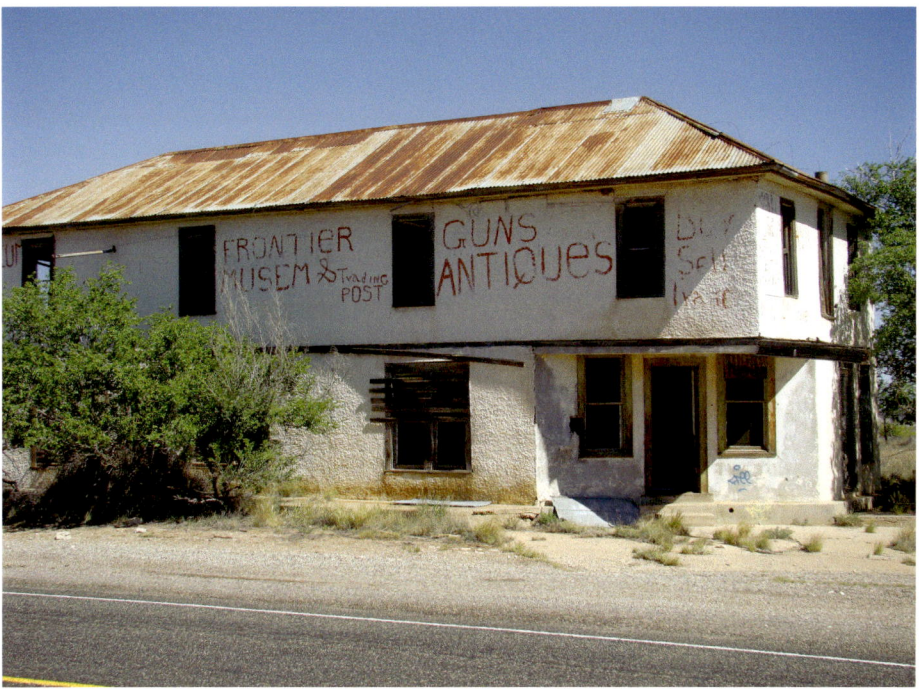

At one time the Frontier Museum and Trading Post in Yeso was a popular place to stop for guns and antiques for which they were willing to "buy, sell, trade."

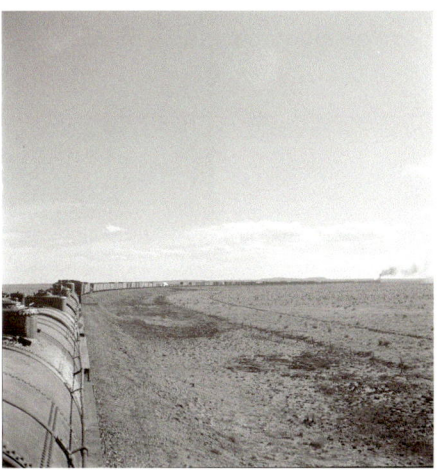 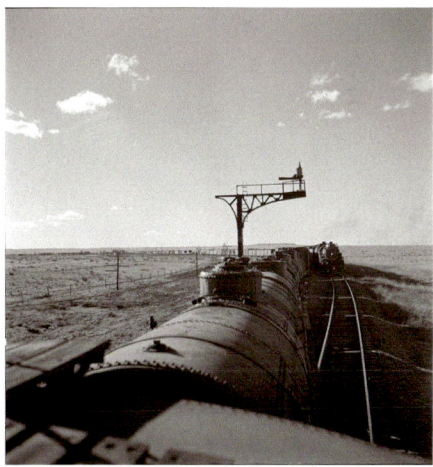

Above left: This photograph shows why Jack Delano liked riding in the caboose since he could photograph the entire length of the train, shown here at the curve at Buchanan. (*Library of Congress, LC-USW3-020662-E*)

Above right: From the caboose of his train, Jack Delano photographed this approaching eastbound train at Buchanan. This view illustrates the heavy traffic of the AT&SF on the Belen Cutoff during World War II. (*Library of Congress, LC-USW3-020666-E*)

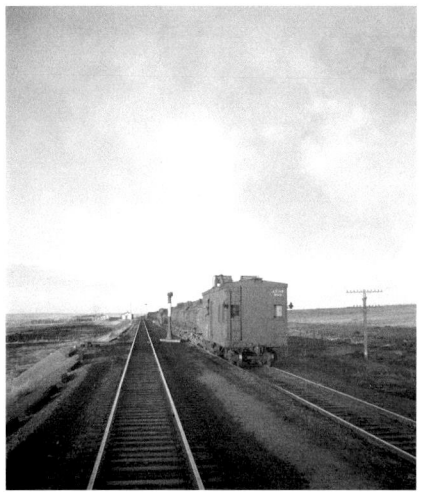 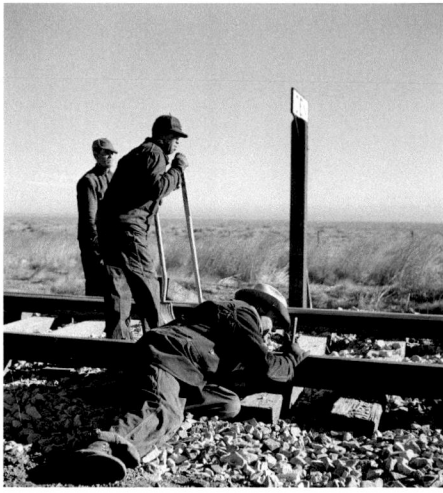

Above left: From the cupola of his caboose, Jack Delano photographed this eastbound water train at Duoro. Water cars were filled at Vaughn and headed east to distribute water to tanks along the line. Notice the boxcar converted to a caboose on the eastbound train. (*Library of Congress, LC-USW3-020677-E*)

Above right: At the Iden track sign, workers are raising, surfacing, and gauging the track. Track workers were primarily Hispanic and Native American. (*Jack Delano photograph, Library of Congress, LC-USW3-020683-E*)

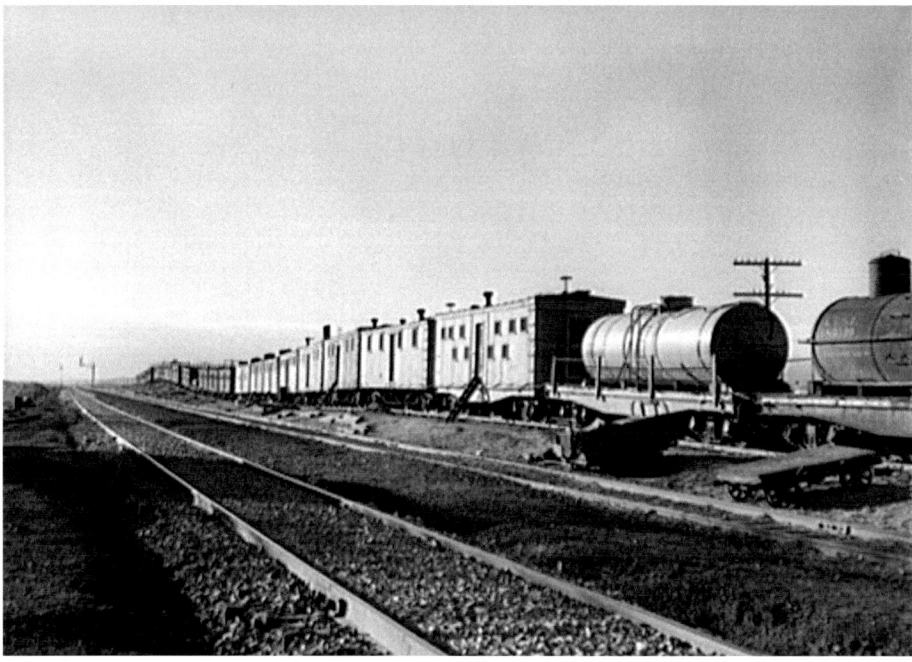

A work train is stopped at Iden with bunk cars and water cars for the track gangs. As a section of track was repaired, the train could move this workers' "hotel" to the next section of track which needed work. (*Jack Delano photograph, Library of Congress, LC-USW3-020529-D*)

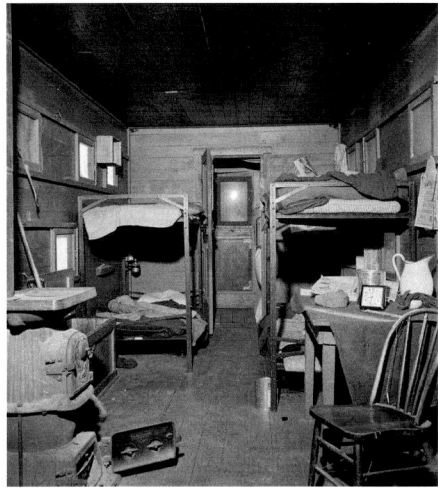 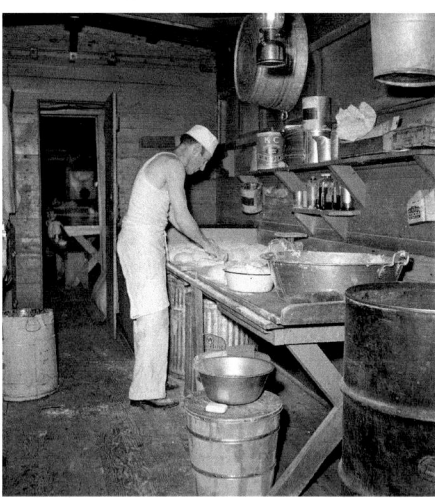

Above left: Inside of a bunk car of the work train at Iden. There were windows for the top and bottom bunks. (*Jack Delano photograph, Library of Congress, LC-USW3-020698-E*)

Above right: Baking bread in the kitchen of a work train at Iden. (*Jack Delano photograph, Library of Congress, LC-USW3-020696-E*)

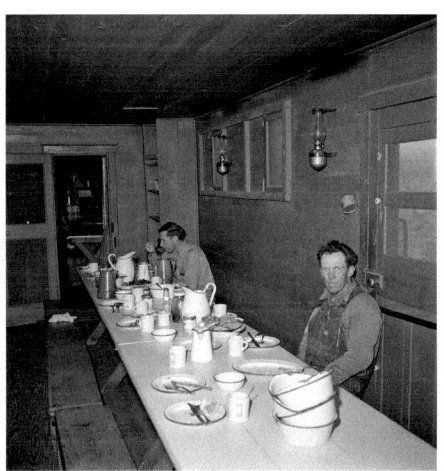 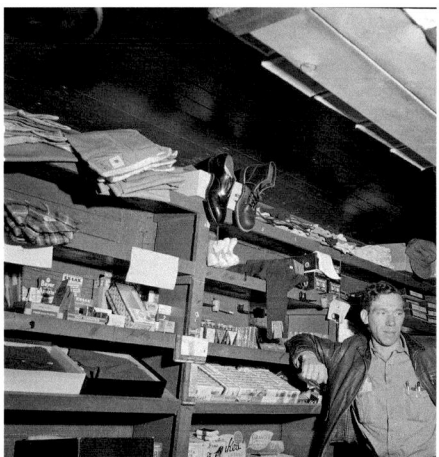

Above left: Track gang eating breakfast in the dining car of the work train at Iden. (*Jack Delano photograph, Library of Congress, LC-USW3-020695-E*)

Above right: The commissary car of the work train at Iden was well stocked with cigarettes, candy, aspirin, Ex-lax, clothing, and shoes. Clerk J. E. Straight of Newton, Kansas, manned the shop. (*Jack Delano photograph, Library of Congress, LC-USW3-020697-E*)

As we have seen, there was a severe shortage of water for steam engines from Vaughn east to Agudo:

> Vaughn was plagued by a lack of water. The Santa Fe built two underground concrete cisterns and a steel water tank in 1908. Water for the reading room, hotel and depot was hauled in tank cars from Willard and Negra. The El Paso & Southwestern Railroad's water [in Vaughn] came from a pipeline to Bonito Creek in Lincoln County a hundred miles away. In late 1909, the Santa Fe signed a contract with the other railroad to siphon water off the pipe into one of its reservoirs at a rate of 24 cents per thousand gallons. This water was for the repair shops and steam engines.[3]

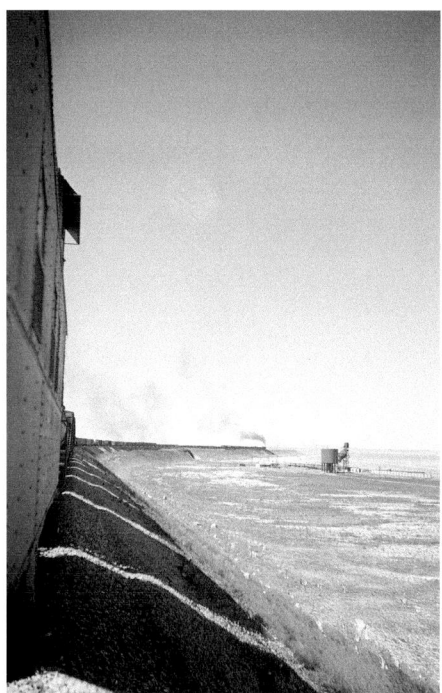 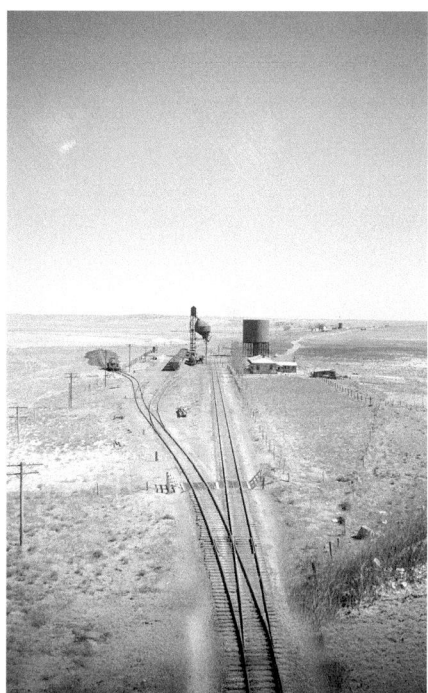

Above left: At Vaughn, Jack Delano's view from the caboose allowed him to photograph his AT&SF train crossing over the tracks of the Southern Pacific (El Paso & Southwestern) Railroad. The Southern Pacific had a water tank and coaling tower at Vaughn. (*Library of Congress, LC-USW3-020717-E*)

Above right: Delano's view of the Southern Pacific facilities at Vaughn, as his train crossed the overpass. The AT&SF purchased water from a Southern Pacific pipeline at Vaughn. (*Library of Congress, LC-USW3-020718-E*)

ALONG THE RAILS: FORT SUMNER TO VAUGHN

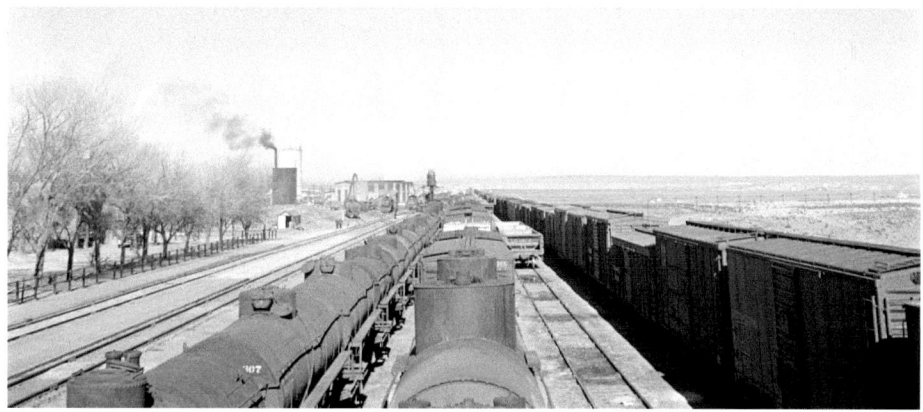

The Vaughn railyard with a string of water cars to the left and freight cars to the right, with the roundhouse in the distance. (*Jack Delano photograph, Library of Congress, LC-USW3-020691-E*)

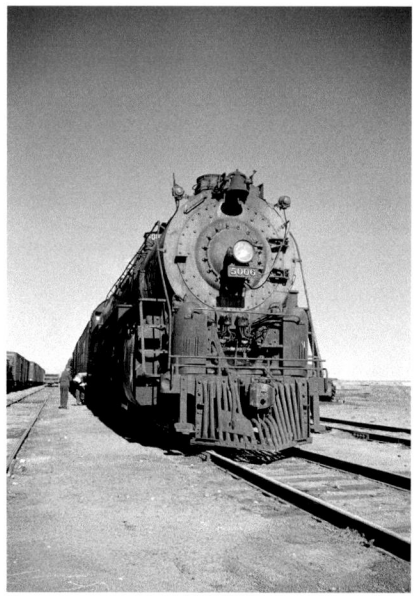 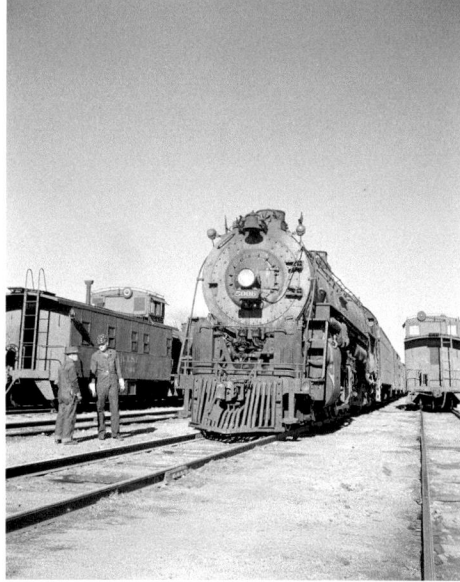

Above left: Inspecting Engine 5006 before departure from Vaughn. (*Jack Delano photograph, Library of Congress, LC-USW3- 020708-E*)

Above right: Engine 5006 was about ready to roll eastbound in this Delano photograph at the Vaughn railyard. (*Library of Congress, LC-USW3-020689-E*)

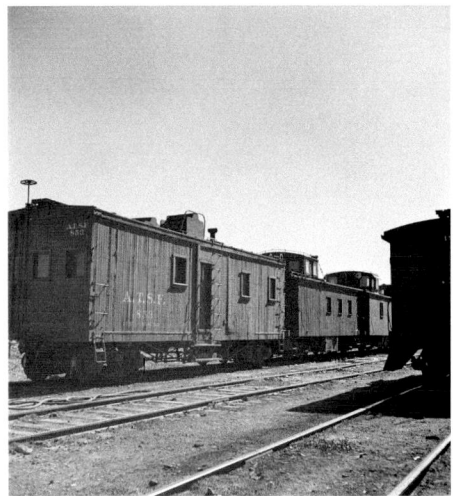 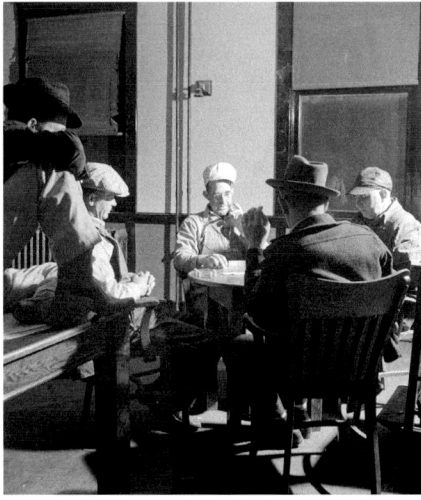

Above left: The AT&SF had a severe shortage of cabooses during World War II, so the railroad converted boxcars to cabooses, such as these shown at Vaughn. The cupola of the caboose was where the conductor and rear brakeman could view their train ahead and spot hot boxes or other signs of trouble, signaling the engineer to stop if necessary. On these converted boxcars, for a cupola a two-sided bench with a common back was installed on top. (*Jack Delano photograph, Library of Congress, LC-USW3-020710-E*)

Above right: The AT&SF provided reading rooms for the relaxation of their crews at some of the stations. Here, Jack Delano witnessed men playing dominoes at Vaughn. (*Library of Congress, LC-USW3-020693-E*)

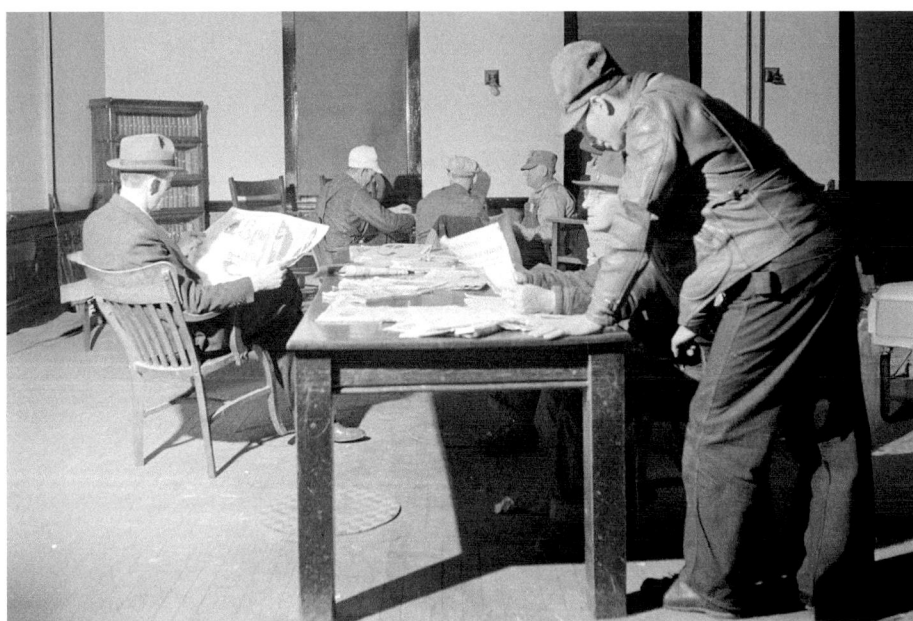

Other activities in the reading room at Vaughn included reading newspapers and books. (*Library of Congress, LC-USW3-020694-E*)

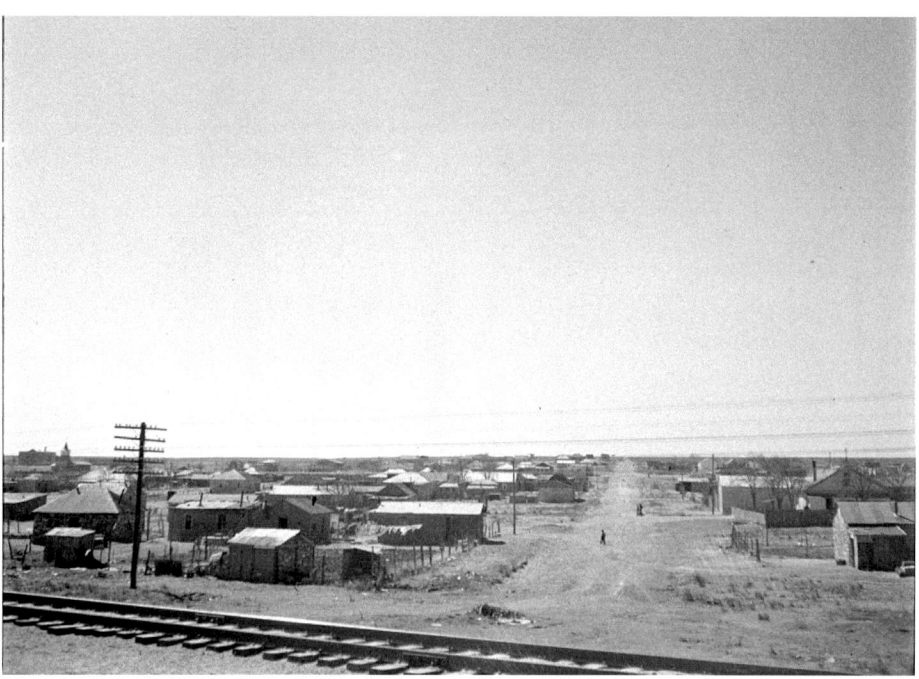

Jack Delano photographed this view of Vaughn, a dusty town on the central New Mexico plains, on March 19, 1943. (*Library of Congress, LC-USW3-020714-E*)

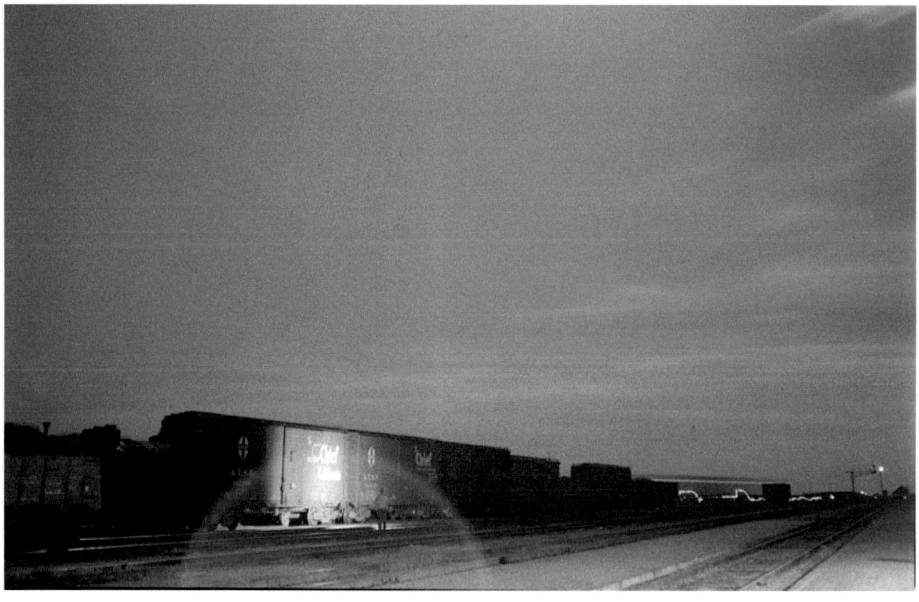

A unique Jack Delano night photograph with a train inspector shining his light in the Vaughn railyard. (*Library of Congress, LC-USW3-020679-E*)

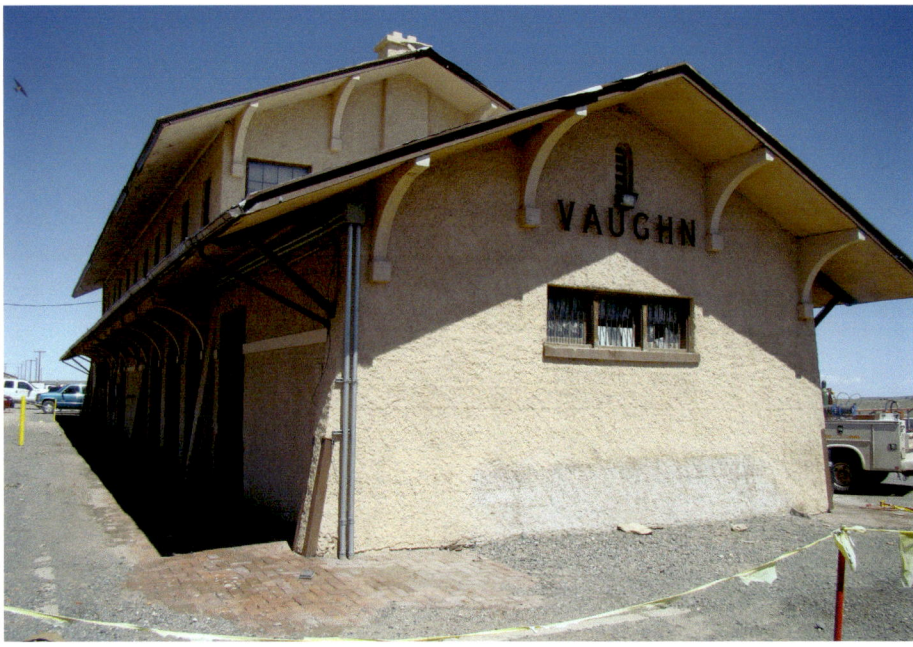

The Vaughn station in 2024 reveals another of Myron Church's Mission Revival-style buildings constructed of concrete, stucco, and arches.

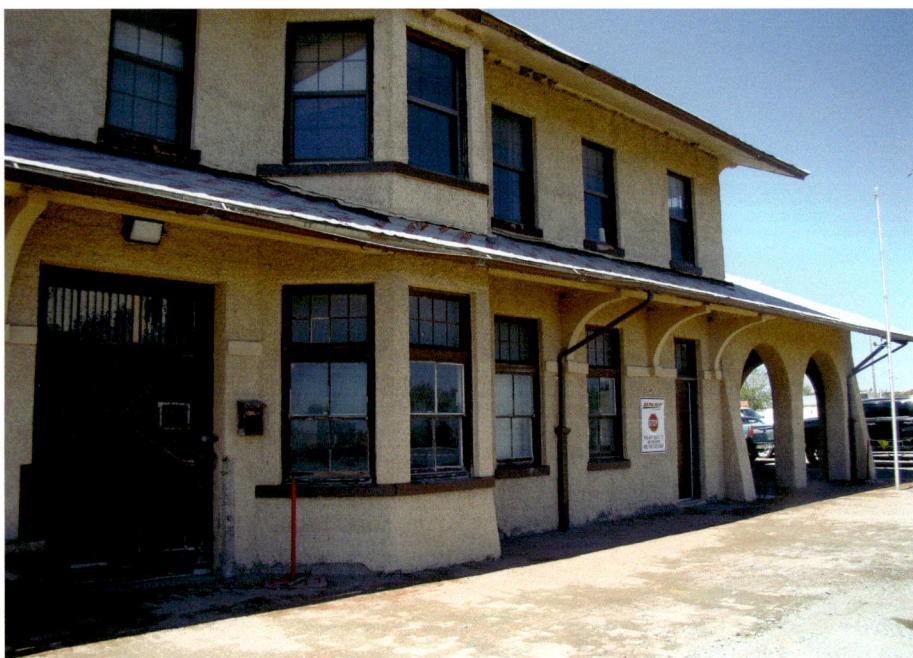

The Vaughn station has a two-story agent's bay window. Vaughn was a busy yard with many trains passing through during World War II just as it is today with the BNSF transcontinental intermodal trains.

7

ALONG THE RAILS: VAUGHN TO BELEN

Traveling west on the AT&SF in March 1943, Jack Delano photographed scenes at Encino, 17 miles west of Vaughn. There was a spring about a mile south of town which supplied water for the thirsty steam engines. "Encino" is Spanish for "oak," referring to the scrub oak that "once was common in the area. Intensive sheep ranching later destroyed this growth."[1] In fact, "both sheep and cattle ranchers settled on the endless plains surrounding the town. Mariano Mondosa had 40,000 head of sheep at one time."[2] The town itself was created in 1904 during construction of the Belen Cutoff. By 1905, a train station had been built. The station closed in 1965, and it marked the decline of Encino. BNSF double-stack container trains roar through the village today, paralleling U.S. Highway 60.

Some 5 miles west of Encino, the rails ran through the little village of Negra, a Spanish word for "black," possibly referring to the soil in the area. Negra had water and it supplied water tank cars sent east to Vaughn. Nothing remains of Negra today.

Other small villages and sidings heading west included Pedernal, Culebria, Lucy, and Silio. Traveling west on U.S. Highway 60 today, there is no sign of these locations. The next village is Willard, and it still exists today with many dilapidated buildings along the highway. Willard was founded in 1902 with the arrival of the AT&SF. "Railroad promoter Willard Samuel Hopewell named the fledgling station for his son, Willard Samuel Hopewell Jr."[3] Willard also had water which was shipped in tank cars to Vaughn. Willard was the center of a vast pinto bean growing area. The *WPA Guide to 1930s New Mexico* noted that "west of Willard are raised most of the pinto beans grown in the United States. New Mexicans eat large quantities of pinto beans and chili, which are very nourishing."[4]

The town of Mountainair (at 6,550 feet elevation), 14 miles west of Willard, is by far the largest town between Vaughn and Belen. Mountainair was founded in 1903 by speculators hoping that the Belen Cutoff would come through there. However, it was not until 1908 when the Cutoff was finally finished, that a depot was built at Mountainair. The town is named after "the delightful summer breezes from the Manzano Mountains nearby to the north."[5] The concrete and masonry depot, designed by Myron Church, was the smallest of the three standard AT&SF depots at 81 feet long. However, "the baggage and freight rooms, with a railcar-level loading platform, were relatively large due to high freight traffic through Mountainair, where prolific bean harvests gave the area the nickname the Pinto Bean Capital of the World."[6]

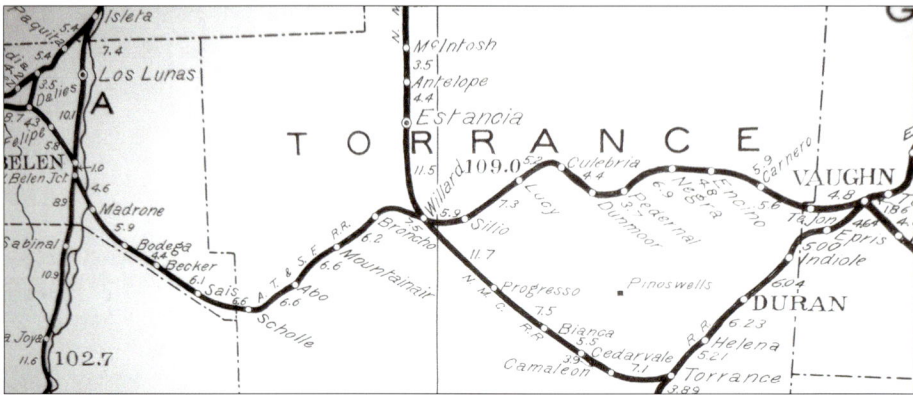

The 1913 railroad map of New Mexico showed the AT&SF route from Vaughn west to Willard, Mountainair and Belen, with the north–south route of the Southern Pacific intersecting and heading south to Duran. (*New Mexico History Museum display*)

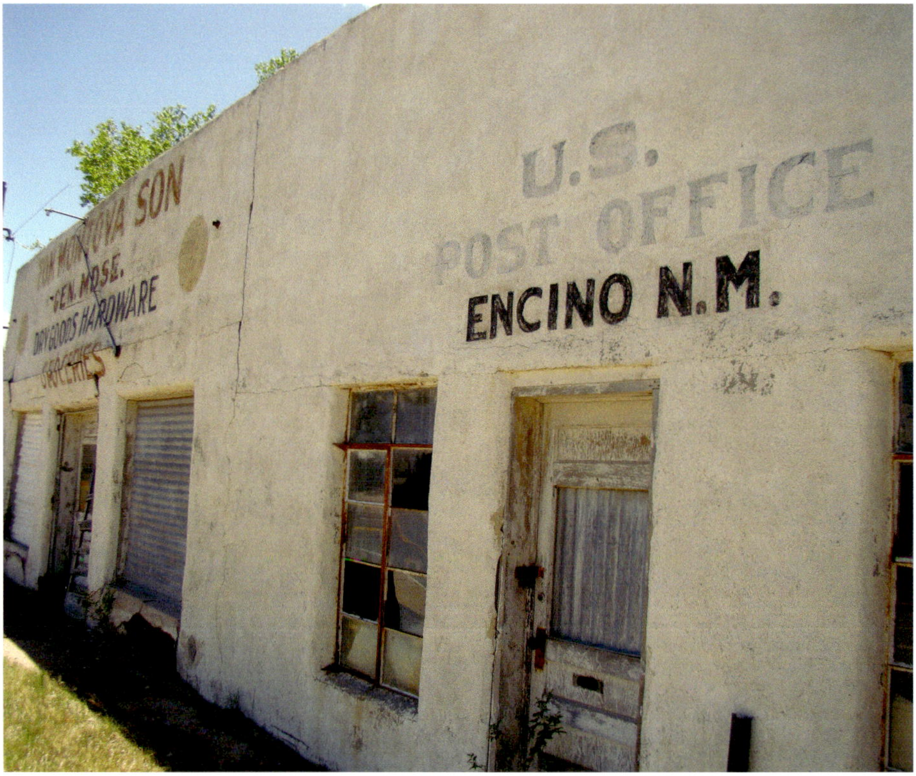

Abandoned Encino post office and Montoya general store seen in 2024. The railroad tracks are one block south of here. There is a new post office across the highway from the abandoned one.

ALONG THE RAILS: VAUGHN TO BELEN 57

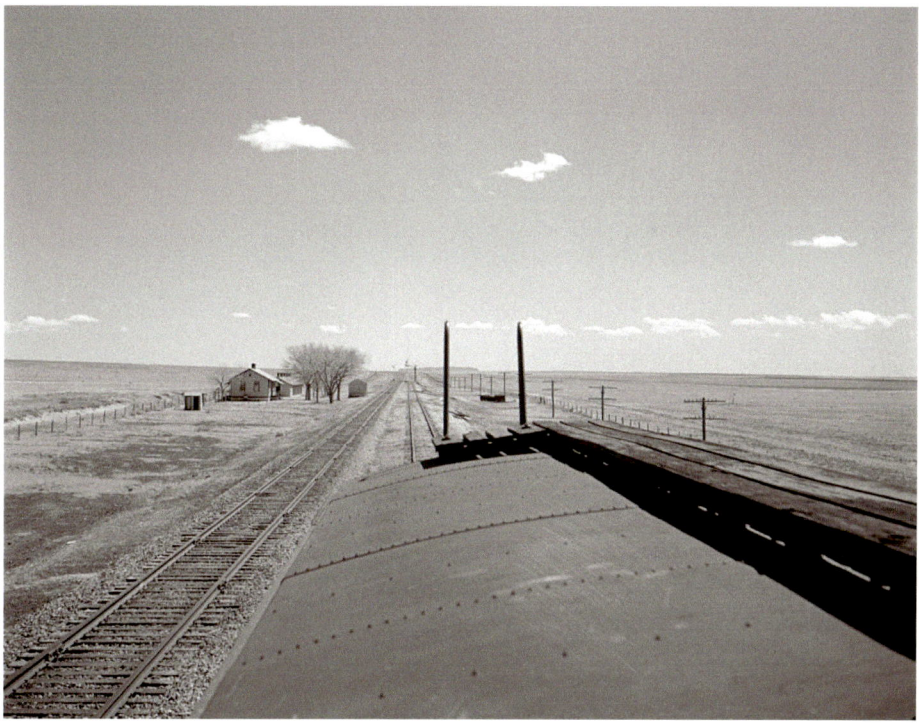

Looking out the rear of the caboose cupola, Jack Delano shot this view of the section house at Dunmoor. (*Library of Congress, LC-USW3-020726-E*)

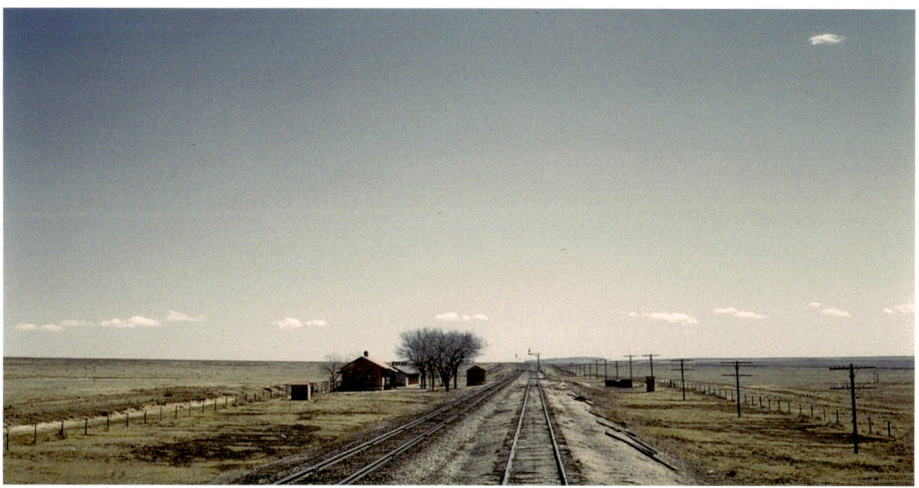

This is Delano's color photograph of the section house at Dunmoor. A section house is where a track section manager and his family lived. (*Library of Congress, LC-USW361-684*)

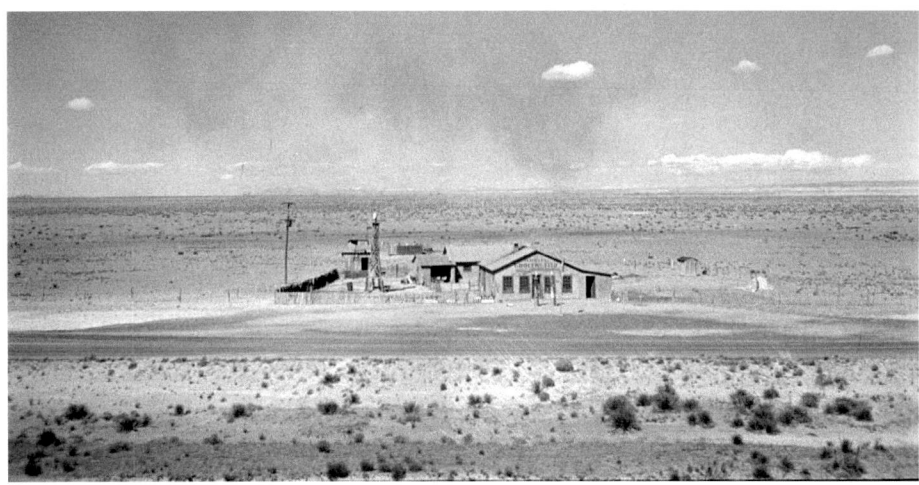

Jack Delano photographed this lonely gas station on the plains at Willard as his AT&SF train passed by heading west. (*Library of Congress, LC-USW3-020737-E*)

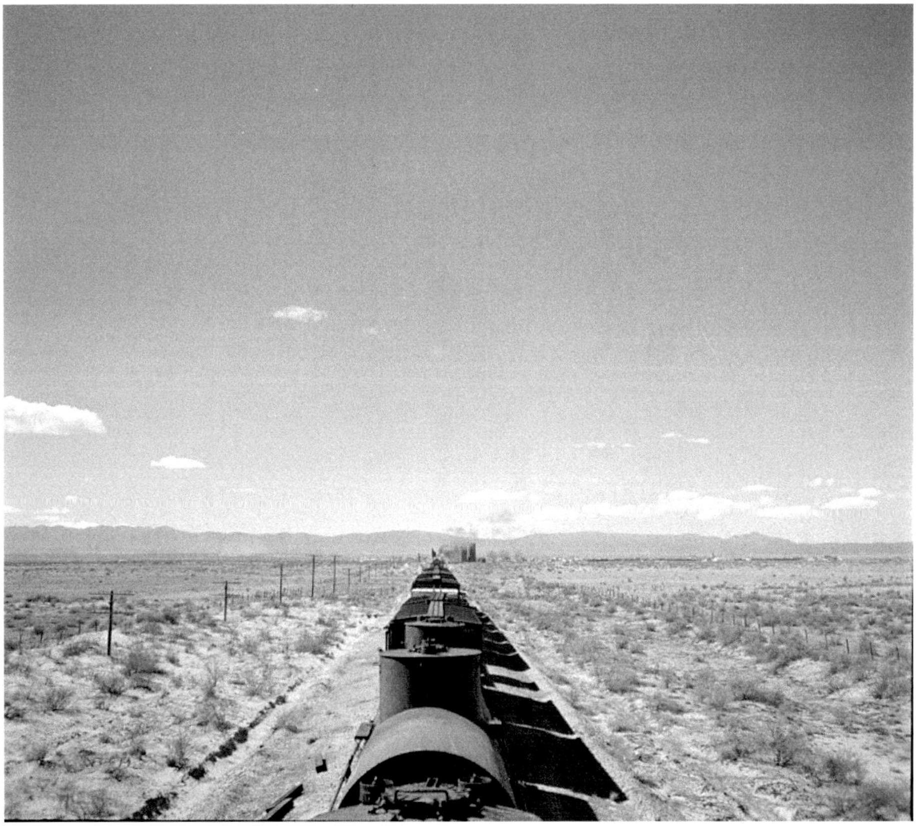

Jack Delano's train stops for water for the engine at Willard with the Manzano Mountains in the distance. (*Library of Congress, LC-USW3-020731-E*)

At the height of the pinto bean era over thirty million pounds of pinto beans were shipped from bean elevators in Mountainair each year.... The Trinidad Bean & Elevator Company from Colorado built elevators in Colorado and New Mexico and had their largest elevator in Mountainair. It was equipped to hold 150 forty thousand-pound cars of pinto beans. The Trinidad Company opened in 1918 and closed in 1945.[7]

Today, Mountainair is somewhat of a tourist destination (offering some relief from the heat of Albuquerque) with art galleries and the quaint Shaffer Hotel, constructed in 1923. Railfans will not be disappointed at Mountainair as BNSF freight trains roar through town every ten to fifteen minutes.

The village of Abo is 7 miles southwest of Mountainair. It is situated at the eastern mouth of Abo Canyon, which presented quite a challenge to the builders of the Belen Cutoff.

On October 30, 1902, the Santa Fe created a subsidiary, the Eastern Railway of New Mexico, specifically to build the line, and grading began in 1903. Since Abo Pass ... was the steepest and therefore most complex portion to build, construction began there early in the year, but by July only twenty miles had been graded.[8]

After years of financial difficulties, the Belen Cutoff was finally completed in 1908. "Abo" is an Ancestral Puebloan word meaning "water bowl." The Abo ruins are a half-mile north of Abo village and today are included in the Salinas Pueblo Missions National Monument. "In 1629 Fray Francisco de Acevedo founded the Mission of San Gregorio here by building adjacent to the pueblo a large church."[9] But the mission church and pueblo could not withstand frequent attacks from the Apache, and they were abandoned by the 1670s with the Puebloans migrating west to the Rio Grande pueblos.

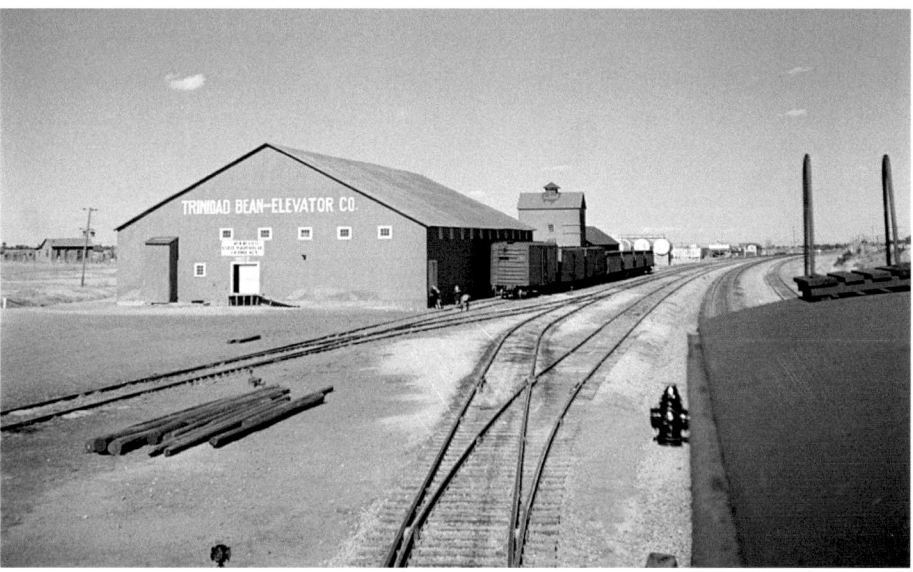

The Trinidad Bean Elevator Company in Mountainair was named after Trinidad, Colorado. The company had bean elevators in Colorado and New Mexico. (*Jack Delano photograph, Library of Congress, LC=USW3-020744-E*)

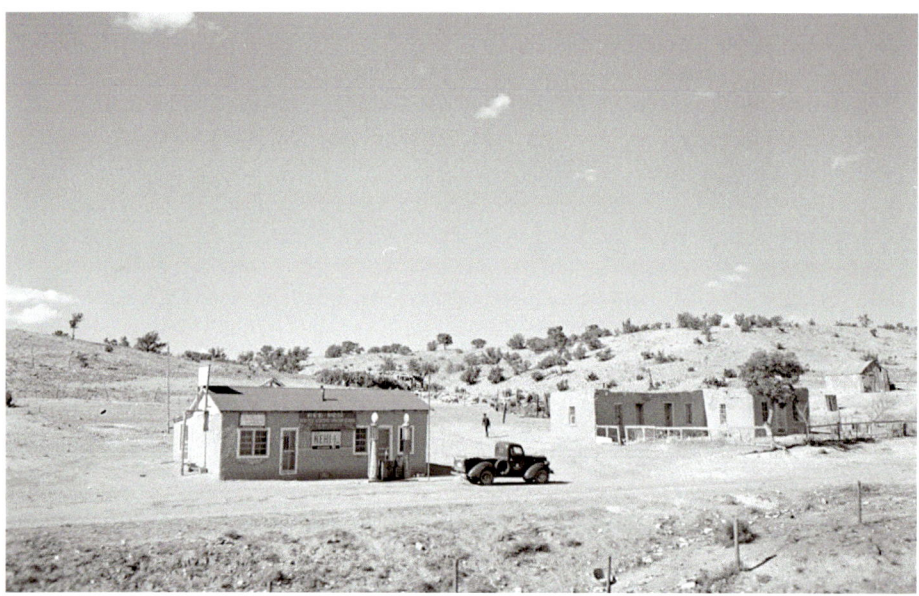

A gas station and homes in Mountainair seen as Jack Delano's train passed by. (*Library of Congress, LC-USW3-020746-E*)

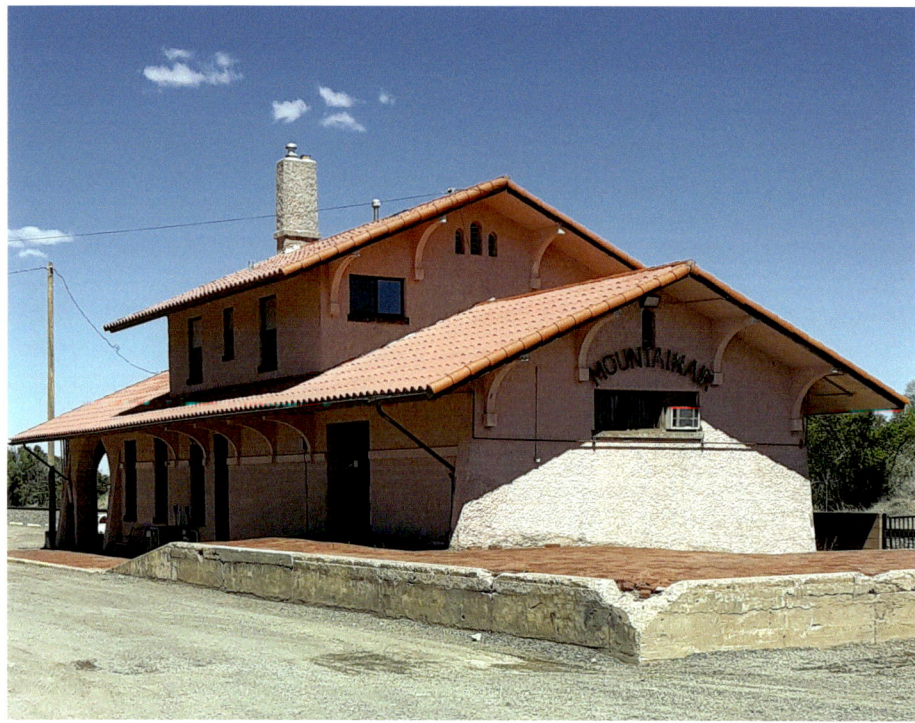

The train station in Mountainair in 2024, is the smallest of the Myron Church designs, being only 81 feet in length. (*Mary Jane Butler photograph*)

During World War II, the AT&SF feared possible enemy sabotage of the bridges in Abo Canyon. B. M. Naylor described the situation:

> In Abo Canyon our track crossed six or seven high bridges and wound through deep rock cuts that were very vulnerable spots to anyone who would want to cripple the railroad. A few shots of explosives at any of the bridges or cuts would have stopped this line of the Santa Fe Railroad for quite a while.... I was to get started at once to provide guards or watchmen for the bridges and other places where sabotage might occur.[10]

Fortunately, there was no sabotage of the line during the war. After World War II, freight traffic on the AT&SF line continued to increase. Abo Canyon became a major bottleneck with its single-track line, causing trains to wait for long periods on sidings at Scholle or Abo.

> By 1990, AT&SF began plans to run double tracks through Abo Pass, which continued when the line became part of the BNSF Railroad.... [The number of trains] had risen to 80–100 trains a day. That's a 100-car train through Abo Pass about every 15 minutes—equivalent to about 35 million semi-truck loads of merchandise and equipment per year.[11]

A twenty-year project was begun to construct a new canyon through Abo Pass, because the original canyon was too narrow to allow for a second track. This massive project was completed in 2011, and the Belen Cutoff was now double-track all the way from Belen to Texico.

Some 7 miles west of the village of Abo, the town of Scholle sat at the eastern entrance of Abo Canyon. The town was named after Fred Scholle, one of the pioneer settlers. The AT&SF built a siding and depot here in 1906:

> Because minerals in the water at Scholle made it unfit for steam engines, the railroad piped in good, mineral-free water from the spring at Abo.... Scholle had a post office by 1908 and the beginnings

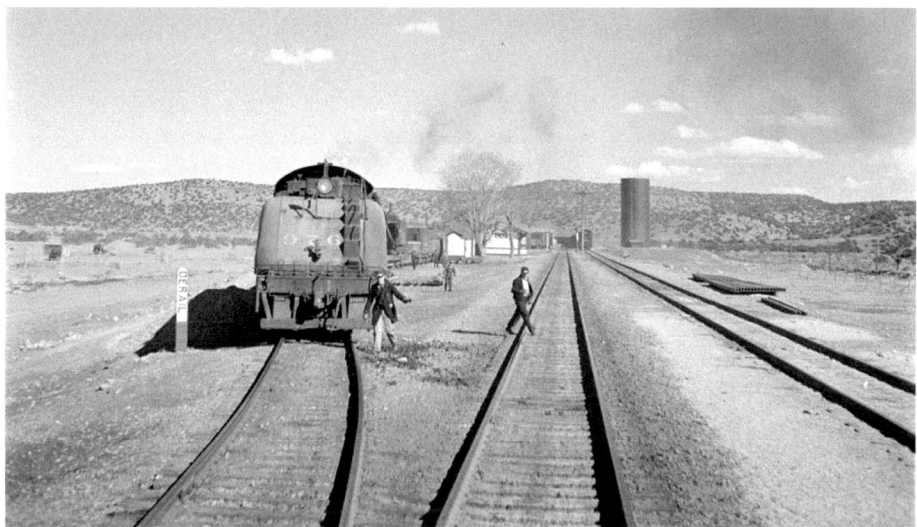

A conductor guides an engine and tender on the siding at Scholle as a train approaches in the distance by the water tank. (*Jack Delano photograph, Library of Congress, LC-USW3-020749-E*)

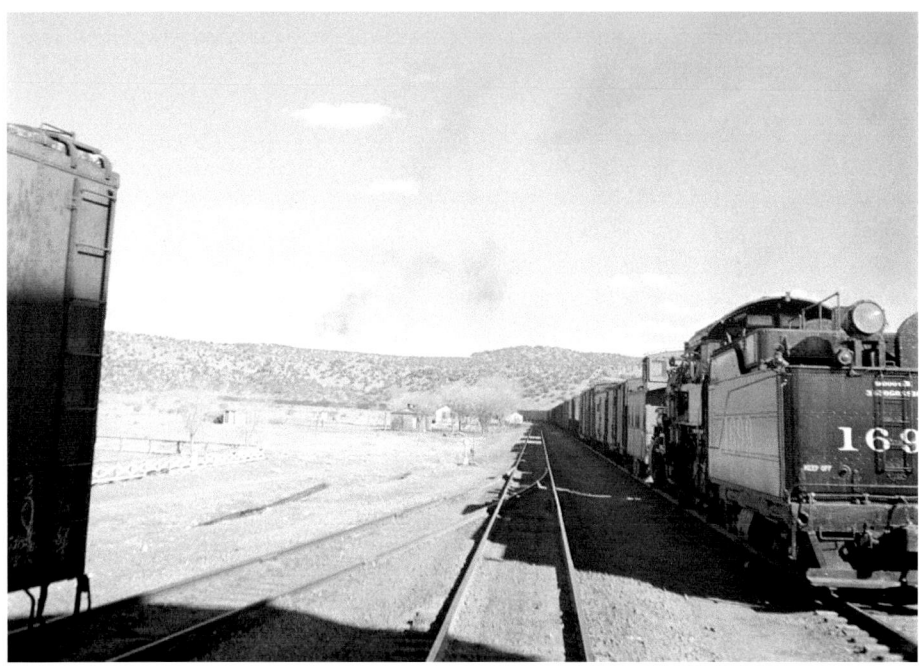

At Scholle, Engine 1699 is a rear-train helper pushing the long freight over Abo Pass to Mountainair where it will be decoupled, turned on the wye, and returned to Belen. (*Jack Delano photograph, Library of Congress, LC-USW3-020748-E*)

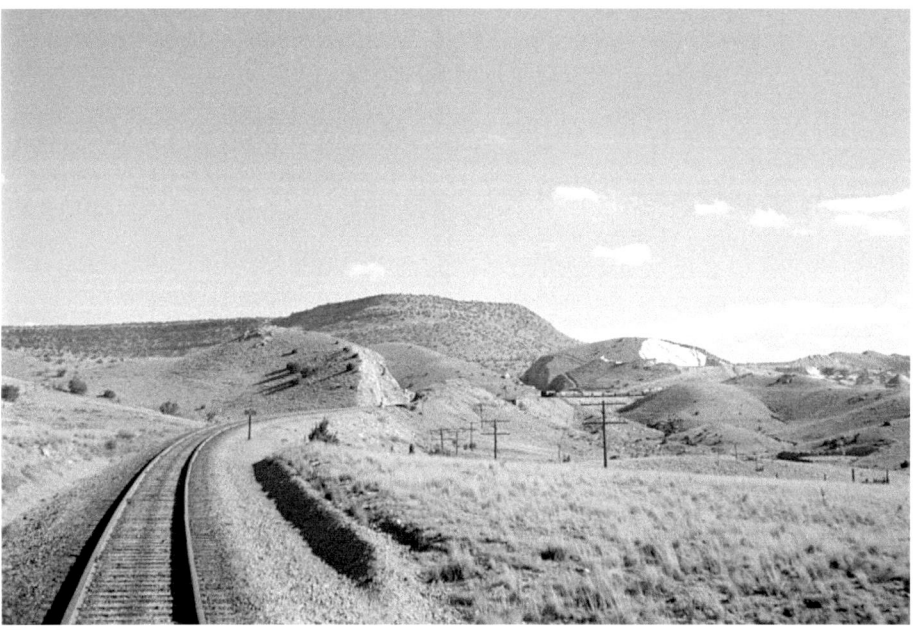

AT&SF track with a gravel mine on the hillside in the distance probably near Sais where there was a crusher. (*Jack Delano photograph, Library of Congress, LC-USW3-020754-E*)

of a community for dozens of families.... Many of these families worked for the railroad on the local section gang that maintained the tracks. Over the next few decades, the settlement grew in size to include a school, various stores, a hotel, a ballroom, a freight depot, station, and scales and loading pens for livestock.... During the late 1940s ... more cattle were shipped from Scholle than any other location in New Mexico.[12]

By the 1950s, drought and better paying jobs elsewhere led to the abandonment of Scholle. The Library of Congress online collection of Jack Delano OWI photographs did not contain any photographs of Scholle from his train trip through there in March 1943.

At the west entrance of Abo Canyon, the village of Sais perched on the high plains. It was named after the Mexican family of Saiz which settled in this area after 1692. Sais had a rock crushing plant which provided ballast for the railroad ties of the AT&SF.

AT&SF stationed some of their employees at the crusher, including an engineer to oversee operations and a brakeman responsible for loading boxcars full of ballast onto trains. Dozens of men would be employed seasonally during blasting and quarry operations. A number of workers lived at the crusher in boxcars or crosstie shacks that served as homes for their families.[13]

Six miles west of Sais and 16 miles southeast of Belen was the village of Becker, a water stop for AT&SF steam engines. It was named for John Becker, a German immigrant who with his partner Paul B. Dalies "formed the Becker-Dalies Co. in Belen and their store was long a local landmark.... Because Becker and Dalies were leaders in having the railroad come through Belen, via the Belen Cutoff, the AT&SF named the first water tank east of Belen for Becker and the first one northwest for Dalies."[14]

Crossing the Rio Grande about a mile south of Belen, the AT&SF headed north to its division point there. The history of Belen dates to 1740 when a land grant known as Nuestra Señora de Belen (Our Lady of Bethlehem) was established. A farming and ranching community soon grew up on the land grant. In 1880 the AT&SF crossed through Belen on its north–south route from Albuquerque to El Paso. When the east–west Belen Cutoff was completed in 1908, Belen became known as "Hub City." Jack Delano rode the rails from Belen to Dalies to Isleta and Albuquerque from March 20–24, 1943. His photographs reveal the great amount of AT&SF activity in Belen during World War II years. Besides the AT&SF depot, Belen had a Harvey House, roundhouse, machine shops, a coaling station and an ice plant, "but now only the depot and Harvey House remain."[15] Diesel fueling stations have replaced the coaling station, and the coupling and uncoupling of freight cars takes place at all hours in the busy Belen classification yard today.

The Belen Harvey House was completed about 1910. It had a forty-five-seat lunchroom and a sixty-four-seat dining room. The upstairs rooms were never hotel rooms but were used as housing for the Harvey Girls who worked in the eating rooms. After World War II "the railroad converted the building into a reading room where railroad workers could socialize, play cards, and read books and magazines. Some may also have boarded in the former Harvey Girl bedrooms upstairs."[16] The AT&SF discontinued use of the building in 1980, and by 1982 planned to demolish it. However, it was saved by a dedicated group of citizens, restored, and today serves as the Belen Harvey House Museum.

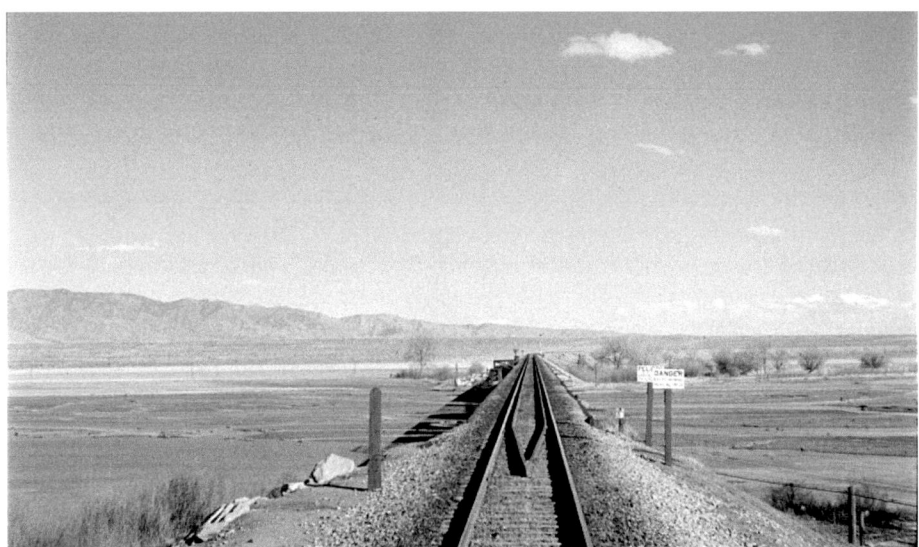

From the caboose, Jack Delano shot this scene of the AT&SF bridge over the Rio Grande as the train proceeded into Belen. The Manzano Mountains are in the distance. (*Library of Congress, LC-USW3-020761-E*)

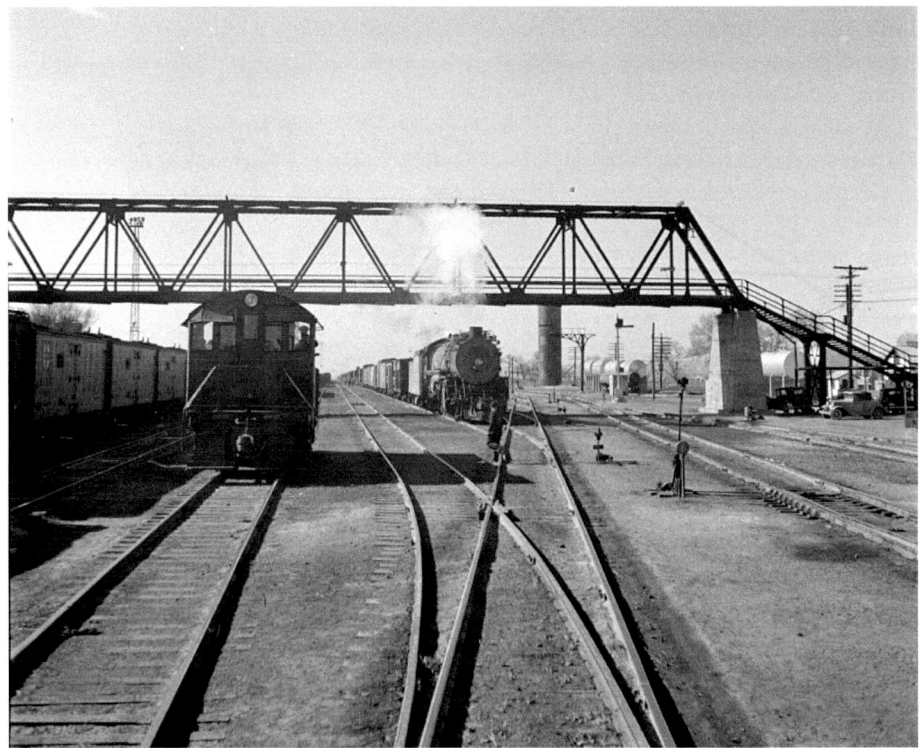

On March 20, 1943, Jack Delano captured this scene in the Belen railyard with a diesel switch engine on the left and a steam locomotive on the right. (*Library of Congress, LC-USW3-021132-E*)

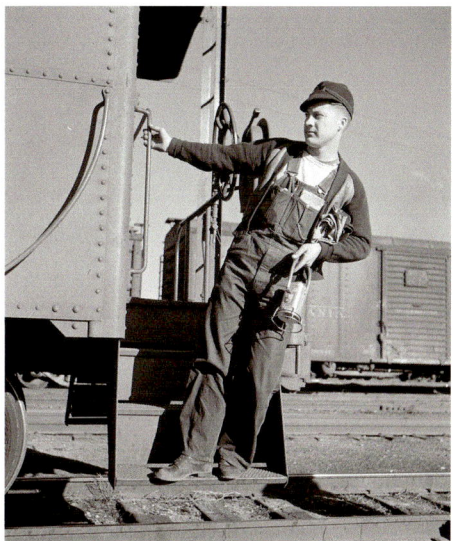 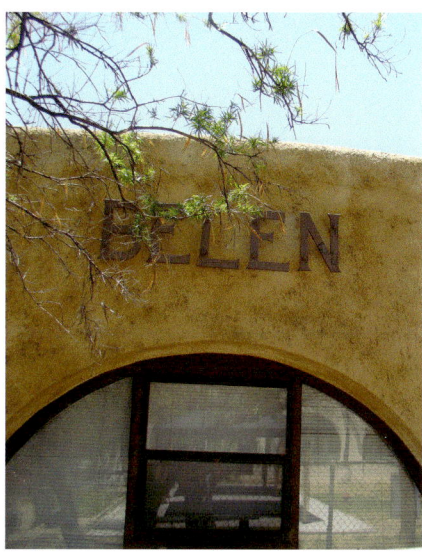

Above left: Brakeman Charlie Kirkland on the caboose in the Belen railyard. (*Jack Delano photograph, Library of Congress, LC-USW3-020762-E*)

Above right: The Belen train station is very difficult to photograph today. It is totally enclosed by BNSF fencing, there is a tree covering the north end of the station, and there is a BNSF building attached to the south end of the station.

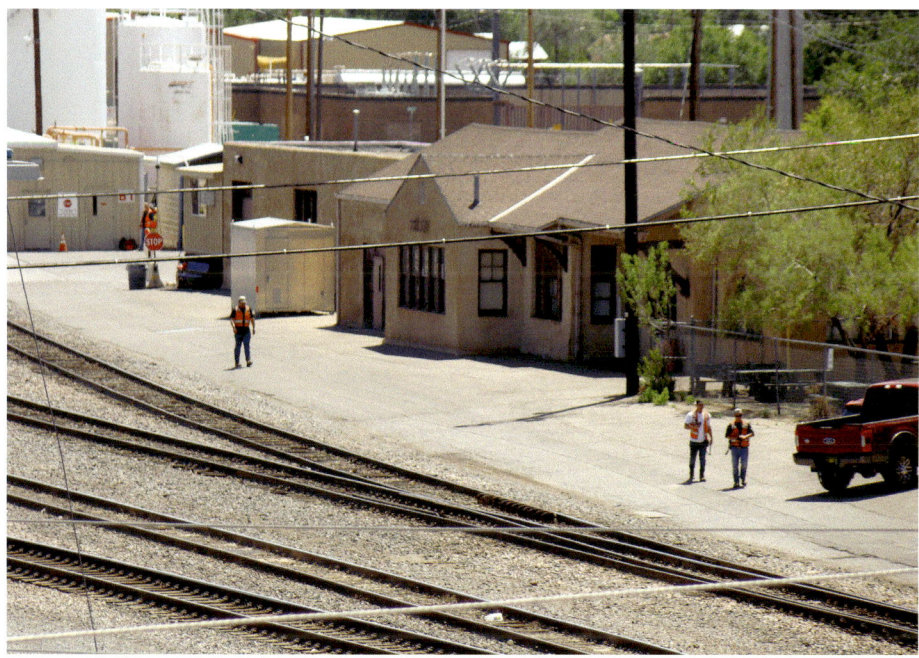

The Belen station seen in 2024 from the roadway overpass of the railyard.

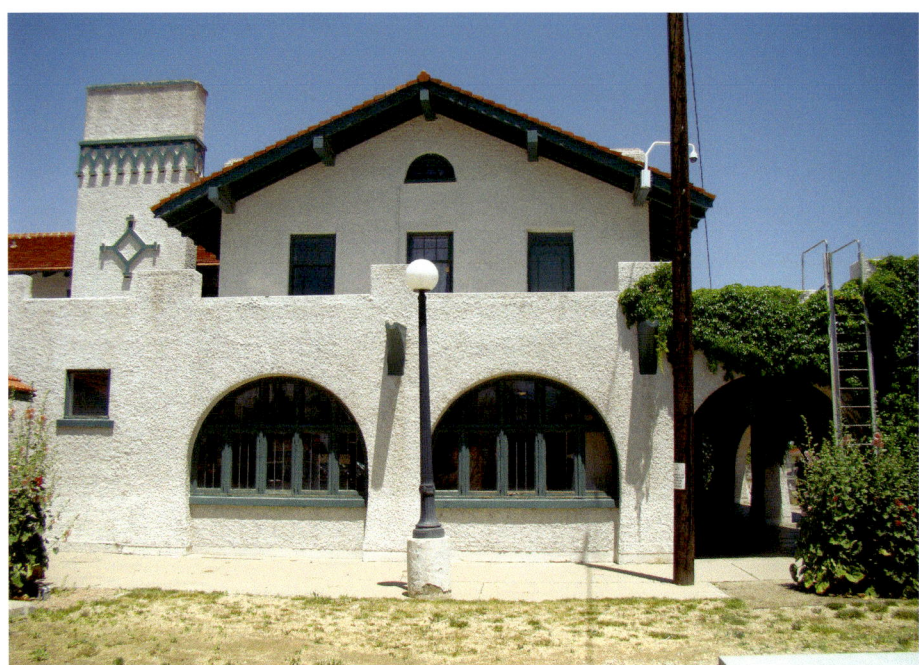

The Belen Harvey House, seen in 2024, has been restored and is now a fine museum paying tribute to the former Fred Harvey lunchroom and dining room inside. Harvey Girl residence rooms were on the second floor and can be viewed on a tour of the museum today.

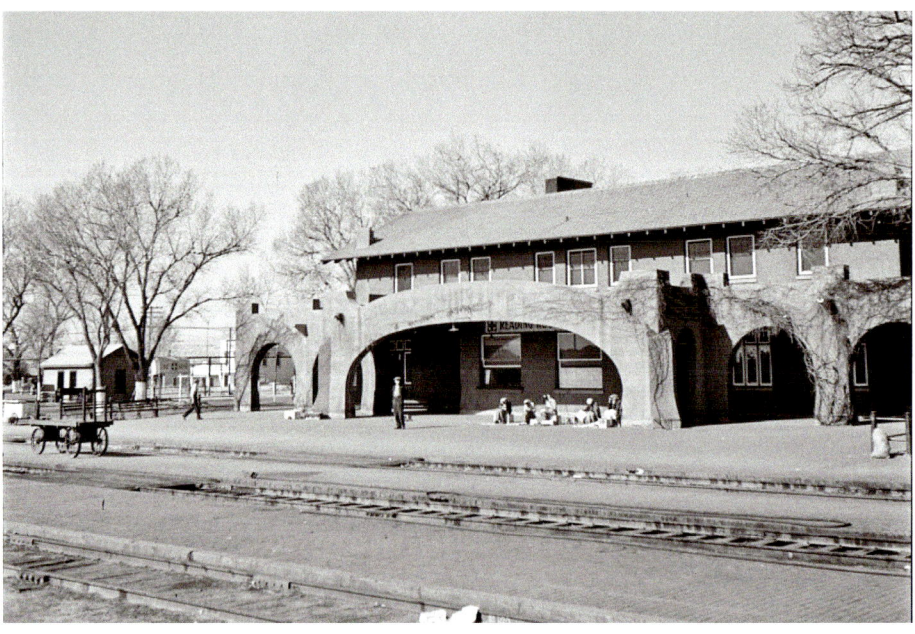

Viewed from the railroad tracks, the large archway at the Harvey House was the entrance to the Reading Room for the AT&SF employees. (*Jack Delano photograph, Library of Congress, LC-USW3-021133-E*)

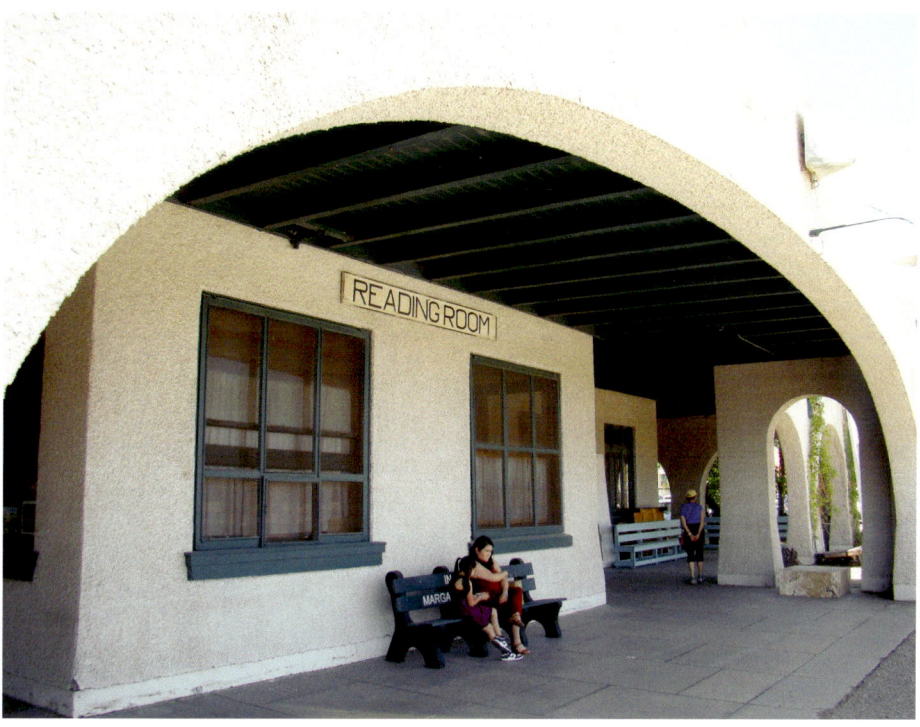

A contemporary view of the entrance to the reading room under the archway at the Belen Harvey House.

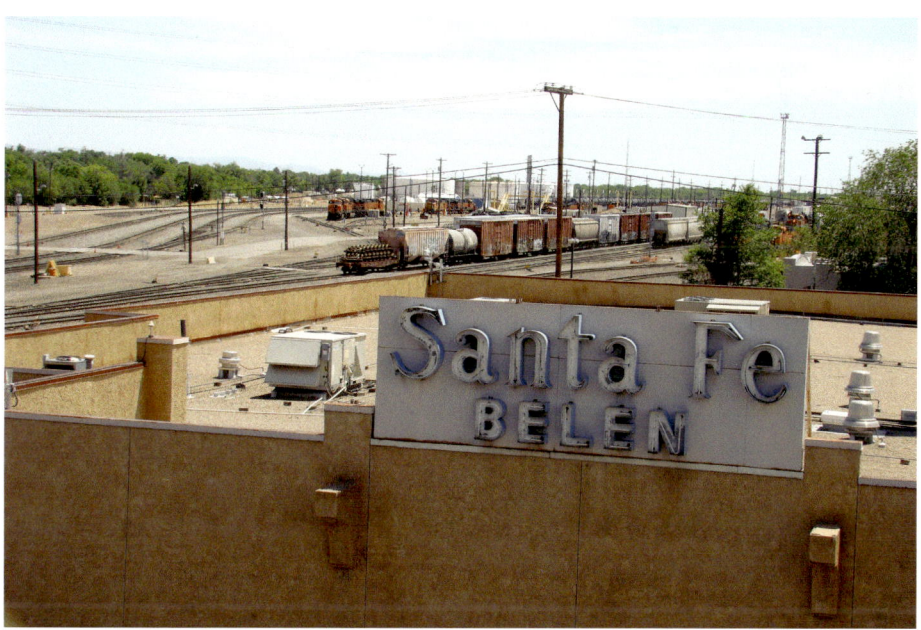

A 2024 view of the Belen railyard with the old Santa Fe Railway sign still there.

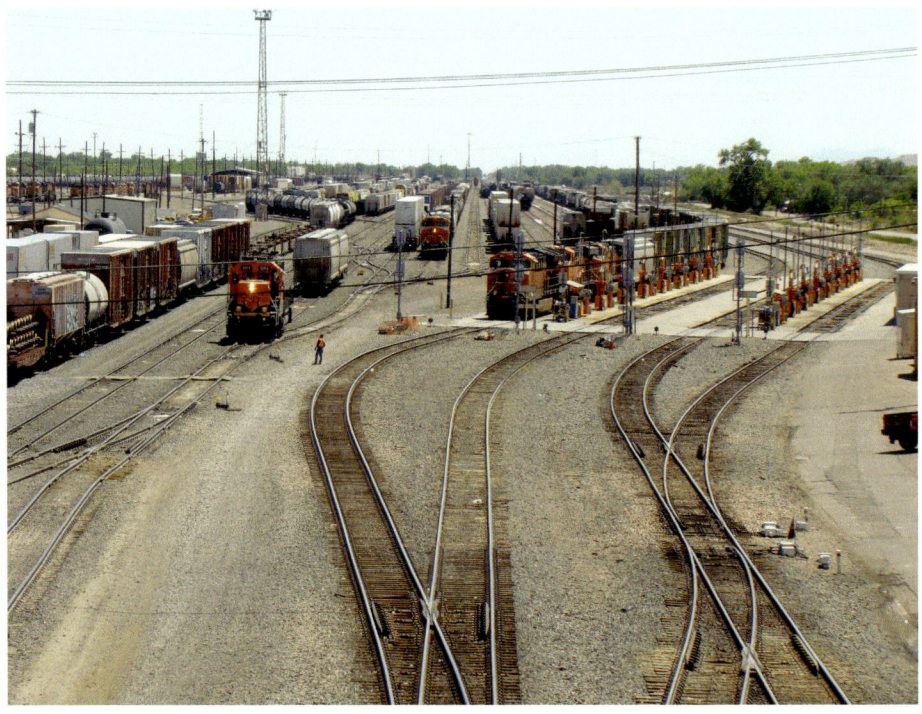

Diesel engines are fueling up in this view toward the south in the Belen railyard in 2024.

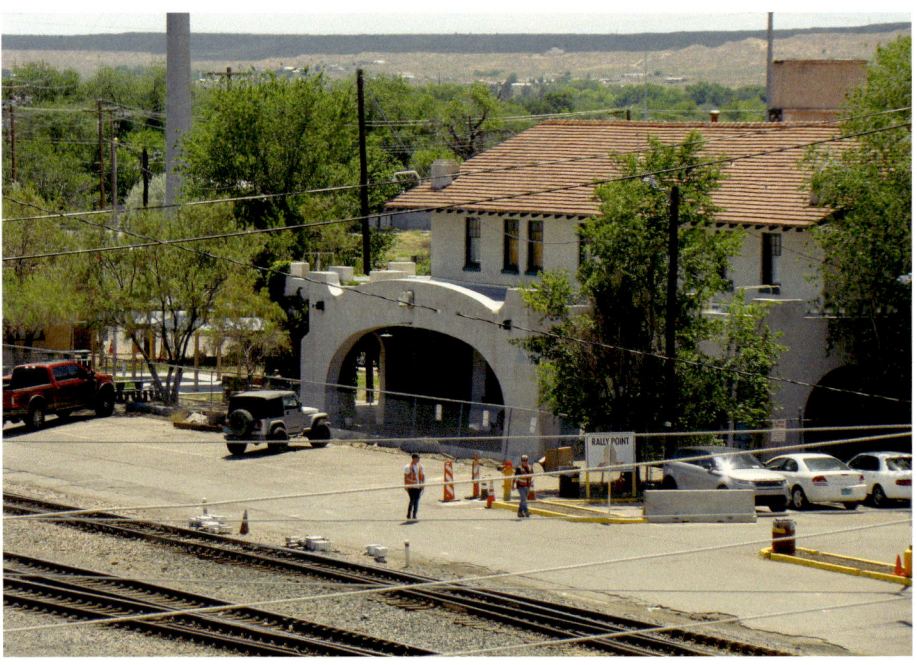

From the roadway overpass of the railyard, the Belen Harvey House can be seen in this 2024 view.

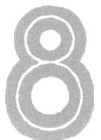

ALONG THE RAILS: A DETOUR TO ALBUQUERQUE

From Belen, AT&SF trains could continue their transcontinental journey west to Dalies or detour north to Albuquerque for repairs in the machine shops there. Jack Delano hopped off his westbound train at Belen and headed to Albuquerque "to see one of the largest locomotive repair facilities in the nation. During the war this complex was of particular strategic importance."[1]

Delano's train pulled into Isleta Pueblo station, 18 miles north of Belen. This was a wooden station, much different from the concrete/stucco Mission Revival-style stations on the Belen Cutoff to the east. Interestingly, this station played a role in Fred Harvey's Southwest Indian Detours:

> By 1932, all Detours from Albuquerque had ceased. To give the cross-country train traveler a taste of the New Mexican pueblos a hurry-up trip to Isleta Pueblo was arranged.... For one dollar, the eastbound train passenger could depart at Isleta station, take fifteen minutes to walk around the church and pueblo, then board a Harveycar for a quick ride north to Albuquerque, where they would rejoin the train which had stopped at the depot for a twenty-minute break. Westbound passengers could depart the train at Albuquerque, hop on a Harveycar to Isleta, walk about, and then reboard the train at the Isleta station.[2]

Jack Delano probably did not take this interesting little detour but continued on to the repair shops in Albuquerque.

The Albuquerque repair shops of the AT&SF were first constructed in 1881, shortly after the railroad reached town. By 1914, it was apparent that the initial facilities were too small for the ever-expanding AT&SF. More land was purchased, old structures demolished, and new construction began, resulting in the facilities that Jack Delano inspected in 1943. In Albuquerque, "The repair and maintenance shops worked around the clock with tens of thousands of spare parts on hand. Each steam locomotive required a careful check of its nearly twenty-five thousand parts, and often needed complete dismantling and reassembly during overhauls."[3]

The parts storehouse was 20,850 square feet in size in a building that was 409 feet long by 50 feet wide. It was built in 1914, and still stands today, housing the Wheels Museum of Albuquerque. Stocking 35,000 items, the storehouse could readily supply parts to the roundhouse, machine shop, and boiler shop. It had "additional outdoor storage on a concrete platform 800 feet x 70 feet, with deck height matching the standard deck height of railroad boxcars and flatcars."[4]

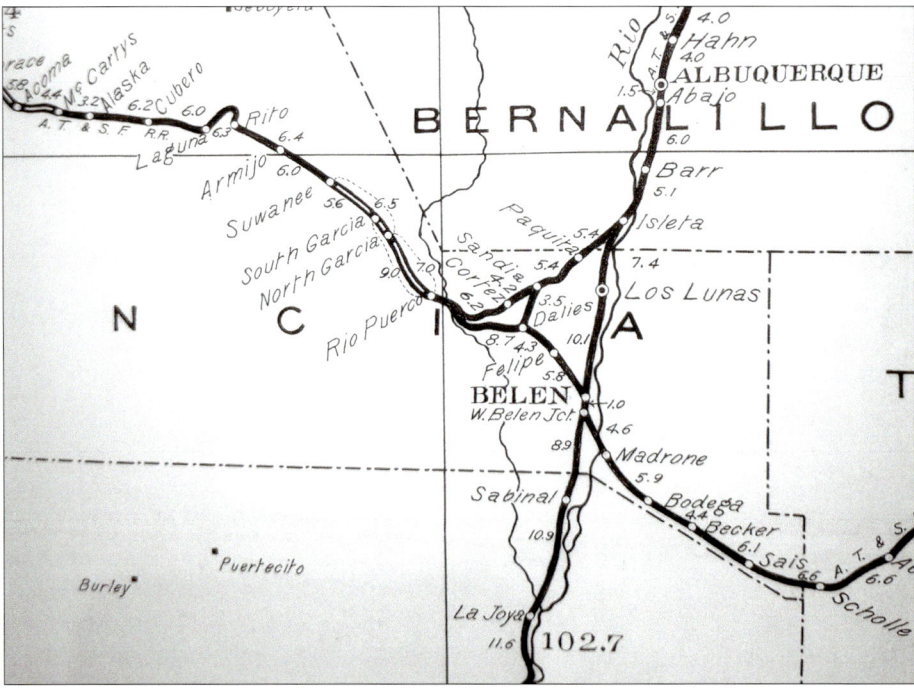

Belen is about 30 miles south of Albuquerque. If a locomotive needed major service, it could be switched out at Belen and sent north to the Albuquerque shops. (*New Mexico History Museum display*)

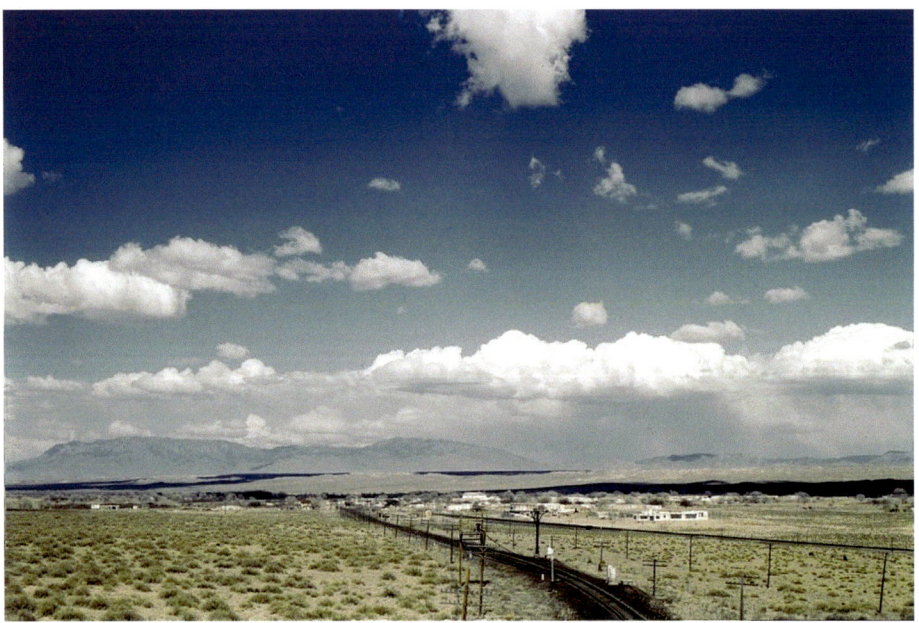

One of Jack Delano's rare color photographs shows Isleta Pueblo coming into view with the Sandia Range in the distance. (*Library of Congress, LC-USW361-712*)

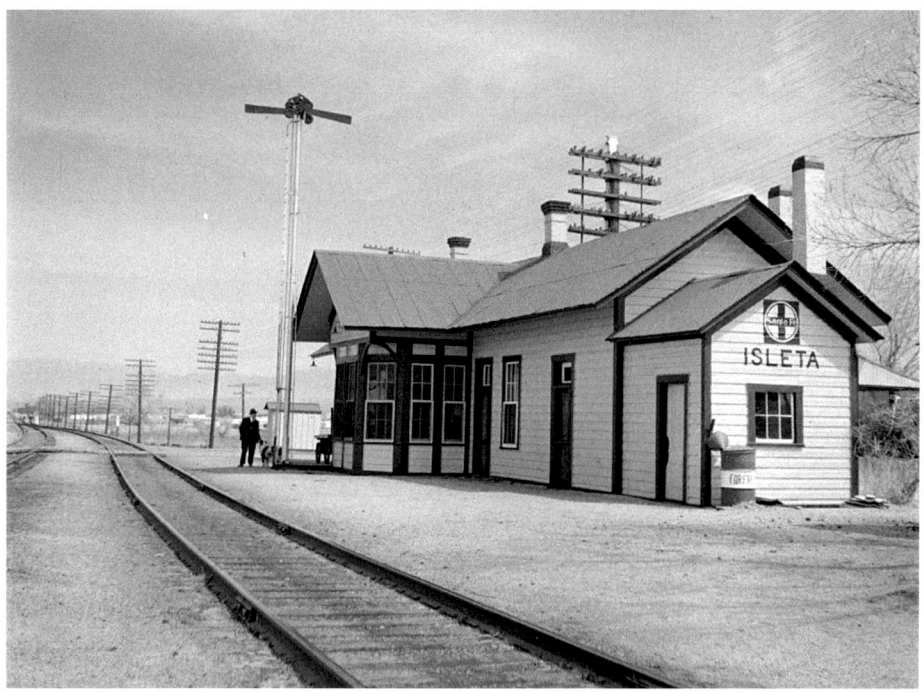

Isleta Station was pretty quiet as Jack Delano passed through on March 21, 1943. (*Library of Congress, LC-USW3-020764-E*)

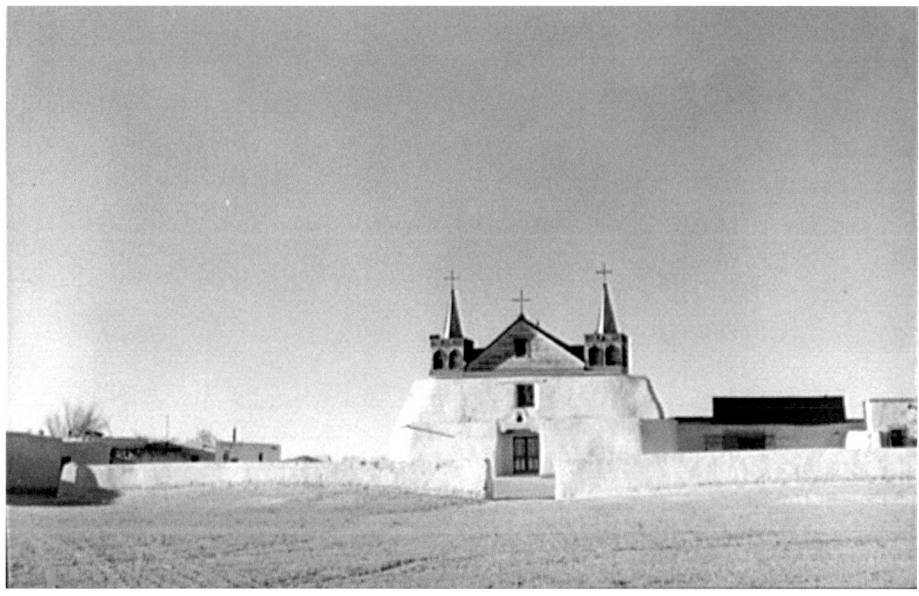

St. Augustine Church in Isleta Pueblo was a destination on Fred Harvey's Indian Detours from Albuquerque. Oddly, there was no one around when Jack Delano photographed it in March 1943. (*Library of Congress, USW3-020537-D*)

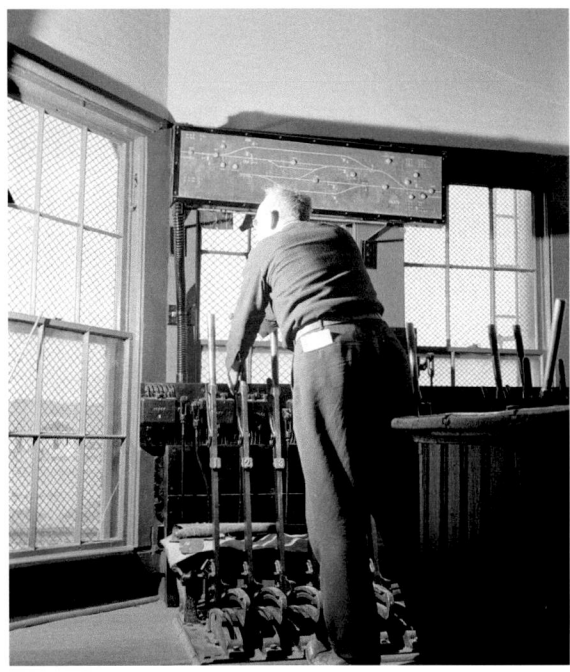

Left: Isleta agent throwing a switch. (*Jack Delano photograph, Library of Congress, LC-USW3-020771-E*)

Below: This "doodlebug" at Isleta was a cross between a locomotive and a passenger car. It served short passenger runs such as between Belen, Isleta, and Albuquerque. (*Jack Delano photograph, Library of Congress, LC-USW3-020770-E*)

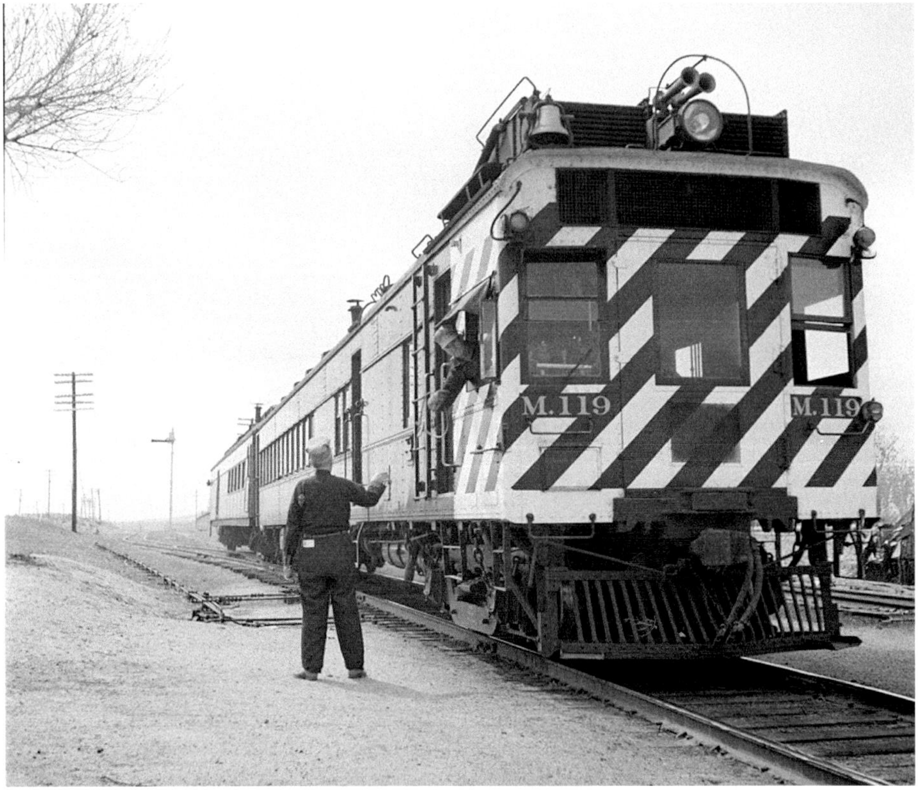

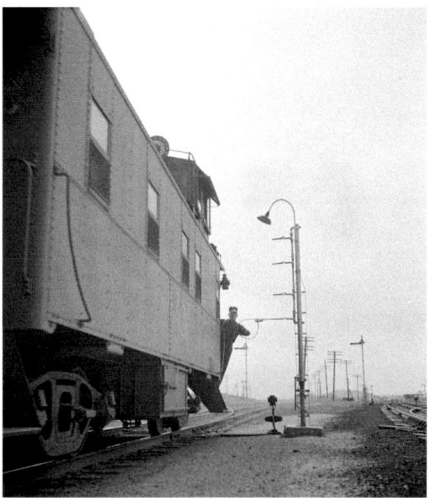 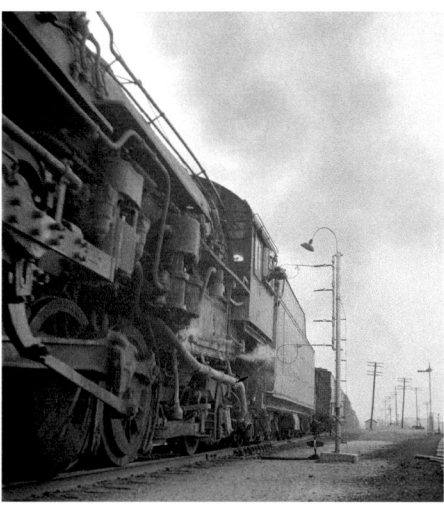

Above left: This train conductor in a caboose at Isleta was picking up a message from the wire loop on the pole as he passed by. (*Jack Delano photograph, Library of Congress, LC-USW3-020769-E*)

Above right: At Isleta, the fireman in the locomotive cab was picking up a message from the upper loop on the pole. (*Jack Delano photograph, Library of Congress, LC-USW3-020768-E*)

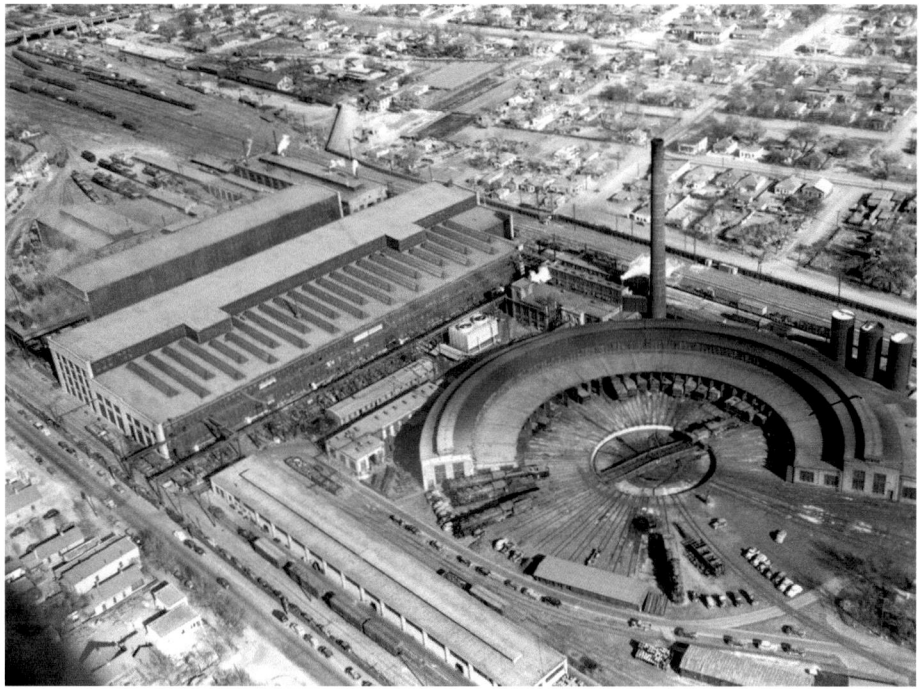

A remarkable aerial photograph of the Albuquerque roundhouse and shops, *circa* 1950. The roundhouse was torn down in 1986, but the other large buildings are still standing today and are identified in the next photograph. (*AT&SF History Archive, Kansas Historical Society*)

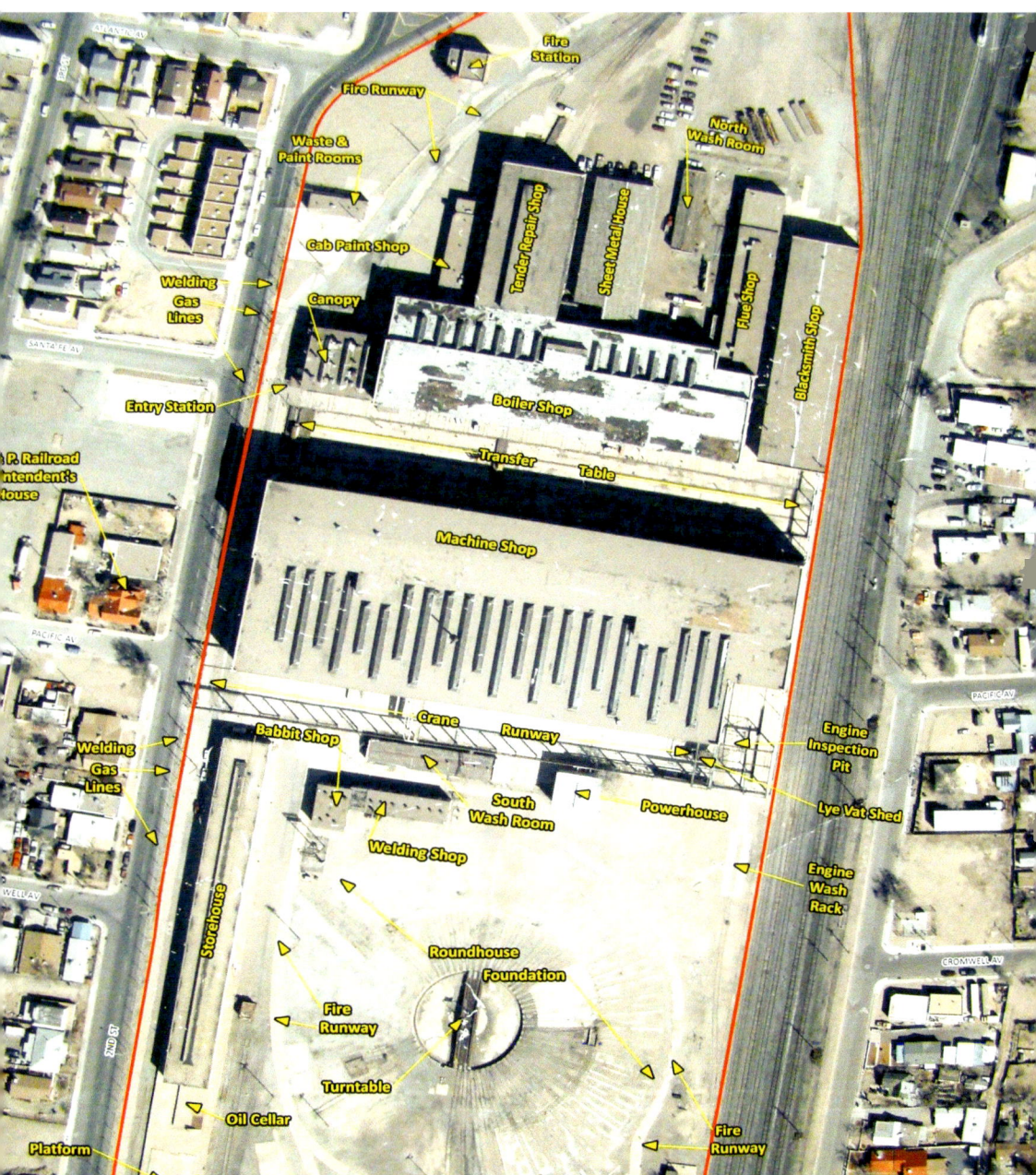

The major buildings which serviced AT&SF locomotives during World War II are identified in the diagram. Notice the transfer table between the machine shop and the boiler shop which allowed for parts, locomotives, and tenders to be transferred from one building to the next. (*Albuquerque Wheels Museum*)

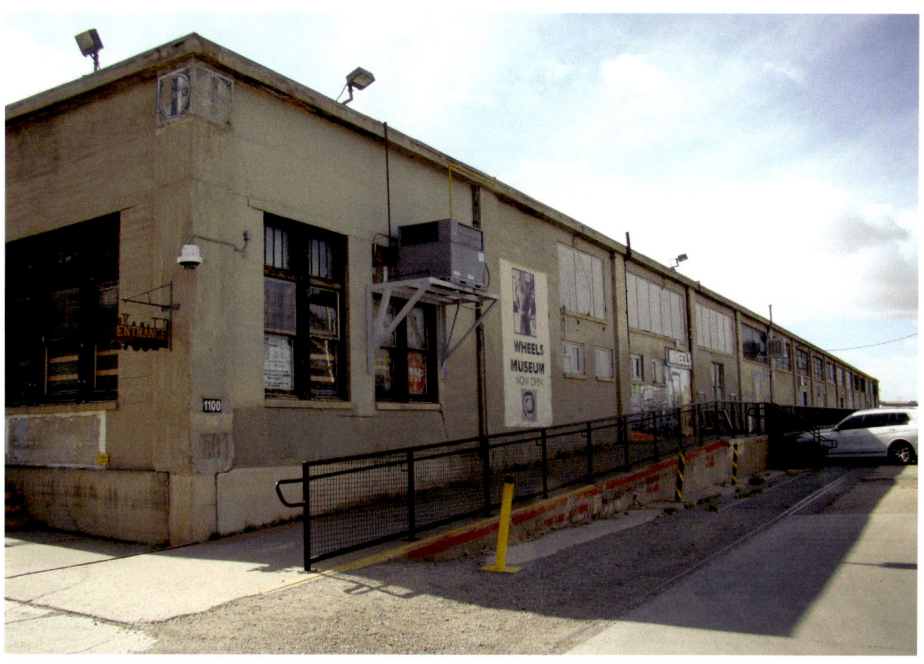

The former storehouse for the Albuquerque shops is now the Wheels Museum. It is 409 feet long.

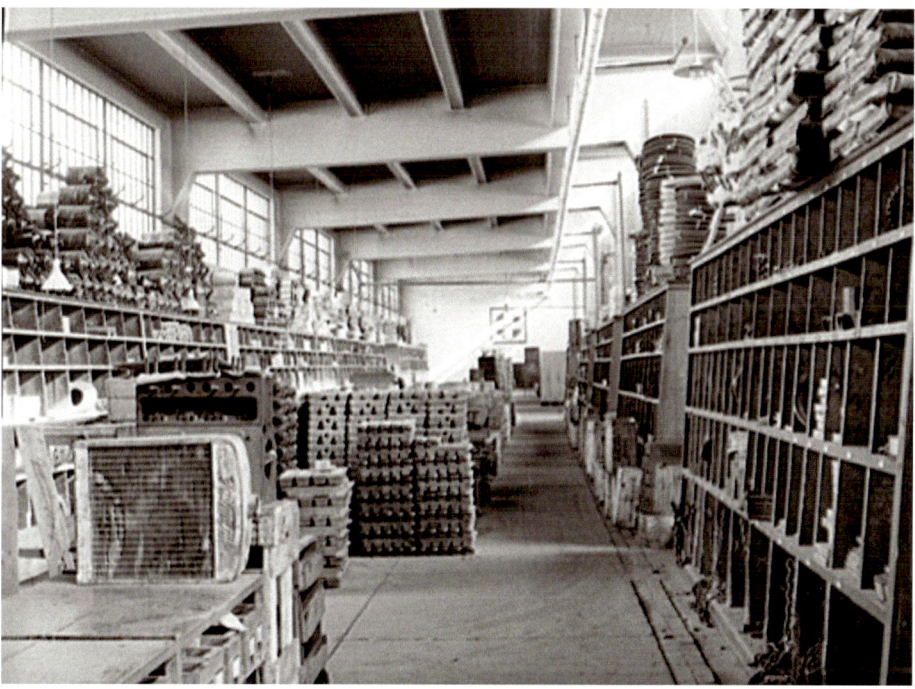

Inside the storehouse was a vast array of shelves containing up to 35,000 different parts for locomotive repairs. (*Jack Delano photograph, Library of Congress, LC-USW3-020480-D*)

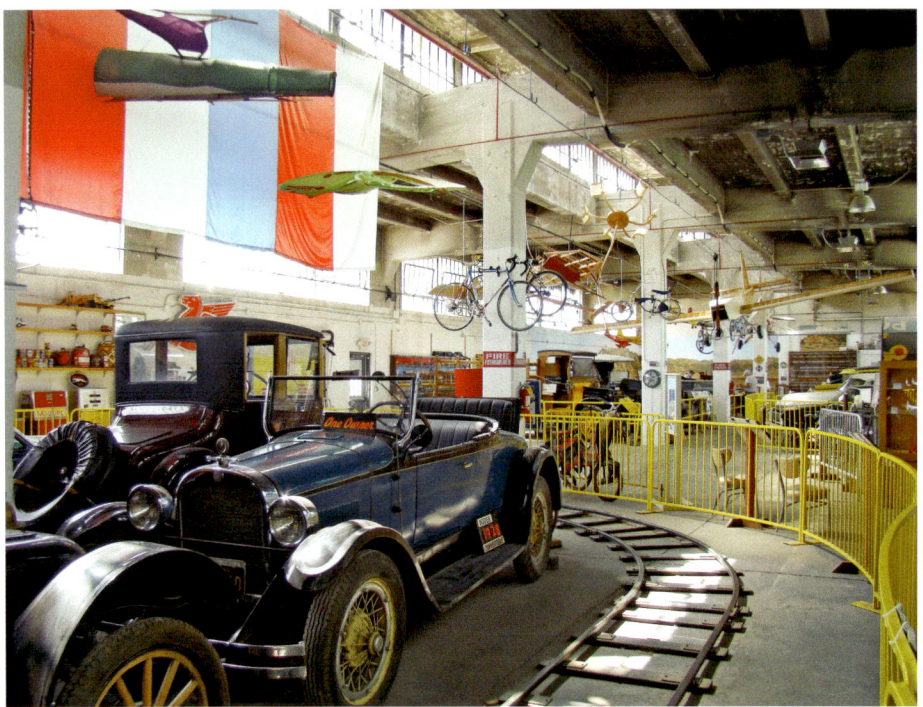

Inside the former storehouse today, the Wheels Museum contains 409 linear feet of wheeled items including automobiles, bicycles, airplanes, and, yes, trains.

Just to the east of the storehouse was the turntable and roundhouse. The roundhouse was built in 1914 and torn down in 1986, but the turntable still exists and is part of the City of Albuquerque's future plans to restore the railyards. The roundhouse had thirty-five stalls where overnight maintenance and cleaning of the steam locomotives took place. "The fire tubes, flues and smoke boxes were cleaned, and boilers were washed out to remove mineral buildup."[5]

Jack Delano took a number of photographs inside the machine shops, and it is important to understand what repairs took place in each building servicing steam engines for World War II freight train transportation across New Mexico. Directly behind the roundhouse was the machine shop built in 1921. It consisted of four bays south to north: bench bay, light machinery bay, heavy machinery bay, and the erecting bay. The first three bays performed repairs on various parts, while the erecting bay had gantry cranes which could lift the entire locomotive off the tracks. There were twenty-six work bays within the erecting bay "each with a pit for working on the underside of a locomotive. All bays were equipped with steam, gas, and electricity. Rails for work bays extended to the north out of the building to the Transfer Table."[6]

The transfer table, built in 1922, was 60 feet wide and 604 feet long. Its purpose was to transfer locomotives, tenders, and large parts between the machine shop to the south and the boiler shop to the north.

> [The transfer table] is the main conveyor of heavy objects between all the major buildings. Rails approach from both sides allowing, for example, a repaired boiler to be loaded from the western-most

ALONG THE RAILS: A DETOUR TO ALBUQUERQUE

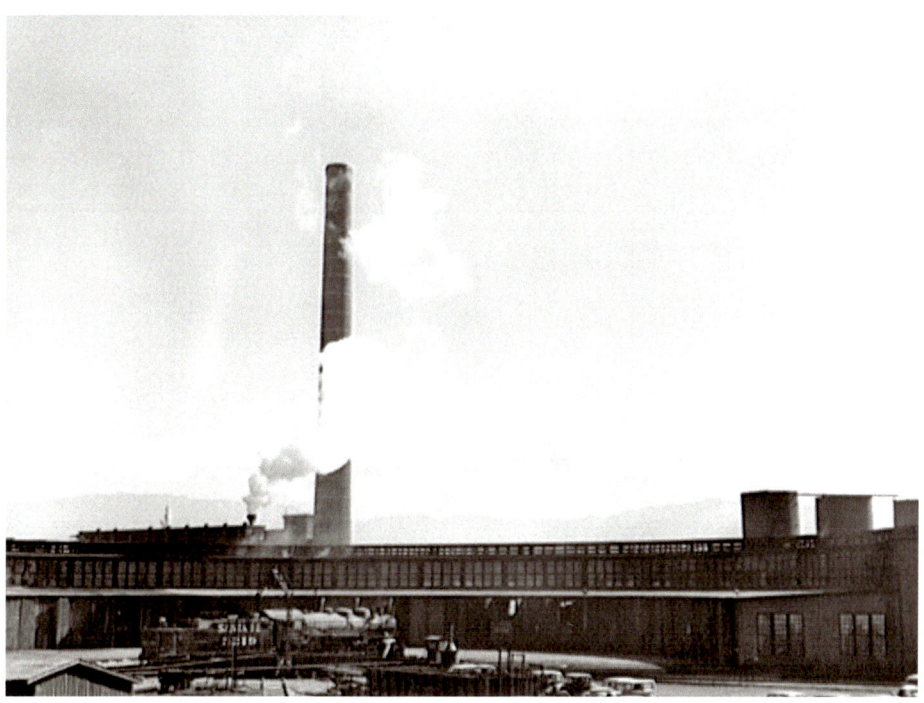

Jack Delano photographed this AT&SF engine and tender on the Albuquerque turntable heading into the roundhouse in March 1943. (*Library of Congress, LC-USW3-020548-D*)

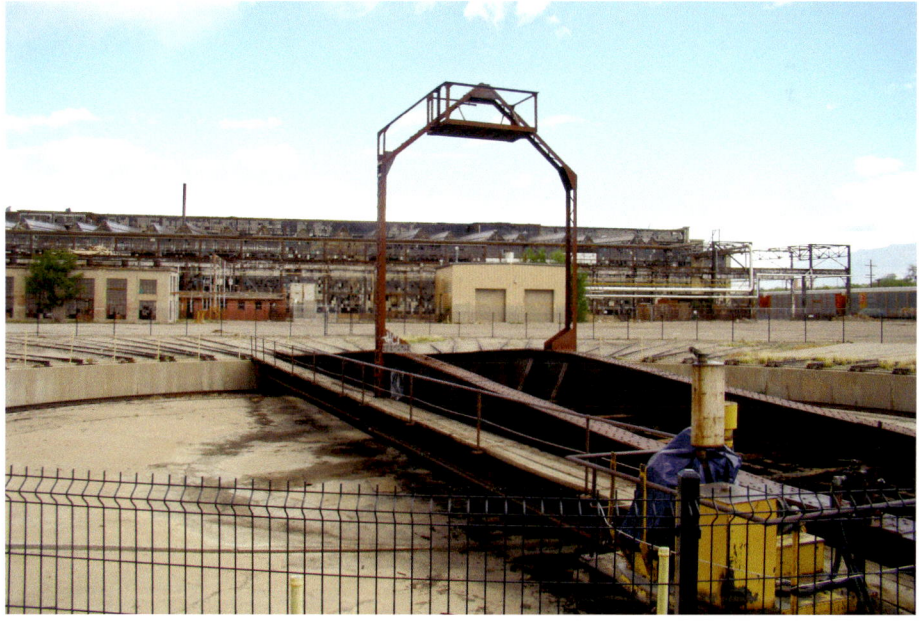

The Albuquerque turntable still stands today, but the roundhouse is long gone. In the distance the large building is the machine shop.

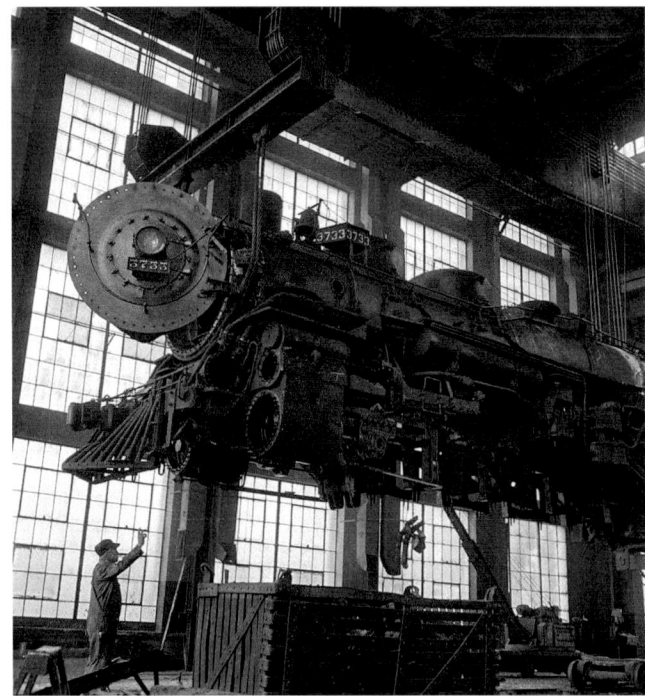

In the machine shop, an overhead gantry crane could lift Engine 3733 for repairs, including obtaining a new set of wheels. (*Jack Delano photograph, Library of Congress, LC-USW3-021127-E*)

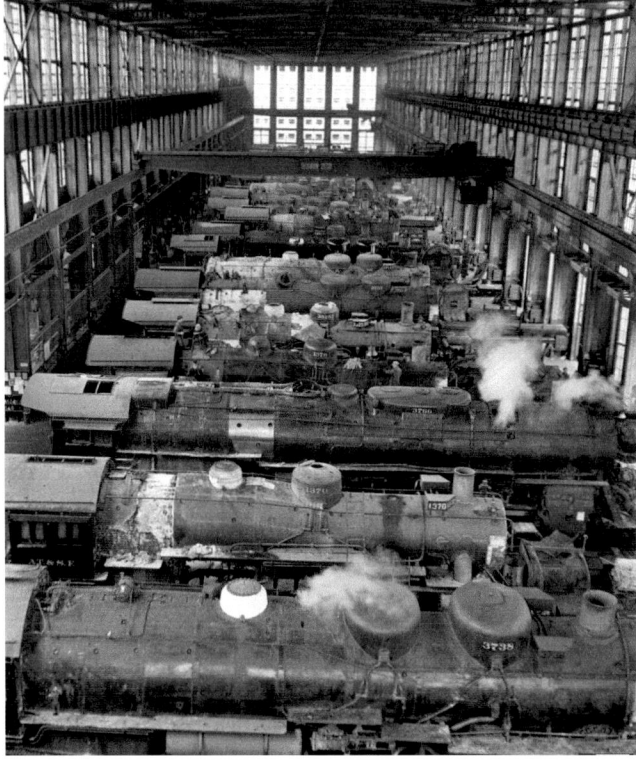

In the machine shop, it appeared that every service bay was filled in this photograph from the collection of the Wheels Museum.

bay in the Boiler Shop and transferred to a centrally located bay in the Machine Shop for reinstallation in a repaired locomotive. Two transfer decks, one with an enclosed cab, travel on four rails mounted at the bottom of the Transfer Table pit.[7]

The boiler shop was completed in 1923, covering 58,000 square feet. Its purpose was to build and repair the boilers of the locomotives. It had "17 workstations, each with rail connection to the Transfer Table. It has a 30-ton bridge crane."[8]

Perpendicular to the boiler shop is the blacksmith shop, constructed in 1917 containing 24,480 square feet. Since it pre-dated the machine shop, transfer table, and boiler shop, it was connected to the roundhouse by outside rails. The blacksmith shop fabricated all types of machine parts in their forges, using new steel and recycled wheels, rails, and other metal parts. The City of Albuquerque purchased all the railyard buildings from BNSF on November 28, 2007, for $8.5 million, however, redevelopment did not begin until 2019.[9] The first building to be rehabilitated was the blacksmith shop, and it now serves as a marketplace for farmers, artists, and craftsmen on weekends during the summer.

Adjacent to the blacksmith shop is the flue shop, constructed in 1920.

> In the Flue Shop, all the pipes in the boilers of the locomotives were repaired or fabricated from scratch, if necessary. The Flue Shop has been remodeled [in 2020] for City-related uses. The work essentially repaired the structural shell and provided all new roof, floors, and windows. New heating, air conditioning, fire suppression, and rest rooms, make the space ready for new occupants.[10]

The tender repair shop abuts the boiler shop. It was built in 1925 to make repairs on locomotive tenders which required maintenance including fixing leaks, repairing valves and cleaning, and working on wheels, axles, and brakes. The tender repair shop has eight bays, and a "track runs from the Transfer Table through the Tender Repair, and outside to the north of the building.... Originally, multiple tracks exited this building to the north."[11]

The AT&SF built a fire station at the north end of the railyard in 1920 to douse any fires that might occur in the structures to the south. It was built of stone originally quarried at Laguna Pueblo. "The two-story building housed two bays for fire trucks and space for other equipment on the first floor and sleeping quarters on the second floor.... The off-center tower provided room for hanging fire hoses to dry."[12] The City of Albuquerque plans to continue restoring other buildings in the railyard over time as funds are acquired.

The importance of the AT&SF maintenance facilities to the city of Albuquerque during World War II cannot be overstated.

> In 1943 ... the AT&SF workforce in Albuquerque reached 1,787.... At $3.5 million a year, the Santa Fe was meeting the largest single payroll in the community other than that of the Federal Government. The Locomotive Repair Shops were busy day and night, running nine-hour shifts and completely overhauling about forty-one locomotives a month.[13]

Another facility on the grounds of the Albuquerque railyard was the tie treatment plant. Here, wood railroad crossties were treated with creosote. The Albuquerque tie treatment plant could treat as many as 80,000 ties a month with creosote.

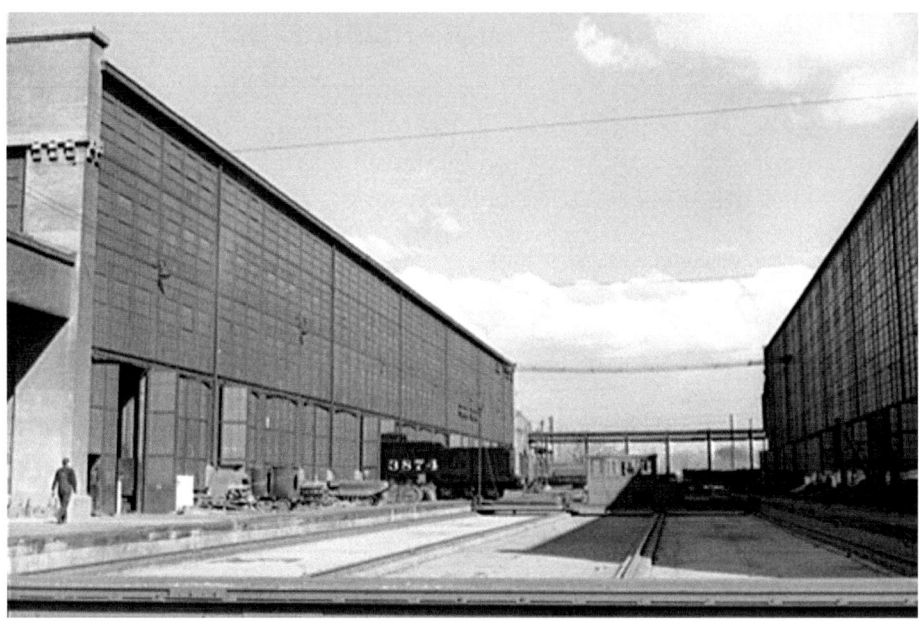

Tender 3874 is moving off the transfer table into the boiler shop, probably headed for passage through to the tender shop which was behind the boiler shop. (*Jack Delano photograph, Library of Congress, LC-USW3-020498-D*)

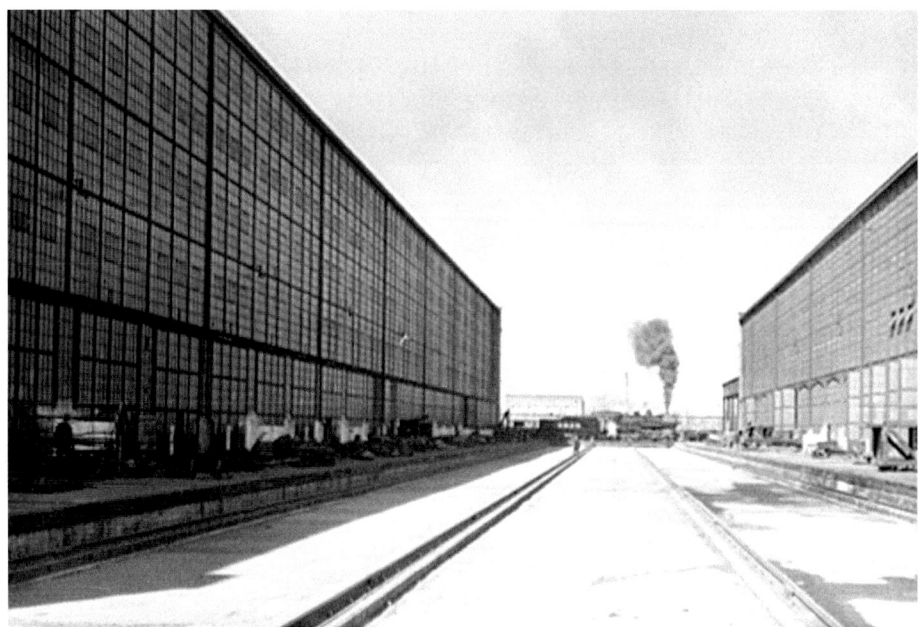

A locomotive and tender on the transfer table which moved east to west between the machine shop on the south (left) and the boiler shop on the north (right). (*Jack Delano photograph, Library of Congress, LC-USW3-020485-D*)

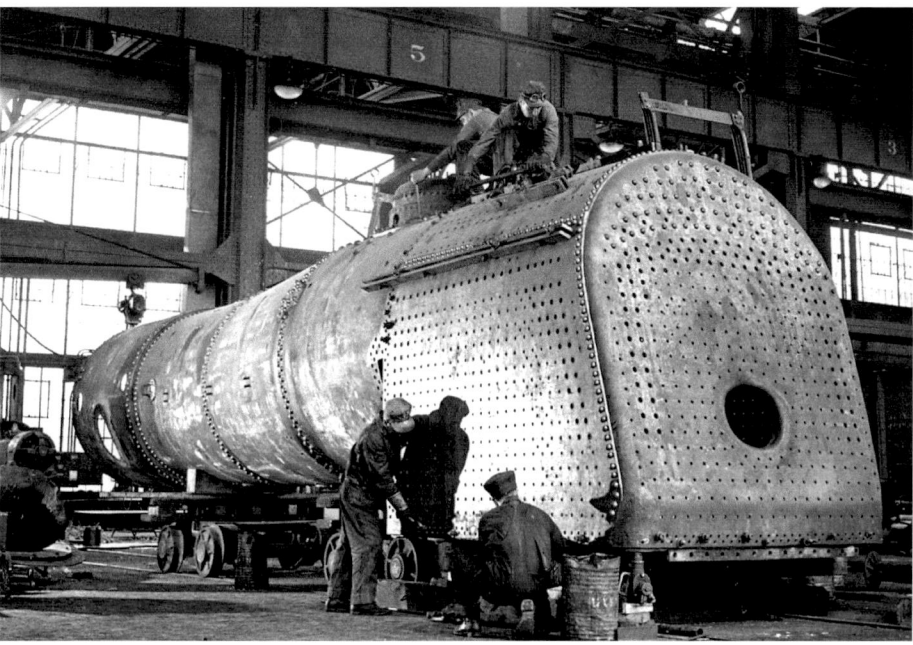

Jack Delano had a close-up view of a crew repairing a boiler in the boiler shop at Albuquerque. (*Library of Congress, LC-USW3-020490-D*)

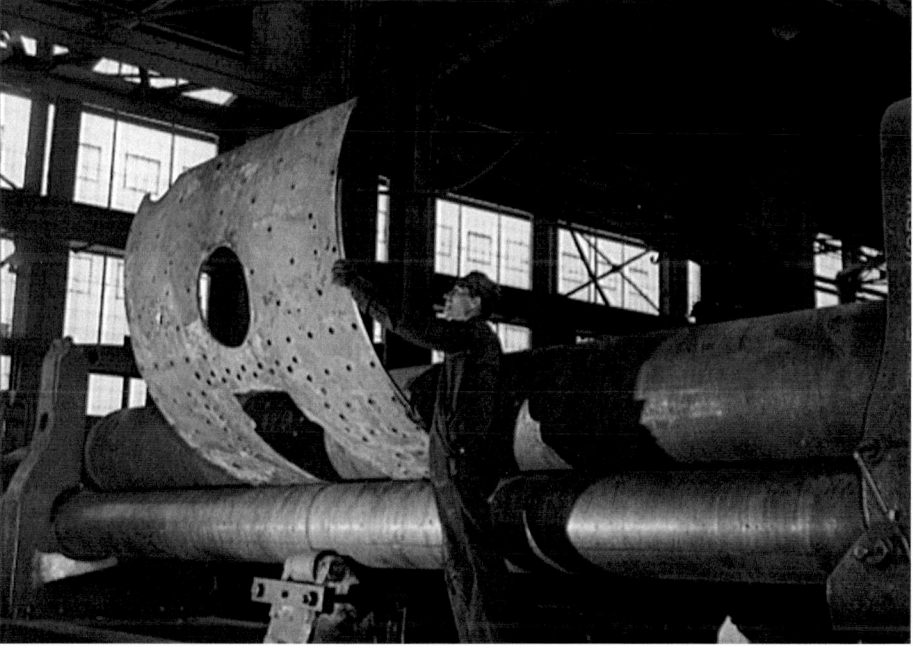

Rolling a boiler sheet in the Albuquerque boiler shop. (*Jack Delano photograph, Library of Congress, LC-USW3-020502-D*)

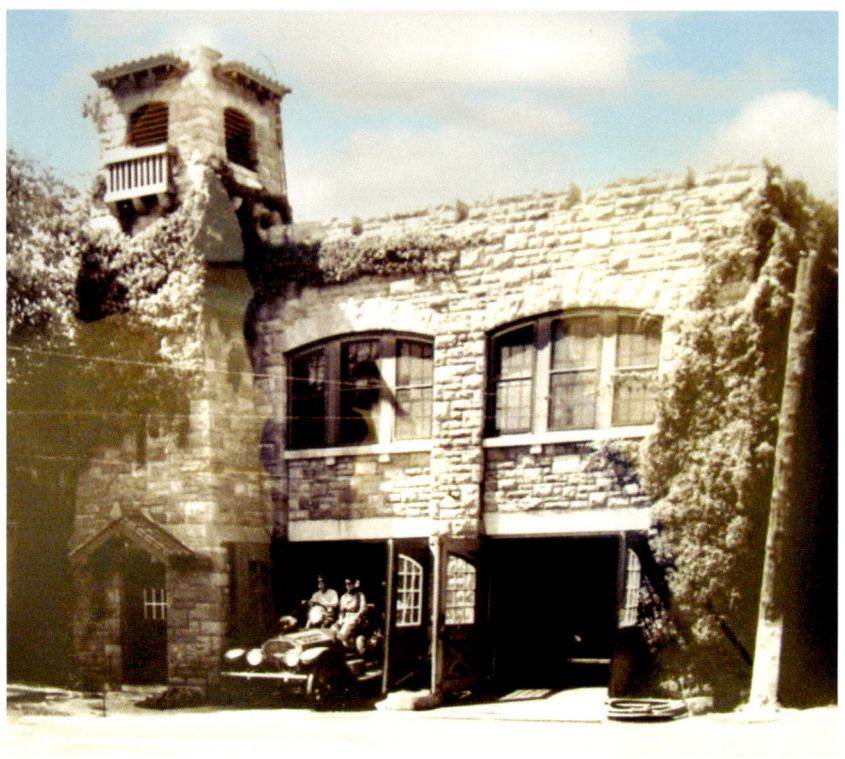

The two-story firehouse was constructed in the Albuquerque railyard in 1920 to provide fire suppression for the shops and yards. (*Albuquerque Wheels Museum*)

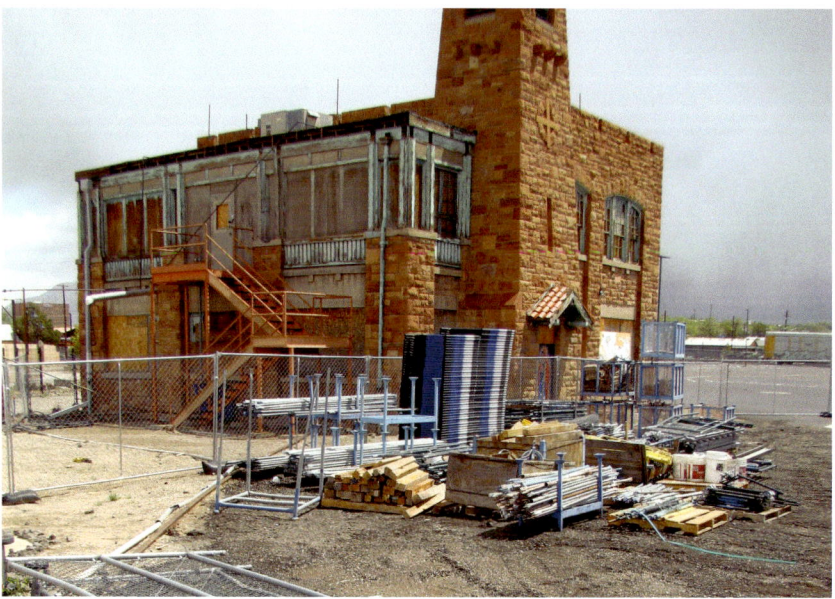

The firehouse is in sad shape in 2024, awaiting future funds for restoration.

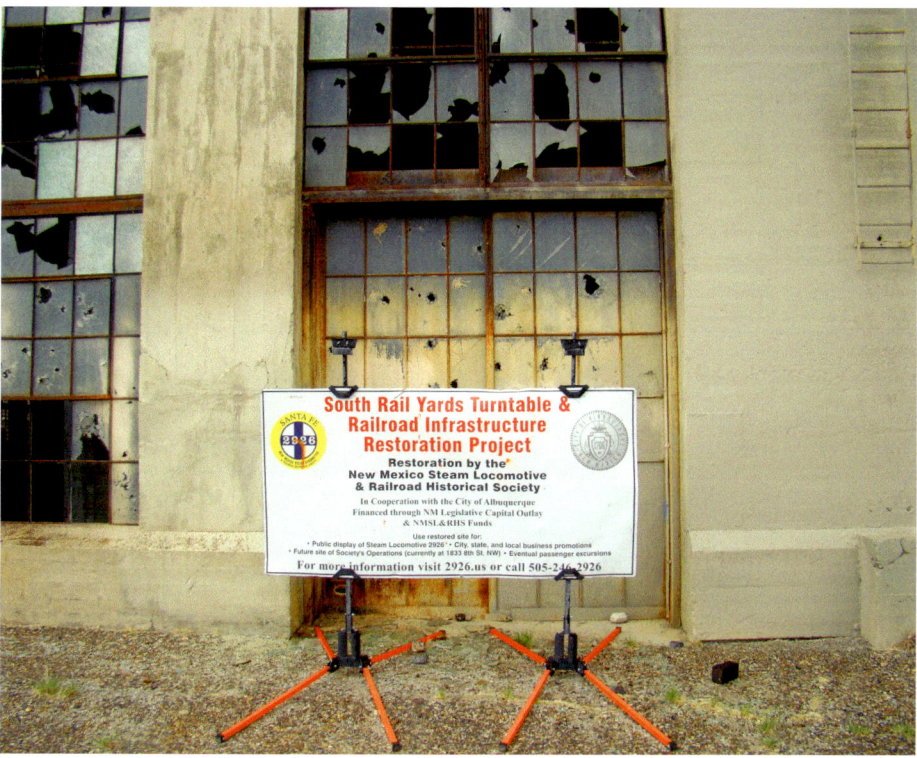

A 2024 sign outside the machine shop illustrates the restoration hopes of the New Mexico Steam Locomotive & Railroad Historical Society.

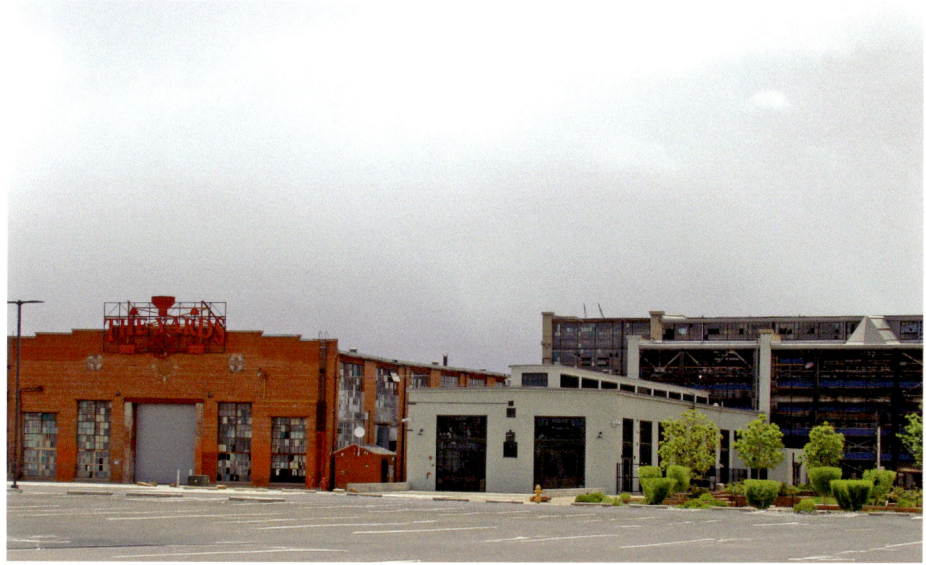

The blacksmith shop with "The Yards" sign and the restored flue shop are shown in 2024, with the boiler shop behind them.

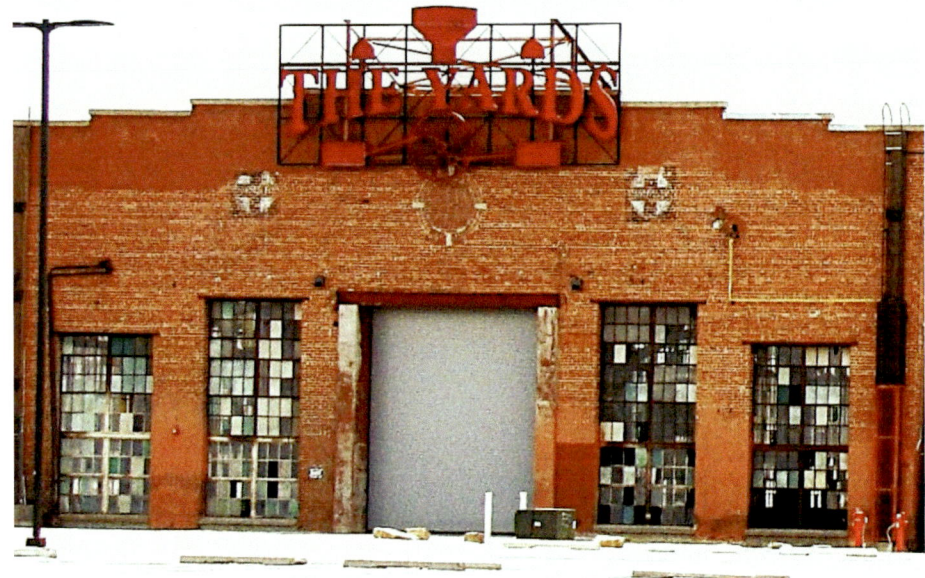

The blacksmith shop awaits further restoration, but in the meantime, its interior is open to farmers market and artist stalls on weekends during the summer.

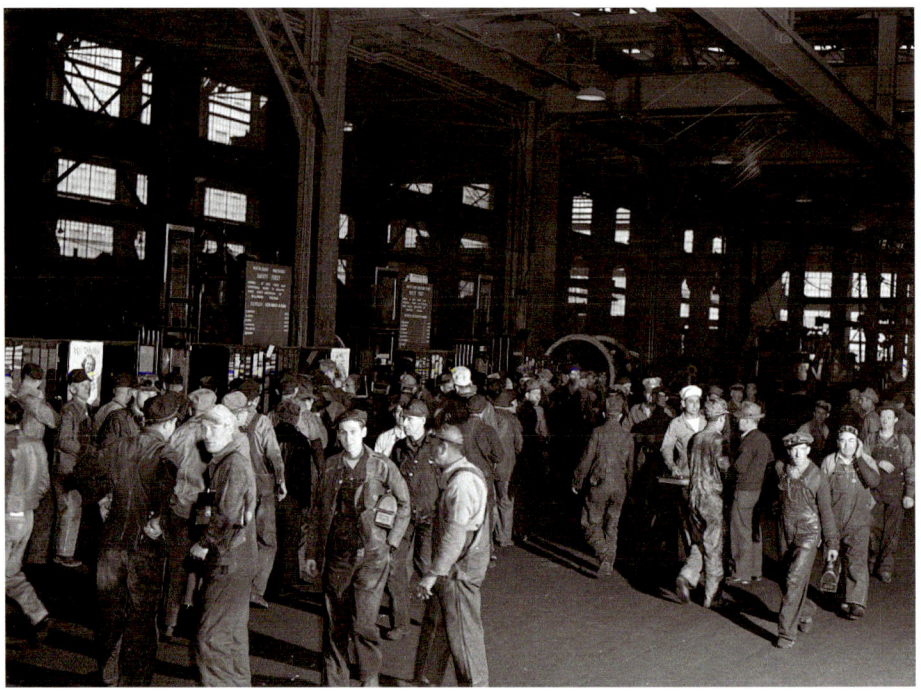

Jack Delano joined the crowd of workers heading out for lunch at the Albuquerque railroad shops in March 1943. (*Library of Congress, LC-USW3-020463-D*)

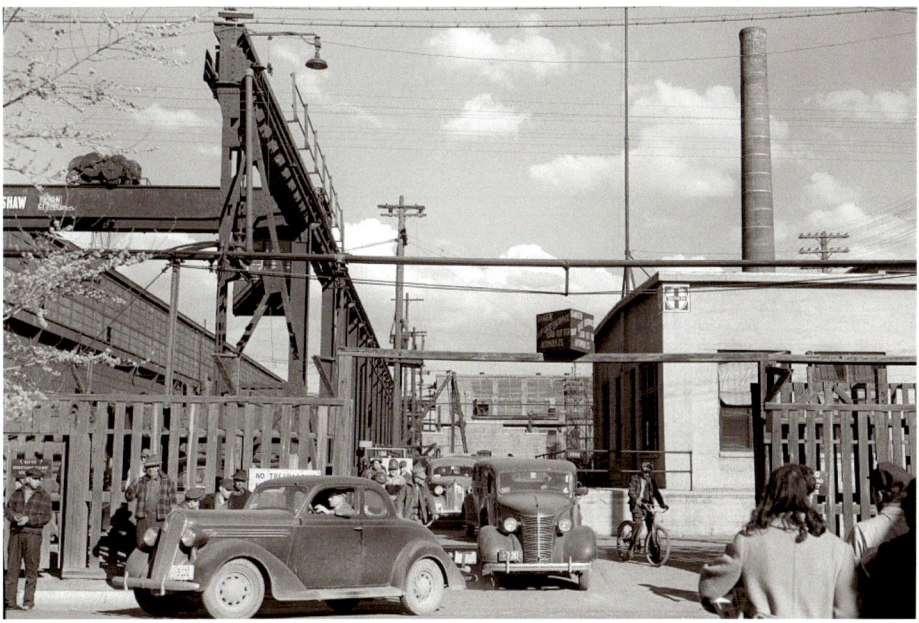

Workers head home after a shift in March 1943, with the storehouse on the right and the machine shop on the left with a gantry crane in front of it. (*Jack Delano photograph, Library of Congress, LC-USW3-022228-D*)

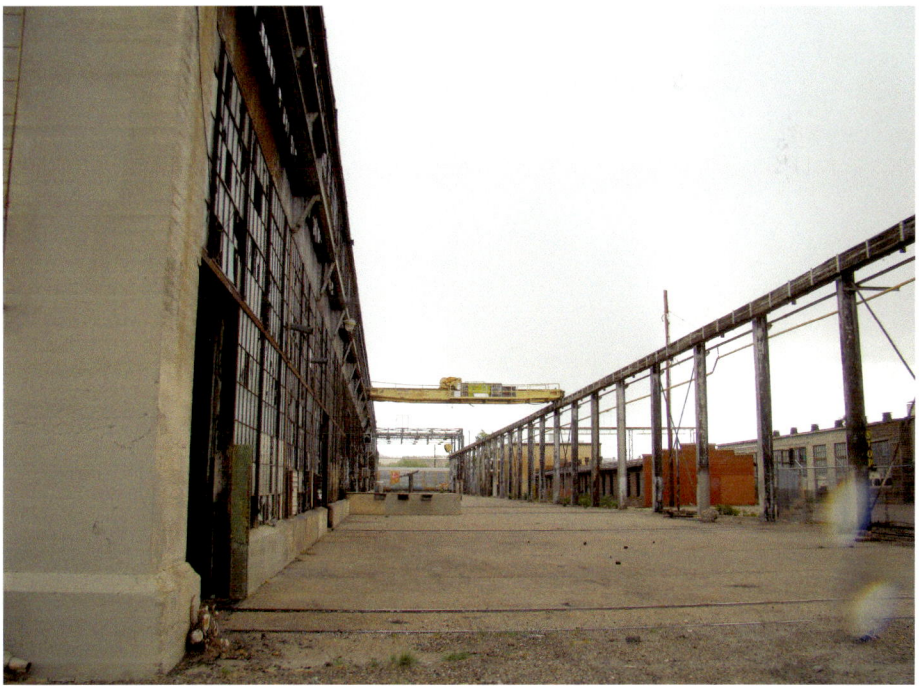

The gantry crane and machine shop as seen by the author in 2024.

The primary problem with wood ties is their tendency to rot, which was addressed with the use of creosote, a gas-tar preservative first used on railroad crossties in 1839. Railroads charted the performance of ties and kept service records by driving date nails into the ends of ties; if a rotted or damaged tie was removed, the date on the nail was noted.... Date nails were used by the Santa Fe Railway from 1901 through 1969.[14]

The AT&SF was also essential in shipping freight in and out of Albuquerque during the war years. Much more freight was shipped in than out. In 1944, 3,742 freight cars were shipped out, and in 1945 freight cars shipped out totaled 4,216. Goods shipped out included lumber, autos and trucks, sand and gravel, and livestock. Inbound freight cars totaled 12,172 in 1944 and 13,770 in 1945. Inbound freight included oil and gasoline, lumber, fruits and vegetables, flour and feed, coal, and 450 cars of beer, greatly appreciated by railyard workers.[15]

Another essential recipient of inbound AT&SF freight was the Albuquerque Army Air Base constructed in 1941. The base provided pilot and bombardier training. It was renamed Kirtland Air Base in 1942. Since it was the largest air base near Los Alamos, where the atomic bomb was developed, it provided training for the pilots who eventually dropped the atomic bombs on Hiroshima and Nagasaki in 1945.

With the AT&SF being the only railroad serving Albuquerque and Kirtland Air Base, it "provided most ground transportation of material and personnel in support of the base. During the construction phase, it transported mostly building materials. Once the base was fully developed, Santa Fe freight trains provided fuel, munitions and the supplies for daily living at the base, while Santa Fe passenger trains provided ground transportation for its personnel."[16]

Fred Harvey's hotels played a huge role in feeding the passengers on the troop trains arriving at all hours of the day and night across the AT&SF system. Harvey had a contract with the military to feed the troops.

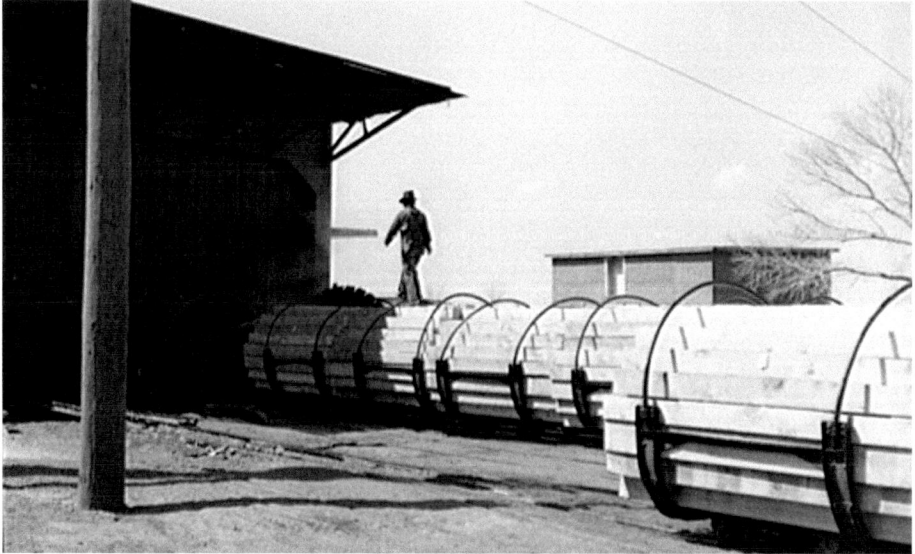

Railroad ties are headed into the retort plant for creosote in the Albuquerque yard in this Jack Delano March 1943 photograph. (*Library of Congress, LC-USW3-020519-D*)

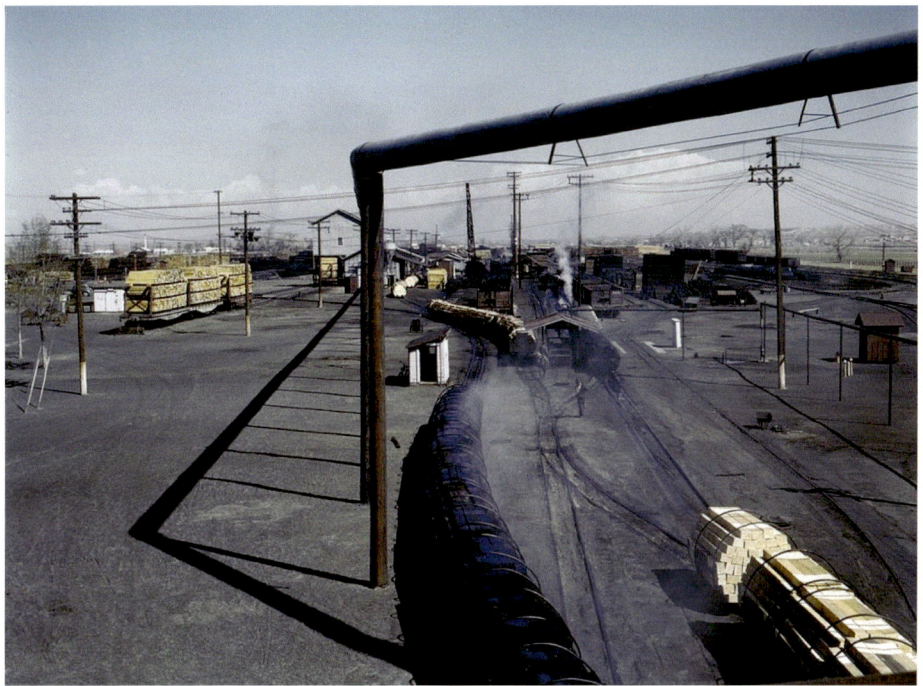

Emerging from the retort plant, the hot, steaming ties are now covered in black creosote, while untreated ties wait to be moved in. (*Jack Delano photograph, Library of Congress, LC-USW361-687*)

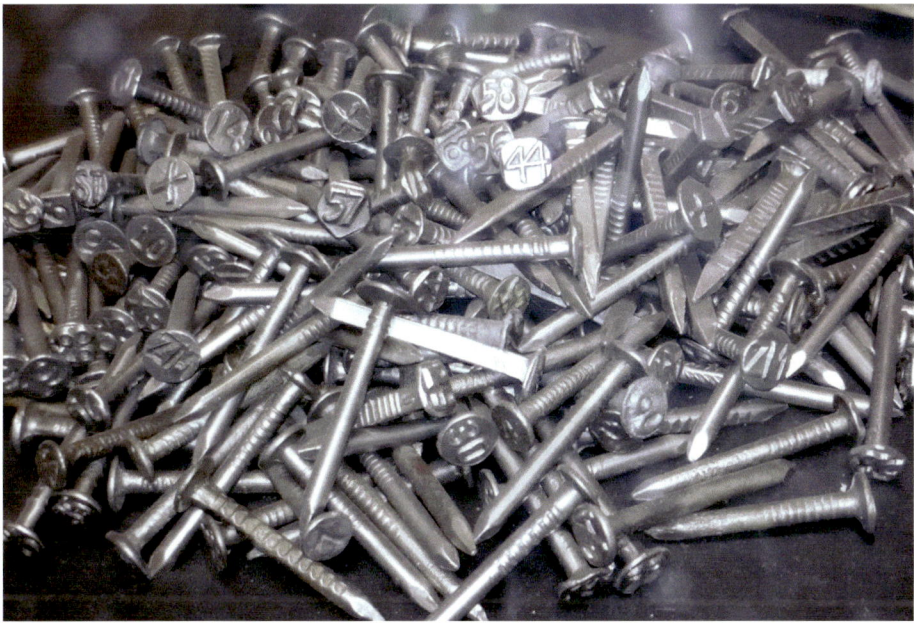

Date nails marked the year in which railroad ties received a creosote treatment. In this collection of nails, the years 1944 and 1958 can be clearly seen. (*New Mexico History Museum display*)

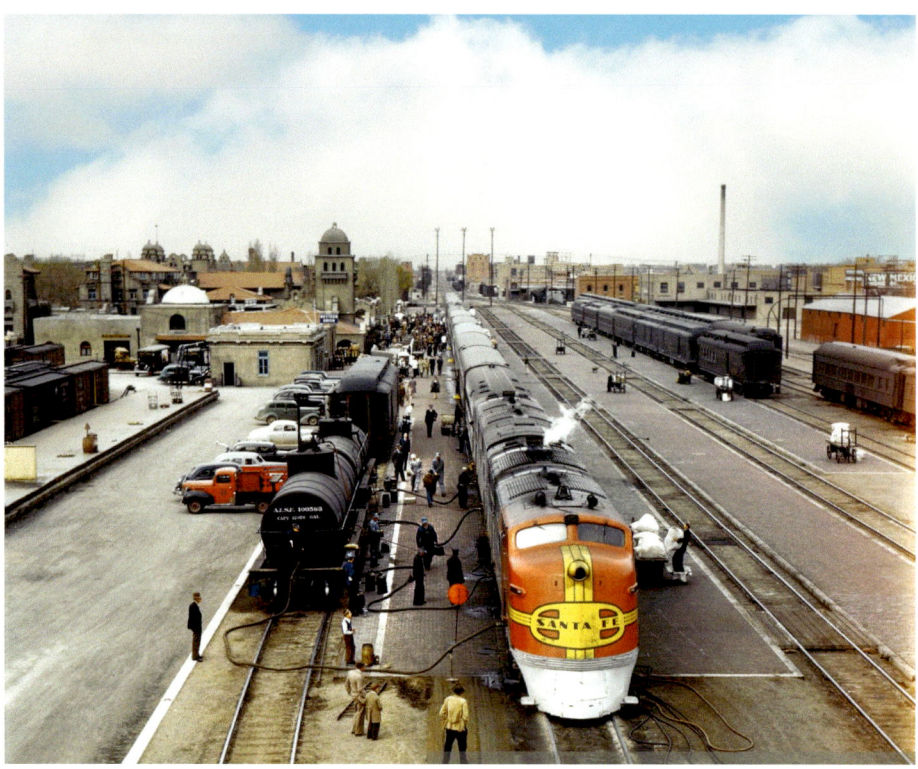

In this colorful March 1943 Jack Delano photograph, the *Super Chief* passenger train is receiving a diesel fill-up at the Albuquerque station. The needs of passengers still had to be met by the AT&SF during World War II along with the constant movement of troop trains. (*Library of Congress, LC-USW361-689*)

With the increased movement of troops, Harvey Houses found the means to feed large numbers of enlisted men and women at the hotels. In 1943 alone, the company served 30 million meals. "Troop-train girls," not trained as Harvey Girls but specialized in serving the military, lived on-site and worked on-call. Many of the troop-train girls were of Hispano descent.... They were provided with white uniforms with a white apron and black ties ... and with room, board, and an hourly wage of 35 cents.[17]

Fred Harvey's Alvarado Hotel in Albuquerque was a major troop train stop. With 500 servicemen departing a train at one time, the hotel had to use every available space to feed them. Extra tables and chairs were set up in the dining room, lunchroom, and out on the patios and walkways. "Box lunches were made by the hundreds in the kitchen for those trains that did not have time to stop for a sit-down meal."[18] In an interview, Harvey Girl Viola Hern Archibeque at the Alvarado recalled the hectic twelve-hour shifts that they worked:

There was no set schedule [for the troop trains]. We never really knew when a train was coming in because it was all very secretive. The average day had a breakfast train at 4 a.m. of five hundred or so men. We had to serve them a standard meal on paper plates. Then there would be a lunch train, usually an evening train, with maybe a couple of trains in between. Sometimes there were so many men we would even set up tables in the lounge. We worked twelve hours a day, easily. We were on call at the hotel for all hours of the day and night. We worked a seven-day week—I couldn't even get away long enough to get away to church![19]

Fred Harvey's La Fonda Hotel in Santa Fe also served meals to the troop trains. The AT&SF trains stopped briefly at Lamy, 18 miles south of Santa Fe. "La Fonda personnel made hundreds of box lunches each day and sent them down to Lamy, where they were picked up by troop trains."[20] Santa Fe also had a role in the Manhattan Project, the secret project at Los Alamos to produce the atomic bomb. Scientists such as "Niels Bohr, Enrico Fermi, Edward Teller, and many hundreds more scientists and technicians stepped off the Santa Fe train in Lamy, boarded a bus or special car, and after a brief stop in Santa Fe, headed up the hill to Los Alamos."[21]

The AT&SF also served other war efforts in Santa Fe. An old Civilian Conservation Corps camp in Santa Fe was turned into an internment camp for Japanese Americans who had been rounded up by President Franklin Roosevelt's Executive Order 9066 signed on February 19, 1942. "From March 1942 until April 1946, 4,555 men of Japanese ancestry were incarcerated [in Santa Fe].… All building materials, supplies and the internees were brought to Santa Fe by the AT&SF."[22]

Also in Santa Fe, the Bruns General Army Hospital was served by the AT&SF. The hospital opened on April 19, 1943. The AT&SF shipped in construction materials and equipment and provided transportation for patients to the hospital. "It is where most members of New Mexico's gallant 200th Coast Artillery Battalion who survived the Bataan Death March were treated."[23] The last patient was discharged from the hospital on December 14, 1946.

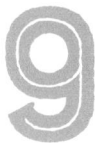

ALONG THE RAILS: BELEN TO GALLUP

Returning to Belen from Albuquerque, Jack Delano boarded a westbound AT&SF train. The first water stop was at Dalies, 10 miles from Belen, where Delano photographed the train conductor on the caboose picking up a message. Delano's next photograph shows the train rounding a curve at Quirk on its way to Laguna.

Laguna Pueblo is unique in New Mexico history in that it was not established until 1699, after the Pueblo Revolt of 1680.

> Following the Spanish reconquest of 1692, residents of Cochiti and Santo Domingo Pueblos fled west and established a new pueblo here along the Rio San Jose. Spanish influence remained strong though, and a mission church, San Jose de la Laguna, was built at the pueblo from 1799–1801. The church still stands.[1]

The AT&SF tracks went right among the Pueblo homes at Laguna. Prior to World War II, trains would stop here briefly to allow the residents to sell their handicrafts to the tourists. Many of the men of Laguna Pueblo worked on the AT&SF during World War II. Laguna is 43 miles west of Albuquerque.

Jack Delano snapped photographs of the action at Acomita, 11 miles west of Laguna. The name means "Little Acoma," and it is named for the Acoma Pueblo to the south. The map accompanying this chapter does not show Acomita. It is 2 miles east of what is shown as "Alaska" on the map. Acomita was settled on the Rio San Jose about 1870 when Navajo and Apache raids in the area subsided. It is part of the Acoma Pueblo Reservation today. Delano photographed troop trains passing through here in 1943.

Some 5 miles west of Acomita, the train passed through McCartys. Delano's photographs here show adobe homes and a church. McCartys is on the Acoma Pueblo Reservation. "AT&SF records say the name was derived from a ranch crossed by the original rail line … describing McCarty as a 'wandering Irishman,' who drifted into these parts, settled, and married a local Hispanic woman."[2]

Jack Delano observed the AT&SF activity at Grants, 15 miles west of McCartys. Grants is "named for the railroad contractors who built the line, the three Grant brothers, Angus, Lewis, and John … in 1880."[3] The exact date of construction of the frame depot in Grants is not known. The logging industry was very important in Grants through the 1940s. A little over 9,000 people live in Grants today.

ALONG THE RAILS: BELEN TO GALLUP

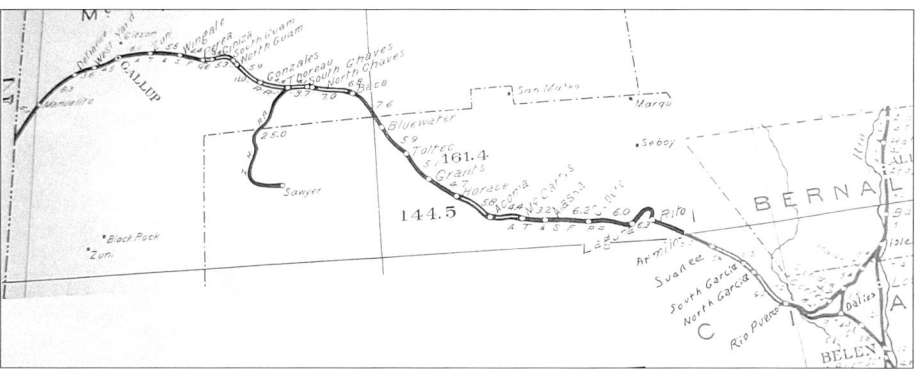

On March 25, 1943, Jack Delano was headed on an AT&SF freight train from Belen to Gallup, a distance of approximately 150 miles. (*New Mexico History Museum display*)

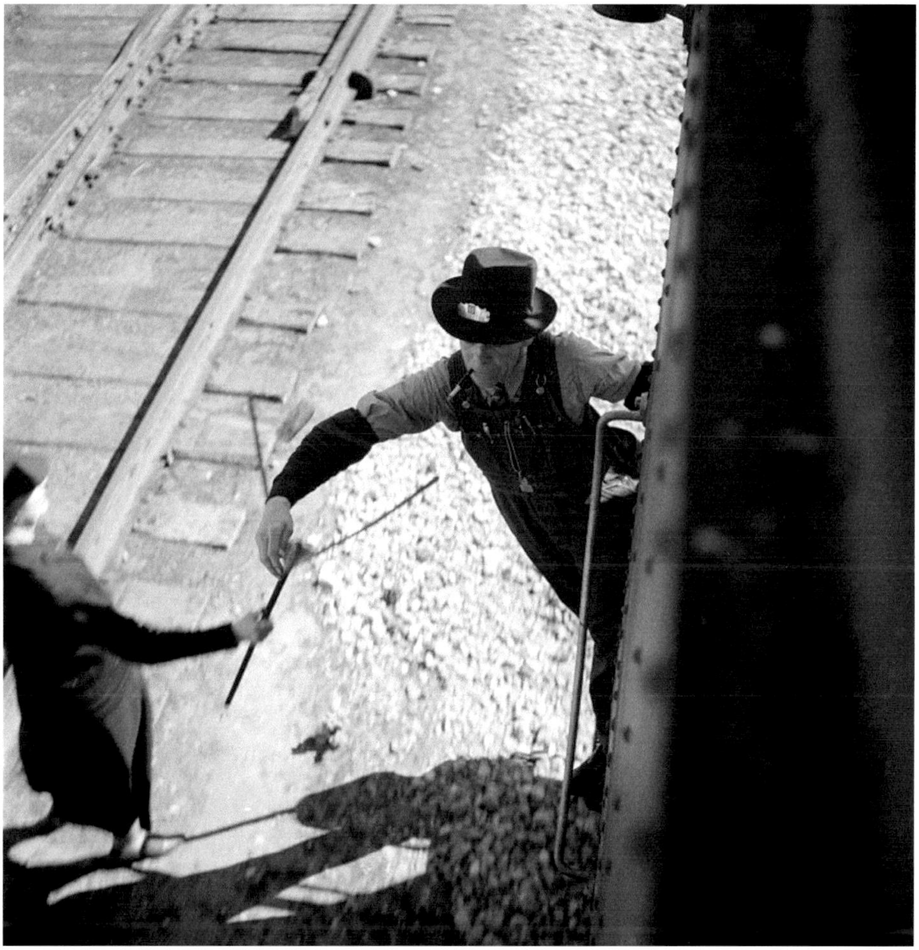

Conductor C. W. Tevis picks up a message from a woman station agent at Dalies. (*Jack Delano photograph, Library of Congress, LC-USW3-021136-E*)

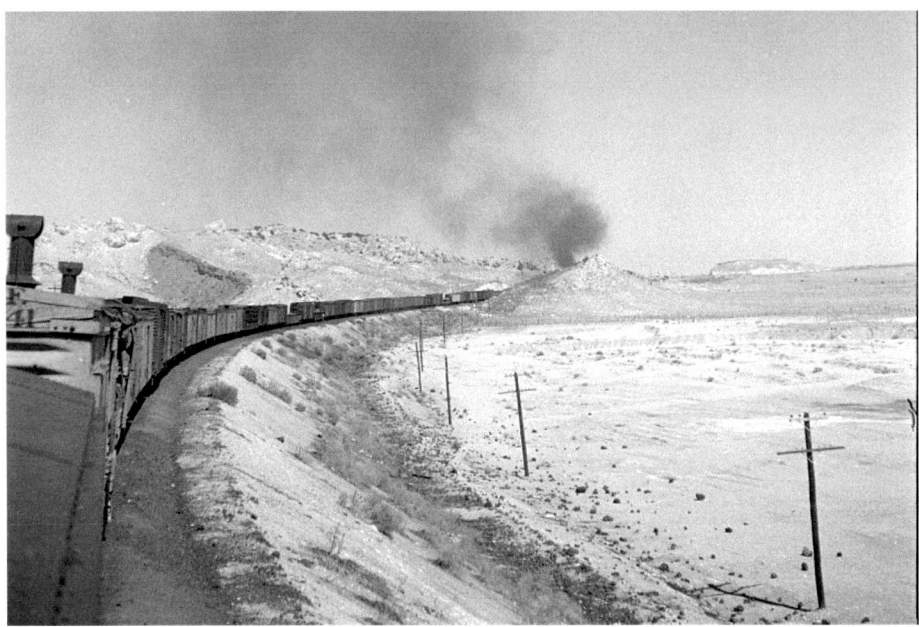

Heading west to Laguna, Jack Delano captioned this photograph as "rounding a curve at Quirk," but Quirk does not appear on a map. (*Library of Congress, LC-USW3-021140-E*)

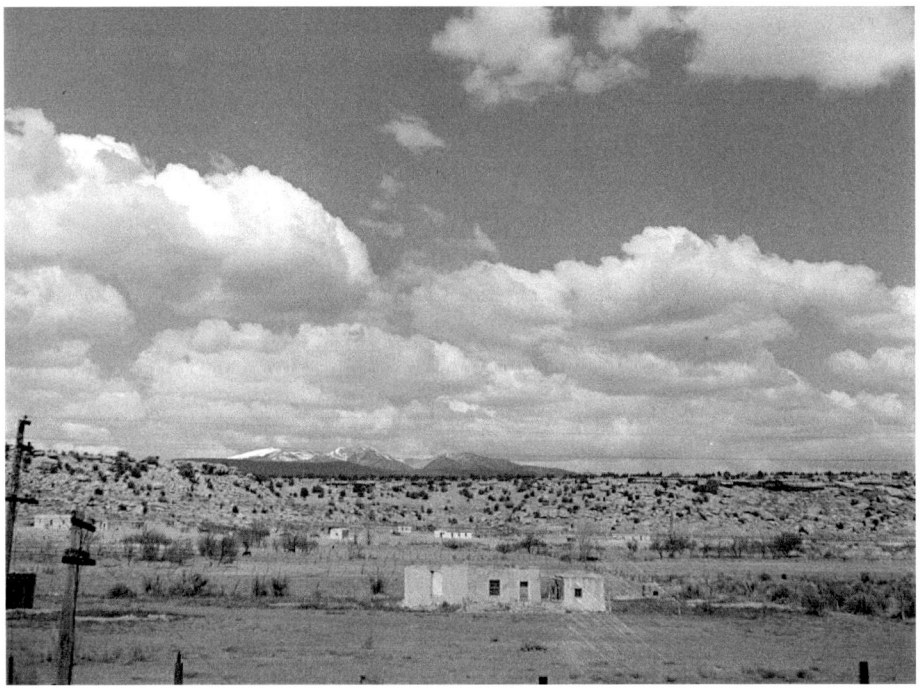

Snow-capped Mt. Taylor rises about thirty miles north of Laguna Pueblo. The Pueblo harvested timber on Mt. Taylor for log beams for their homes. (*Jack Delano photograph, Library of Congress, LC-USW3-021152-E*)

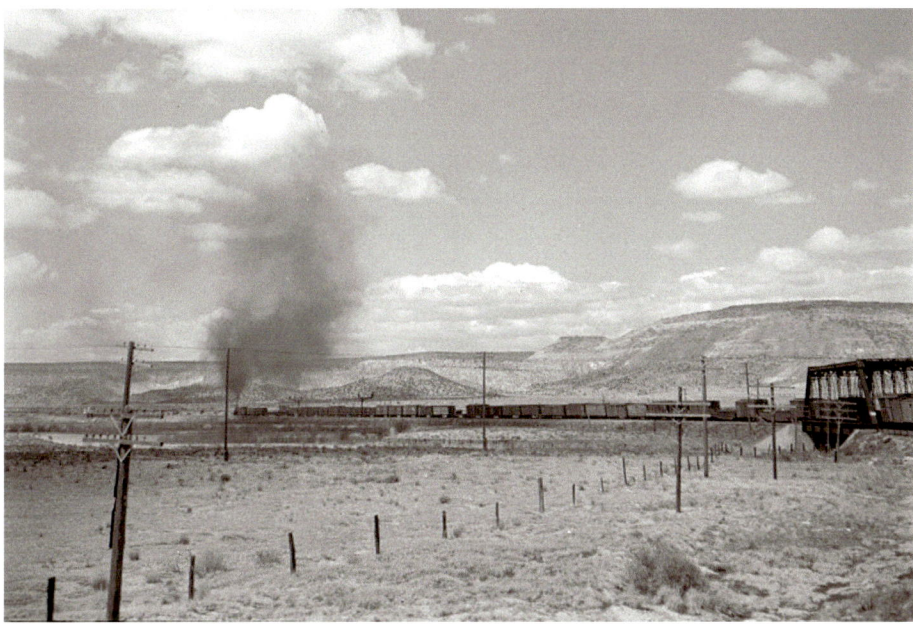

Jack Delano's train crosses the Rio San Jose bridge at Laguna on March 25, 1943. (*Library of Congress, LC-USW3-021145-E*)

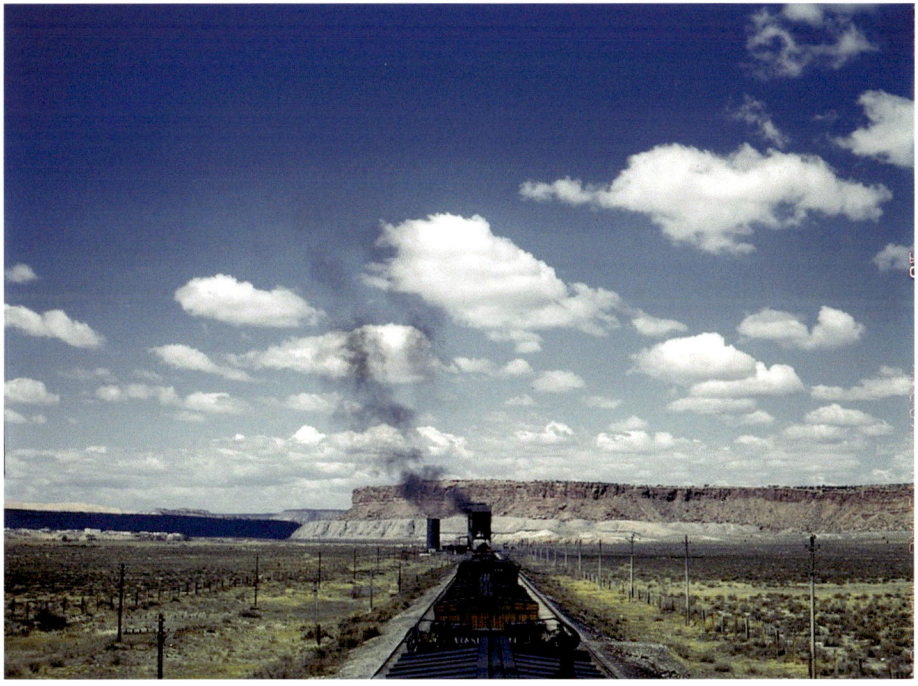

Another Jack Delano color photograph shows his train stopping at Laguna for water and coal. (*Library of Congress, LC-USW361-714*)

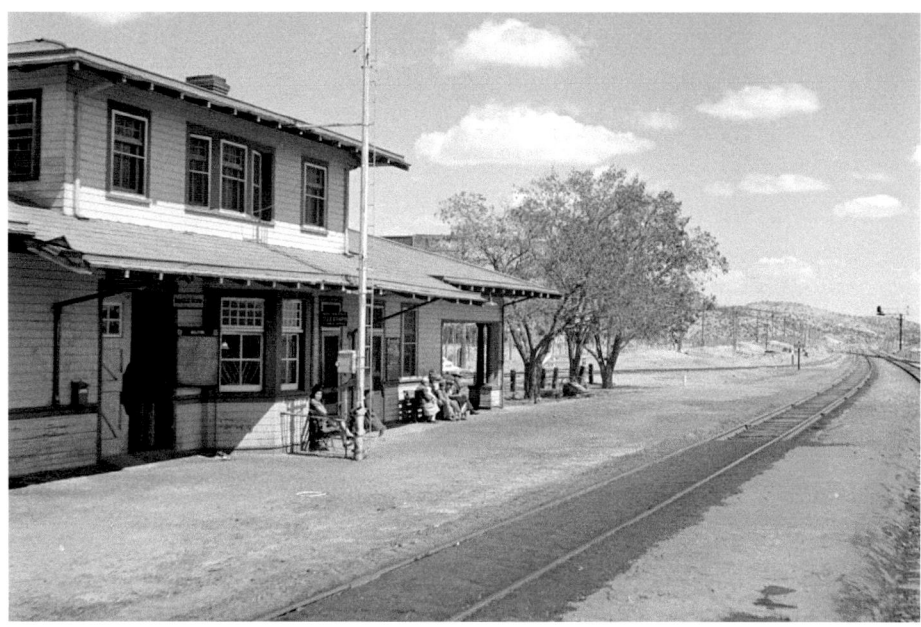

Passengers waiting at the Laguna station. (*Jack Delano photograph, Library of Congress, LC-USW3-021147-E*)

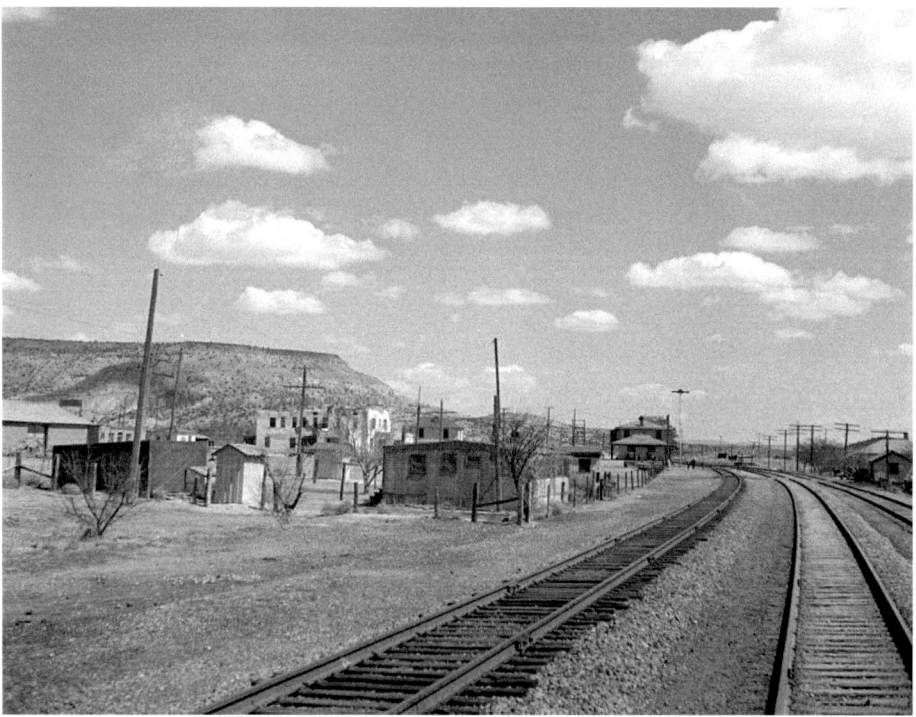

Heading west, Jack Delano took this parting shot of the tracks and buildings at Laguna. (*Library of Congress, LC-USW3-021148-E*)

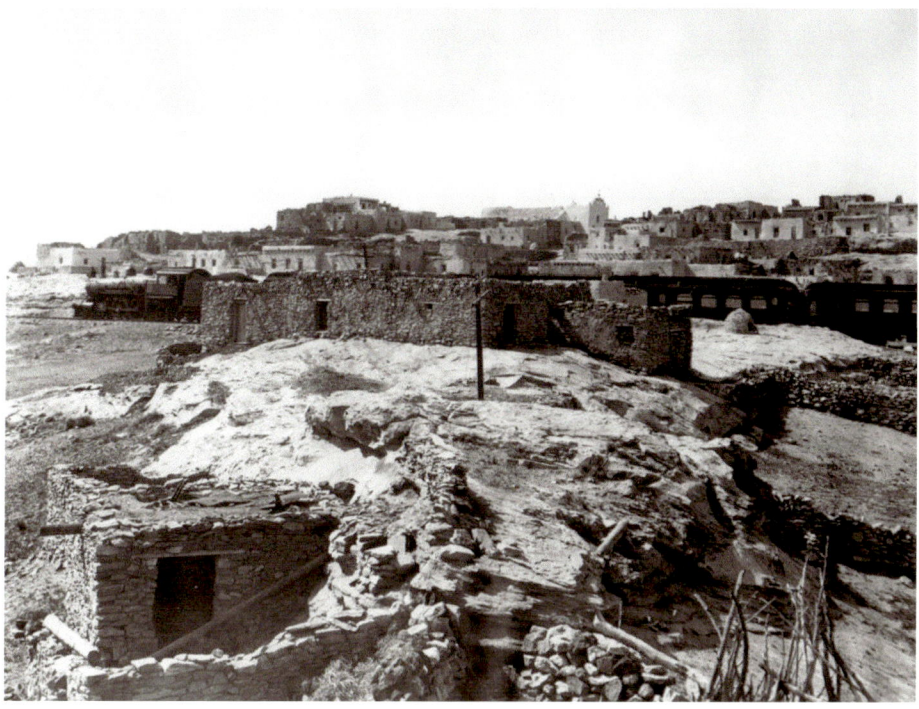

AT&SF trains roared right through the heart of Laguna Pueblo in the early 1900s until the tracks were rerouted in 1909. The San Jose de la Laguna mission church can be seen at the top right center of the photograph. (*AT&SF History Archive, Kansas Historical Society*)

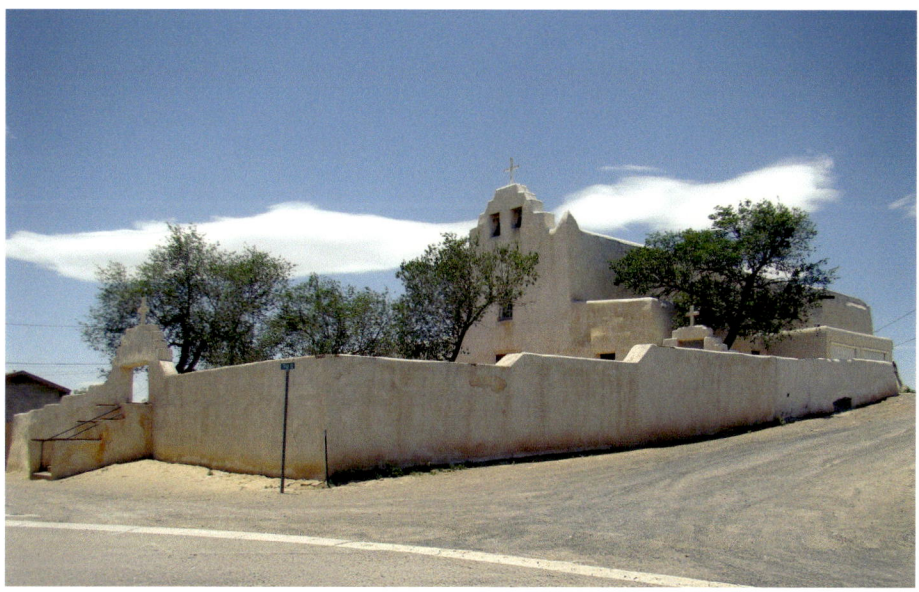

San Jose de la Laguna mission church still stands at Laguna Pueblo today.

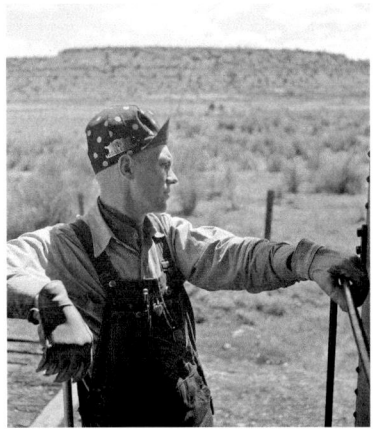 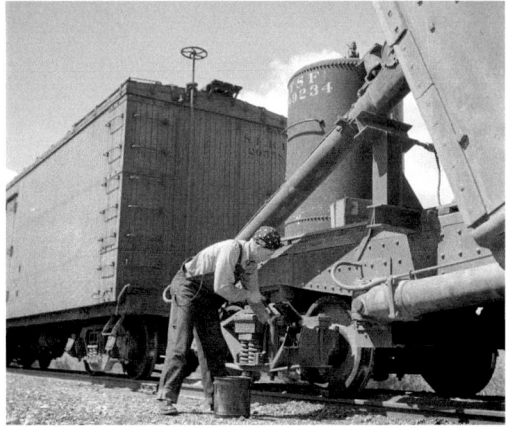

Above left: Brakeman R. E. Capsey views the scenery at Acomita from the caboose. (*Jack Delano photograph, Library of Congress, LC-USW3-021154-E*)

Above right: Brakeman R. E. Capsey repacks a journal box with grease on a special military car at Acomita. (*Jack Delano photograph, Library of Congress, LC-USW3-021157-E*)

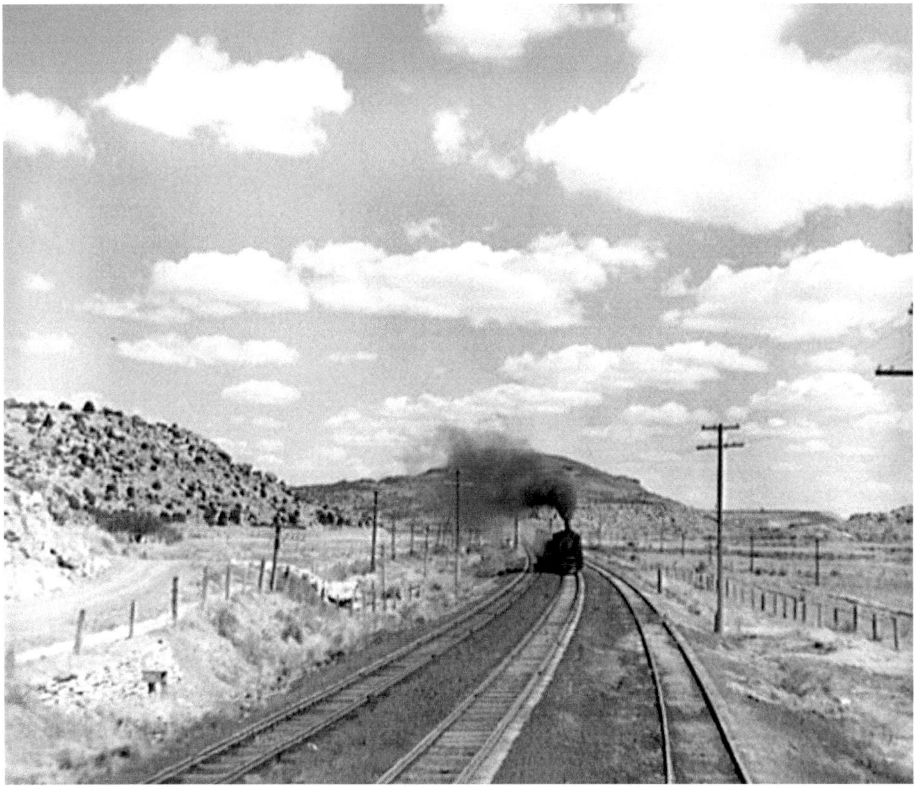

Parked on a siding at Acomita, Jack Delano photographed an oncoming freight train. (*Library of Congress, LC-USW3-022277-D*)

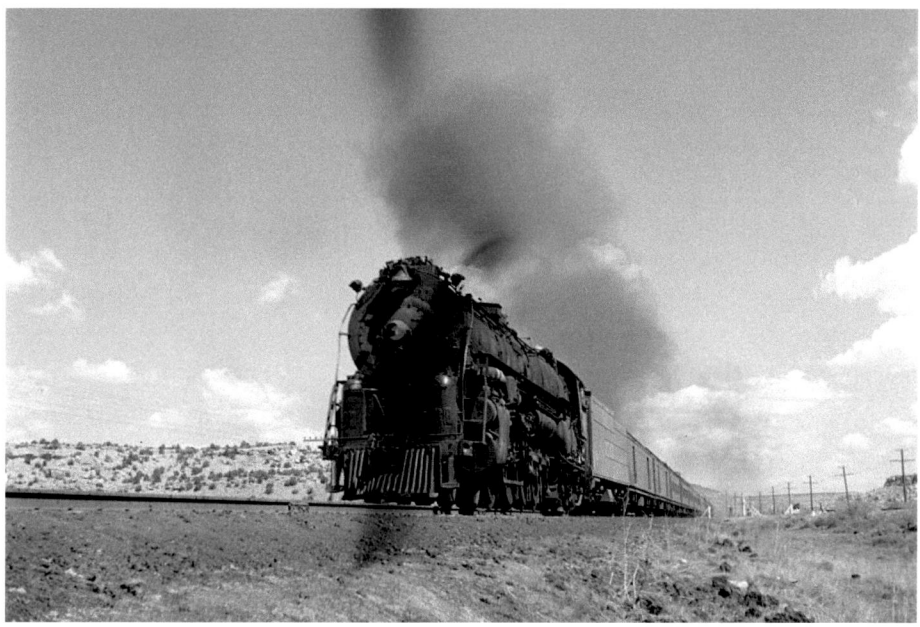

A westbound troop train steams through Acomita, passing Jack Delano's freight train on a siding. (*Library of Congress, LC-USW3-021160-E*)

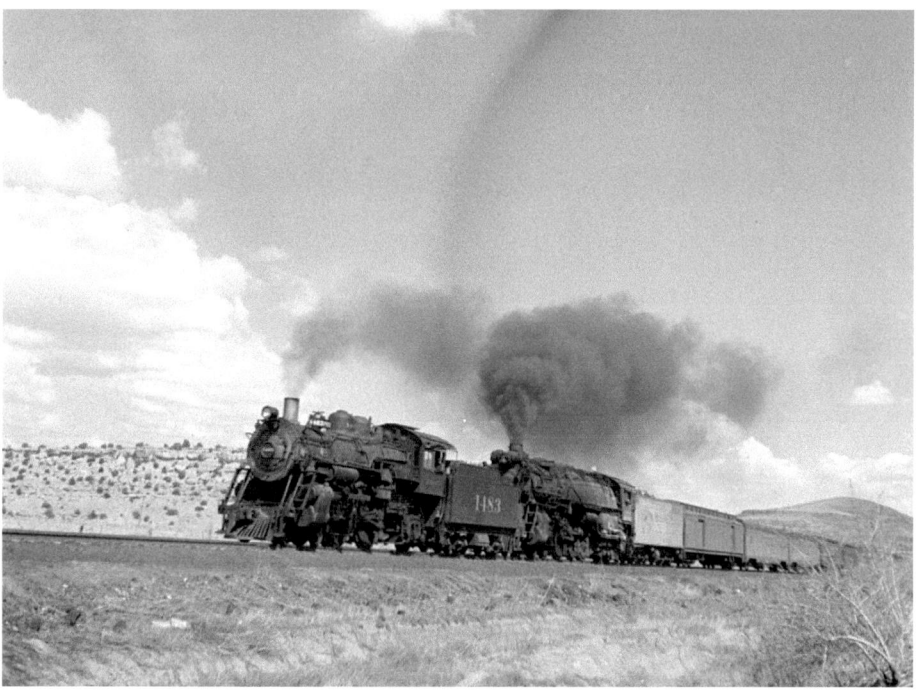

A rare double-header charging west at Acomita with a troop train. (*Jack Delano photograph, Library of Congress, LC-USW3-021161-E*)

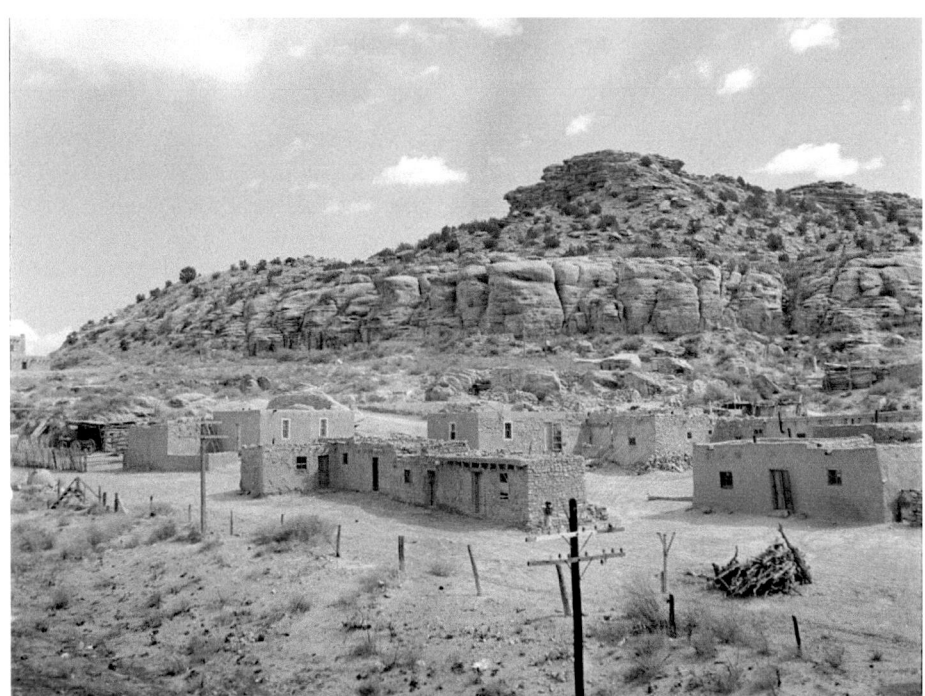

Adobe homes at the base of a rugged cliff at McCartys on the Acoma Pueblo Reservation. (*Jack Delano photograph, Library of Congress, LC-USW3-021163-E*)

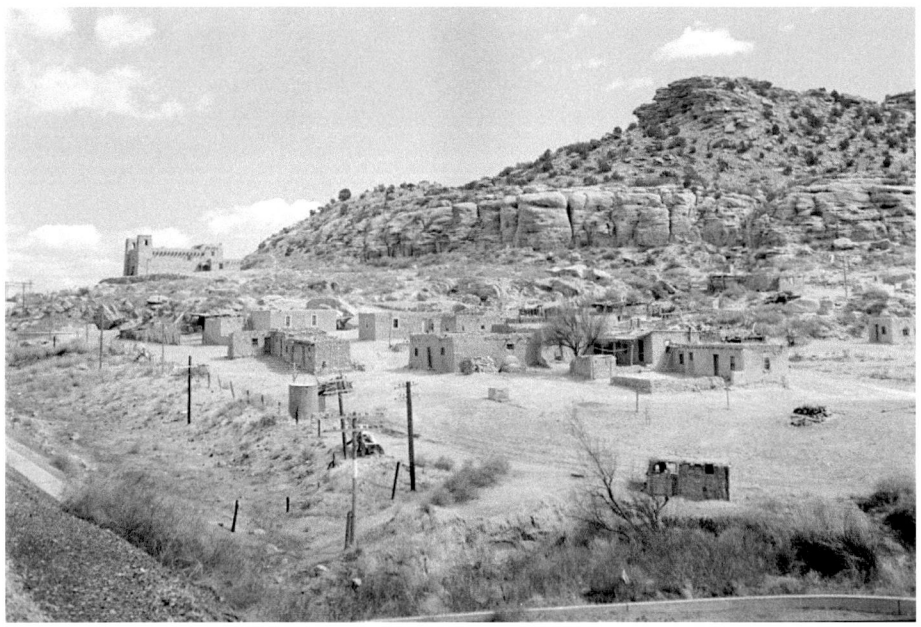

Another Jack Delano view of McCartys with adobe homes and a church in the distance. (*Library of Congress, LC-USW3-021164-E*)

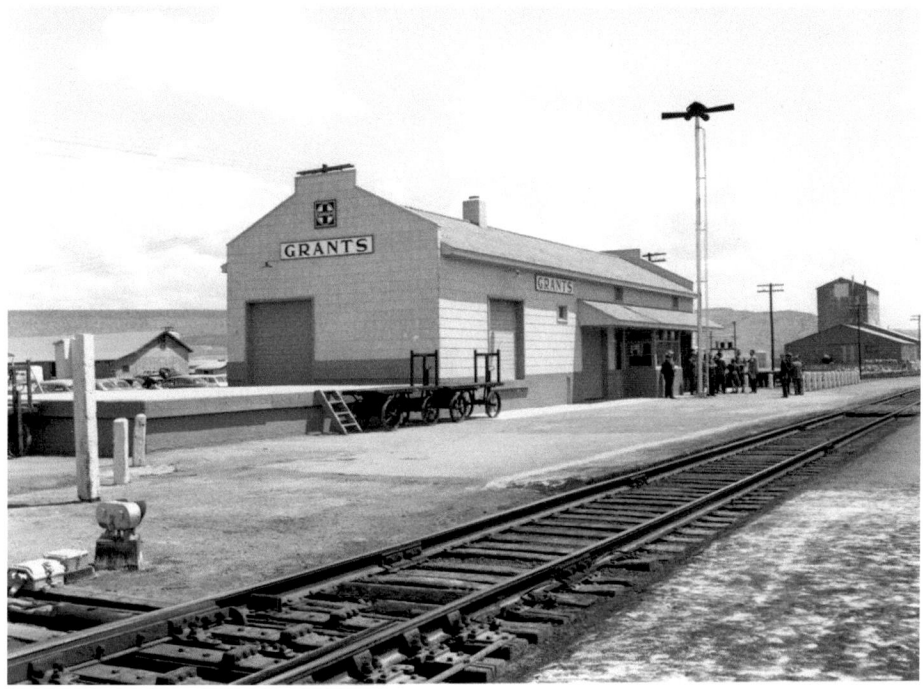

Passengers at the frame depot in Grants wait for the next train to arrive. With troop trains dominating AT&SF traffic, passenger trains were fairly rare. (*AT&SF History Archive, Kansas Historical Society*)

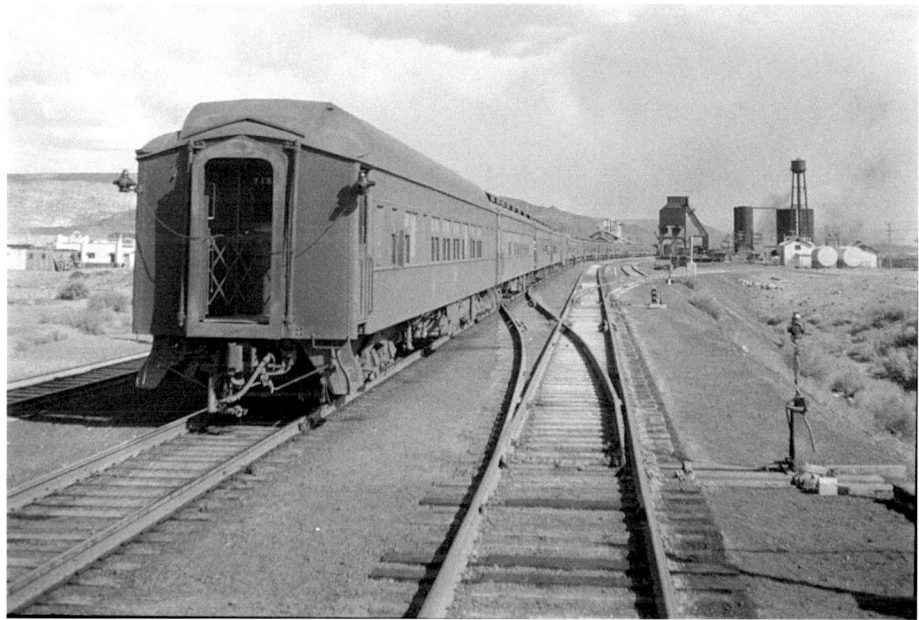

A troop train taking on coal and water at Grants. (*Jack Delano photograph, Library of Congress, LC-USW3-020175-E*)

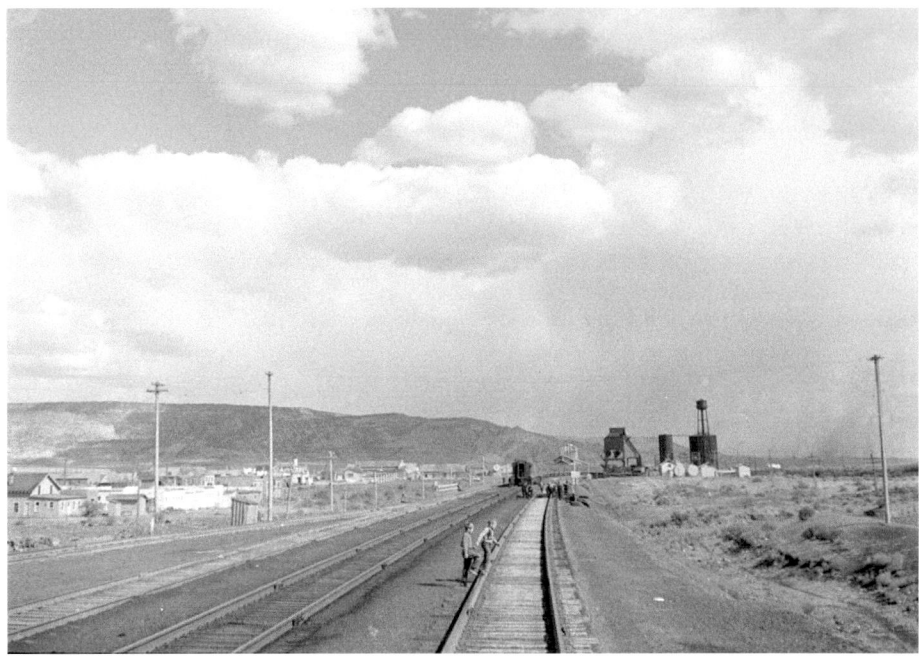

From his caboose at Grants, Jack Delano witnessed two small boys crossing the siding while a track crew and a troop train were in the distance. (*Library of Congress, LC-USW3-020174-E*)

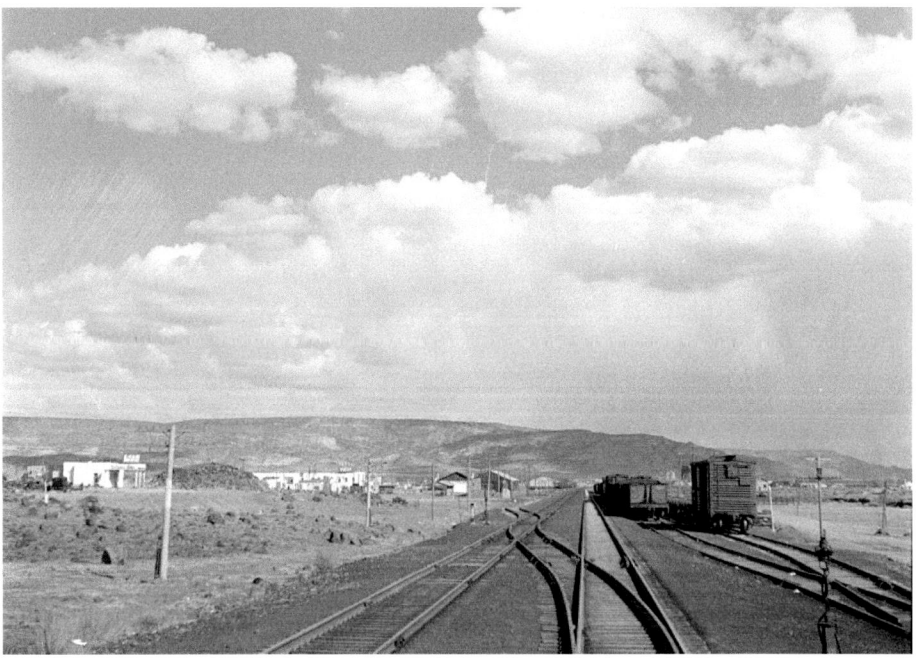

Jack Delano's view from the caboose at Grants with freight cars on the siding. (*Library of Congress, LC-USW3-021176-E*)

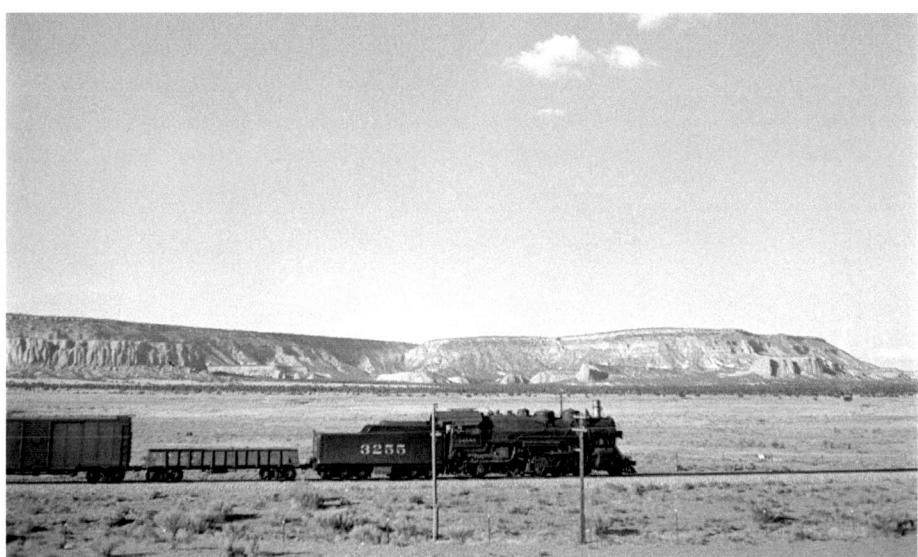

Locomotive 3255 pulled this freight train eastbound at South Chaves on March 25, 1943. (Jack Delano photograph, *Library of Congress, LC-USW3-021183-E*)

Approximately 25 miles northwest of Grants, the AT&SF had water stops at sidings at North and South Chaves. The sidings took on "the name of the Chaves family who kept a store here."[4]

Thoreau is about 4 miles west of the Chaves sidings. It began in 1881 with the arrival of the railroad. Its name has several derivations. The most likely is that it was named after the naturalist Henry David Thoreau. But some locals say it was named after an army paymaster or a railroad contractor. "Locals have altered the pronunciation ... to THROO."[5] Whichever way it is pronounced, the town today has a population of just less than 2,000.

Jack Delano's photographs continue with scenes of Gallup, 31 miles northwest of Thoreau. Undoubtedly there were water stops and sidings between the two towns, but Delano did not record them. "David L. Gallup in 1880 was auditor and paymaster for the Atlantic & Pacific Railroad [later acquired by the AT&SF], and on payday railroad workers would announce they were 'going to Gallup's' to collect their money."[6] Gallup became a major trading center for the nearby Navajo Nation. The *WPA Guide to 1930s New Mexico* noted:

> [Gallup is] the main shipping point and buying center for the Navajo wool clip, thousands of pounds being shipped annually ... and the shipping of sheep and cattle from the grazing lands of the Zuni mountains are important activities here. The town serves as a trading point for the Zuni and Navajo from the nearby reservations.[7]

As far as railway facilities are concerned, Gallup was chosen as a division point in 1895:

> ... and once had a full complement of shops and repair facilities. The depot and El Navajo Harvey House ... were designed in 1916 by the Harvey Company's Mary Colter.... Both were built concurrently but were not completed until 1923 because of World War I.... The two-story depot was made of concrete, and, at over 16,000 square feet, provided space not only for passenger waiting

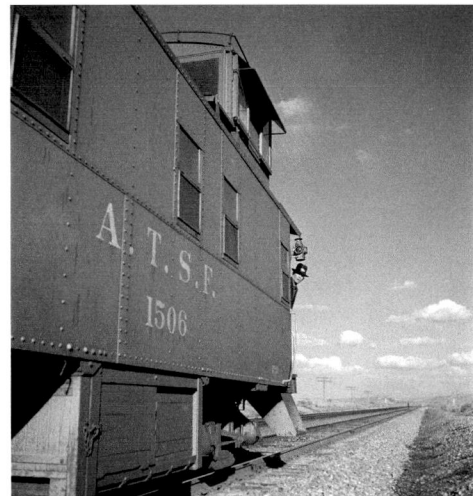
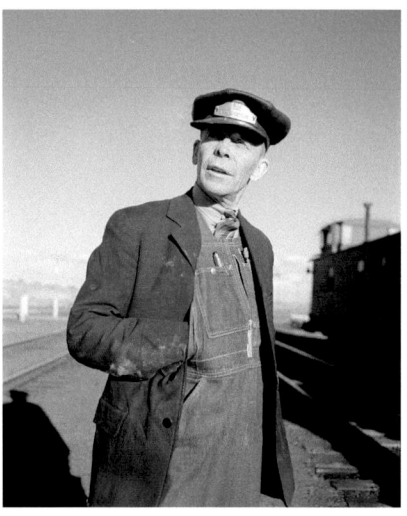

Above left: Conductor C. W. Tevis views the scene from the caboose at Thoreau, watching for any problems with the train. (*Jack Delano photograph, Library of Congress, LC-USW3-021184-E*)

Above right: Jack Delano photographed a contemplative conductor C. W. Tevis at Thoreau on March 25, 1943. (*Library of Congress, LC-USW3-021190-E*)

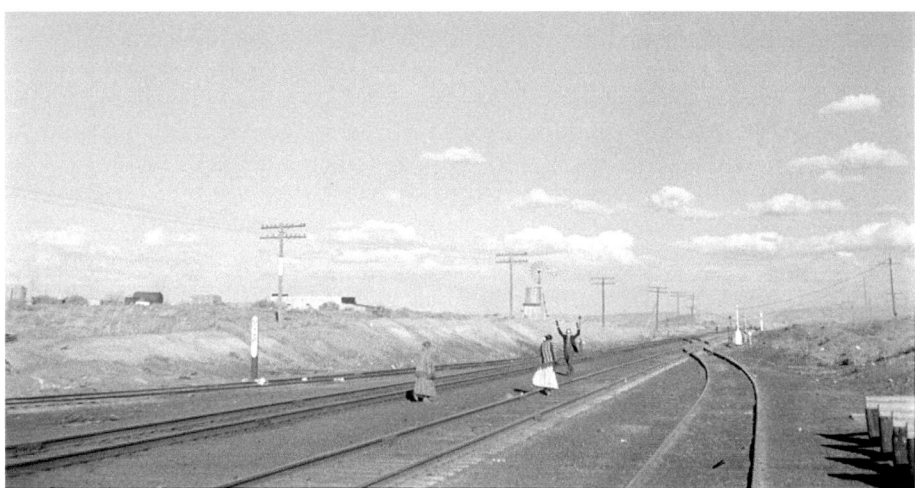

Conductor C. W. Tevis signaling the engineer at Thoreau as Native American women cross the tracks. (*Jack Delano photograph, Library of Congress, Lc-USW3-021185-E*)

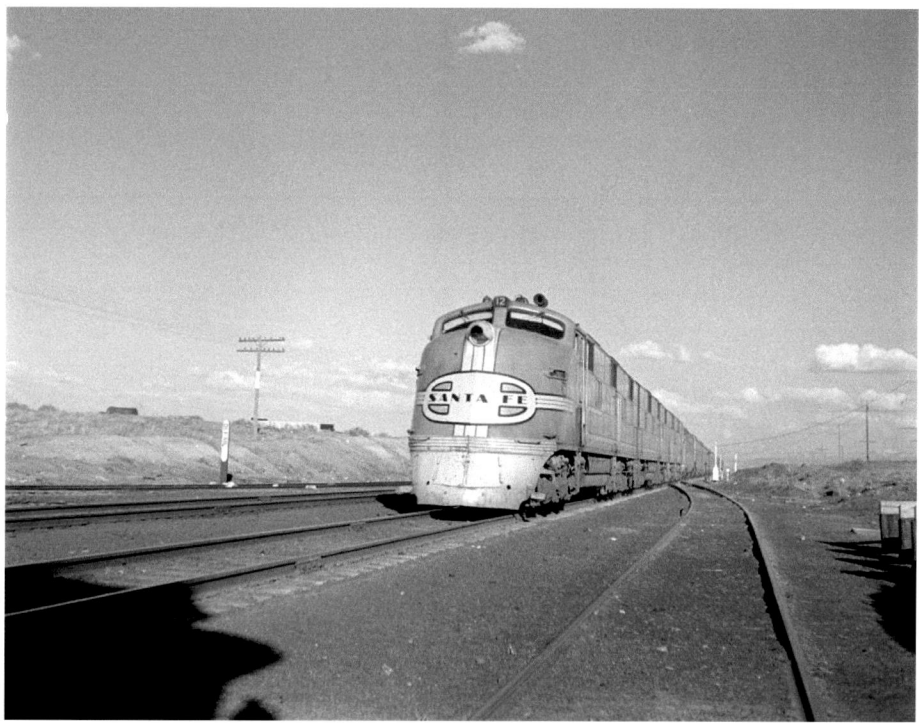

Jack Delano's caboose at Thoreau casts a shadow on the tracks in front of the approaching *Super Chief* passenger train heading west. (*Library of Congress, LC-USW3-021187-E*)

and ticket purchases but also for railroad operations, a telegraph office, and a Railway Express Agency. The station name and Santa Fe logo were formed into the stucco.[8]

El Navajo Hotel was a Mary Colter design masterpiece built in Pueblo Revival style with thick walls and inset windows. The interior was decorated with Navajo sand paintings. Fred Harvey's El Navajo Hotel served meals to the troop trains passing by, just as did the Alvarado Hotel in Albuquerque. After the war, tourist traffic to the hotel declined and it was demolished in 1957. The depot still stands and serves as an Amtrak station today. Gallup has approximately 22,000 residents today.

Jack Delano photographed Navajo homes in the village of Manuelito, 16 miles southwest of Gallup. Manuelito is 2.5 miles east of the Arizona border. "Manuelito was a famous 19th century Navajo leader.... His abiding interest was the return of traditional tribal lands to his people."[9]

As Jack Delano crossed the Arizona border on an AT&SF train on March 25, 1943, he could reflect on his journey all the way across New Mexico from Clovis to Gallup. Delano had captured on film World War II railroad operations across the state illustrating railyards, machine shops, freight trains, troop trains, passenger trains, water stops, sidings, and the diverse population that contributed to New Mexico's heroic efforts to keep the trains rolling. Jack Delano's son Pablo commented on the lesson we can learn from his father's photographs: "what it means to work for the common good, to take pride in a job well done, to respect one another."[10] That is what it took for America and her allies to win the war.

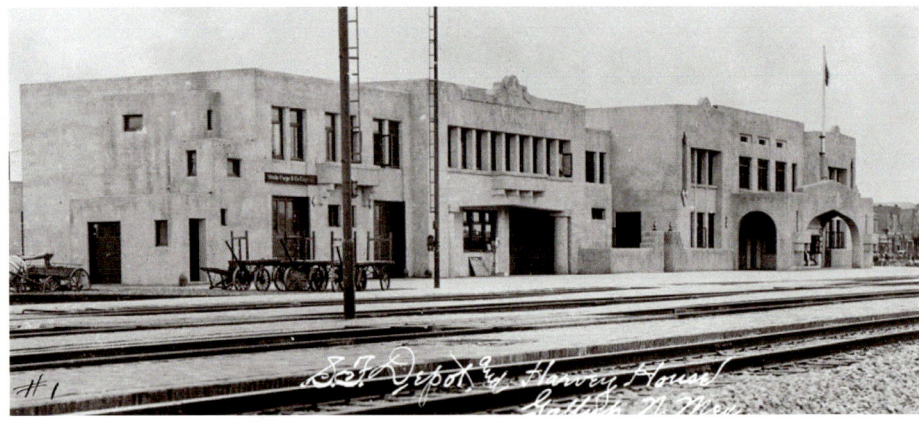

The Santa Fe depot and Harvey House in Gallup in 1918, were designed by Fred Harvey architect Mary Colter in 1916 in a Pueblo Revival style. (*Library of Congress, LC-DIG-pcrd-1d0428*)

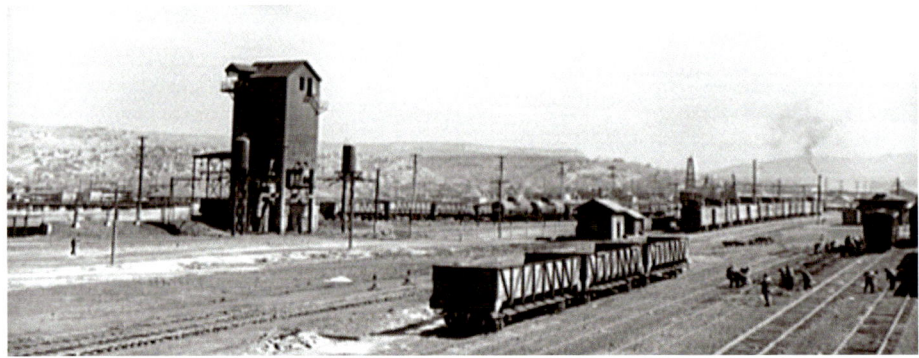

The coal tower and freight yard in Gallup on March 25, 1943. (*Jack Delano photograph, Library of Congress, LC-USW3-022177-D*)

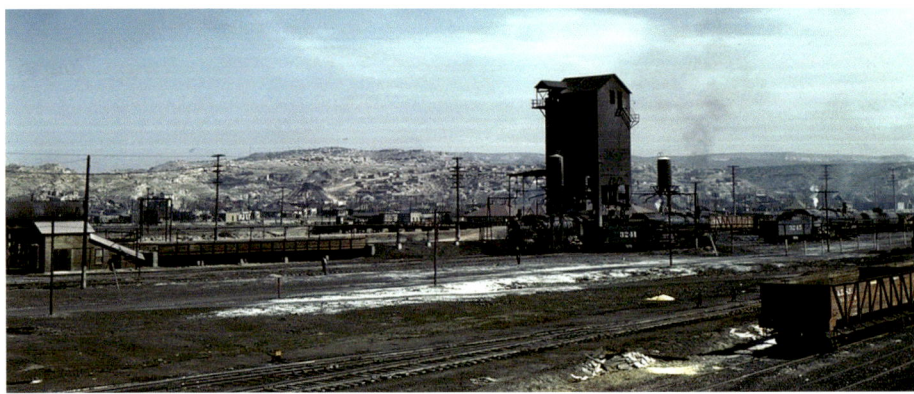

Jack Delano's color photograph of the coal tower and freight yard in Gallup shows snow on the ground and several locomotives near the coal tower. (*Library of Congress, LC-USW361-681*)

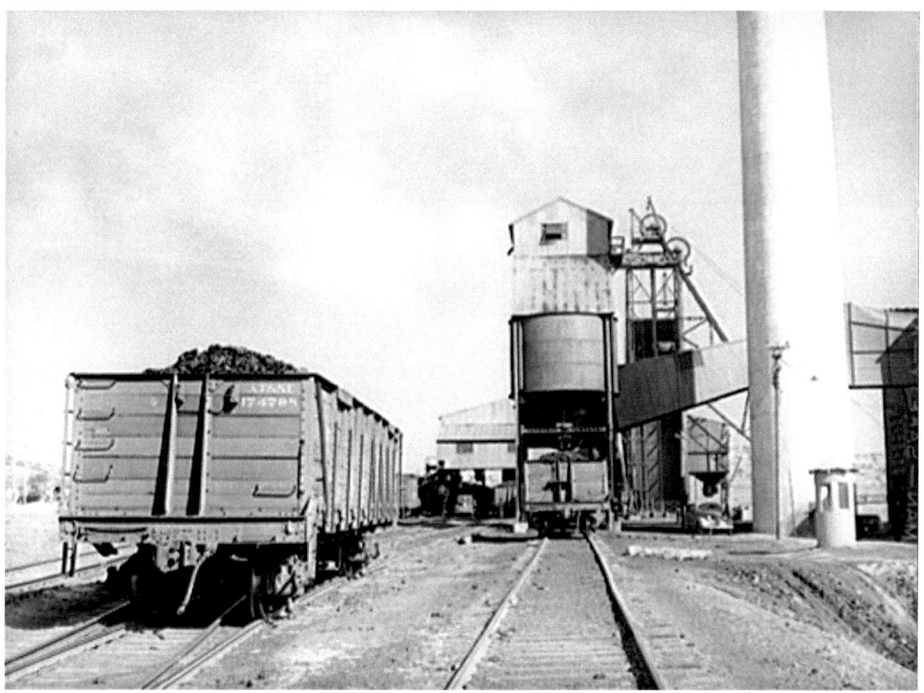

Coal cars being loaded at the American Mining Company at Gallup. (*Jack Delano photograph, Library of Congress, LC-USW3-0221183-D*)

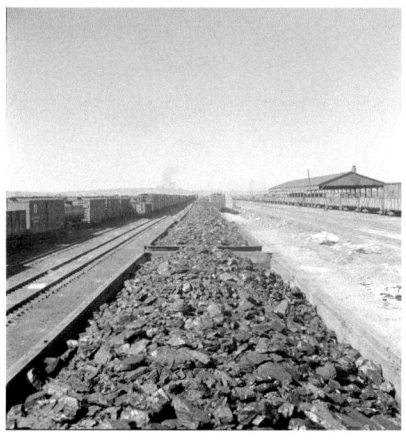
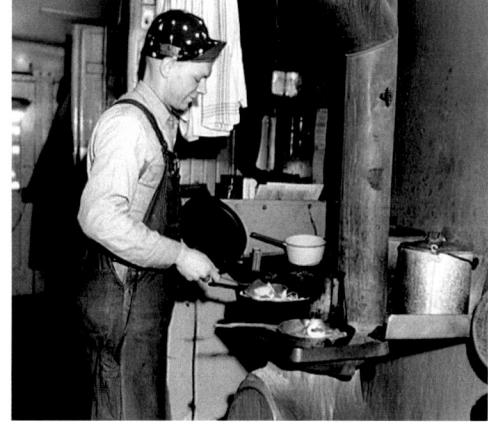

Above left: Loaded coal cars in the Gallup railyard await shipment to coal towers along the AT&SF line across New Mexico. (*Jack Delano photograph, Library of Congress, LC-USW3-021198-E*)

Above right: Jack Delano was probably waiting to share this meal with brakeman R. E. Capsey in the caboose at Gallup on March 25, 1943. (*Library of Congress, LC-USW3-022223-D*)

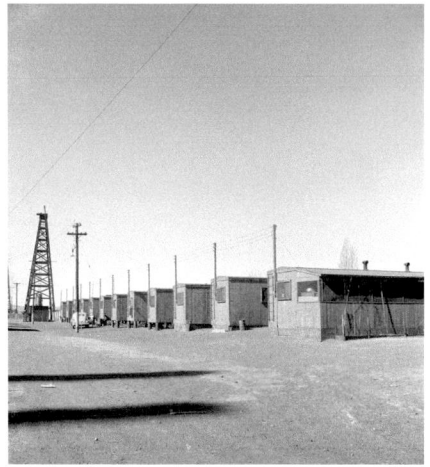 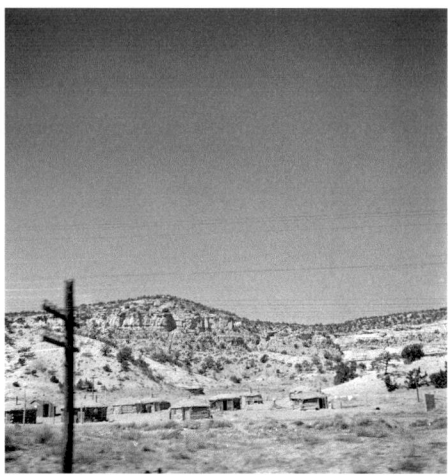

Above left: AT&SF provided these converted boxcars for worker housing at Gallup. (*Jack Delano photograph, Library of Congress, LC-USW3-021197-E*)

Above right: Jack Delano snapped this photograph of Navajo hogans at Manuelito as his train passed by. (*Library of Congress, LC-USW3-021207-E*)

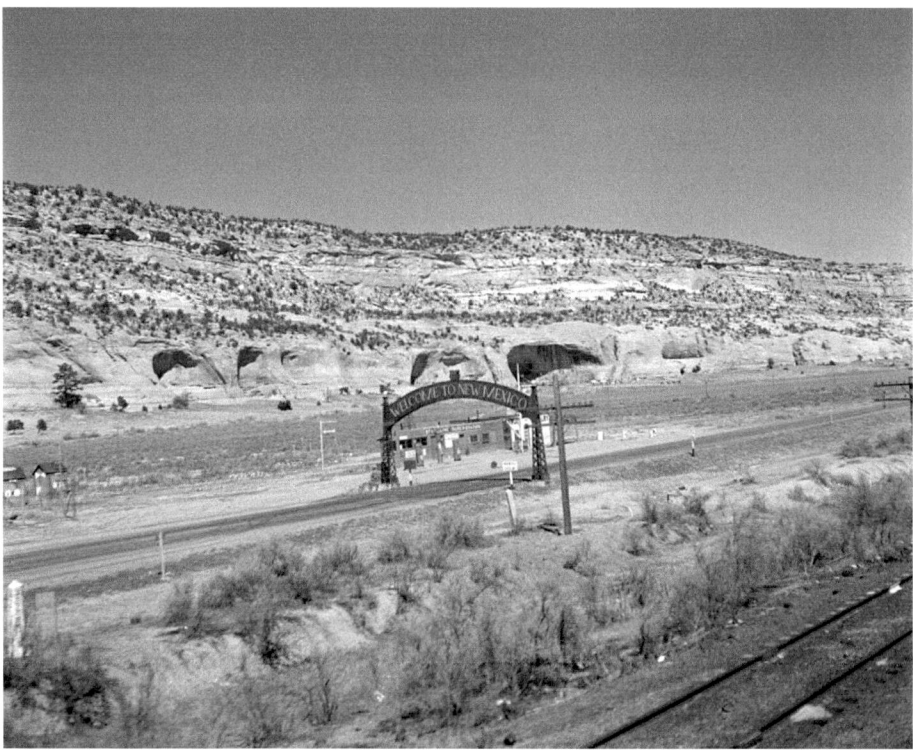

Jack Delano bade farewell to New Mexico as his train crossed the Arizona border on March 26, 1943. (*Library of Congress, LC-USW3-021208-E*)

ENDNOTES

Chapter 1

1. Rabinowitz, J., *Far from Main Street: Three Photographers in Depression Era New Mexico* (Santa Fe, NM: Museum of New Mexico Press, 1994), p. 23.
2. Hurley, F.J., *Portrait of a Decade: Roy Stryker and the Development of Documentary Photography in the Thirties* (Baton Rouge, LA: Louisiana State University Press,1972), p. 185.
3. Reevy, T., *The Railroad Photography of Jack Delano* (Bloomington, IN: Indiana University Press, 2015), p. 4.
4. *Ibid*., p. 7.
5. *Ibid*.
6. *Ibid*., p. 8.
7. Flynn, K., *The New Deal: A 75th Anniversary Celebration* (Layton, UT: Gibbs Smith, 2008), p. 86.
8. Rabinowitz, *op. cit*., p. 27.
9. Reevy, *op. cit*., p. 14.

Chapter 2

1. DeNevi, D., *America's Fighting Railroads: A World War II Pictorial History* (Missoula, MT: Pictorial Histories Publishing Company, 1997), p. v.
2. Ball, D. Jr., and Whitaker, R., *Decade of the Trains: The 1940s* (Boston, MA: New York Graphic Society, 1977), p. 16.
3. Valle, J., *The Iron Horse At War* (Berkeley, CA: Howell-North Books, 1978), p. 5.
4. Ball, *op. cit*., p. 111.
5. *Ibid*., p. 103.
6. Heimburger, D., and Kelly, J., *Trains to Victory: America's Railroads in World War II* (Forest Park, IL: Heimburger House Publishing Company, 2009), p. 9.
7. Riskin, M., *The Train Stops Here: New Mexico's Railway Legacy* (Albuquerque, NM: University of New Mexico Press, 2005), p. 30.
8. DeNevi, *op. cit*., p. 1.
9. *Ibid*.
10. Ball, *op. cit*., p. 11.
11. Heimburger, *op. cit*., p. 46.
12. Ball, *op. cit*., p. 183.
13. Heimburger, *op. cit*., p. 15.

Chapter 3

1. Valle, *The Iron Horse At War*, p. 6.
2. Myrick, D., *New Mexico's Railroads* (Albuquerque, NM: University of New Mexico Press, 1990), p. 18.
3. *Ibid.*
4. Bryant, K., *History of the Atchison, Topeka & Santa Fe Railway* (Lincoln, NE: University of Nebraska Press, 1982), pp. 192–193.
5. *Ibid.*, p. 193.
6. Riskin, *The Train Stops Here*, p. 71.
7. Penner, W., et al., *Ho! To the Land of Sunshine: A History of the Belen* Cutoff (Albuquerque, NM: P3Planning, 2013), p. 12.
8. Naylor, B., *Forty Years on the Santa Fe Railroad: 1921–1961* (Midwest City, OK: Santa Fe Railway Historical and Modeling Society, 2022), p. 55.
9. *Ibid.*, p. 54.
10. *Ibid.*, p. 55.
11. *Ibid.*, p. 54.
12. *Ibid.*, pp. 56–57.
13. *Ibid.*, p. 70.
14. *Ibid.*, p. 78.
15. *Ibid.*, pp. 93, 97.

Chapter 4

1. Naylor, *Forty Years on the Santa Fe Railroad*, pp. 67, 70.
2. Armyhistory.org.
3. *Ibid.*
4. Ball, *Decade of the Trains*, p. 127.
5. Quoted in Valle, *The Iron Horse At War*, p. 255.
6. Heimburger, *Trains to Victory*, p. 12.
7. Reevy, *The Railroad Photography of Jack Delano*, p. 162.
8. *Ibid.*, p. 113.
9. Valle, p. 6.
10. Bryant, *History of the Atchison, Topeka & Santa Fe Railway*, p. 273.
11. Naylor, *Forty Years on the Santa Fe Railroad*, pp. 76, 78.
12. Rabinowitz, *Far From Main Street*, p. 27.
13. Reevy, *op. cit.*, p.114.

Chapter 5

1. Valle, *The Iron Horse At War*, p. 169.
2. Riskin, *The Train Stops Here*, pp. 90–91.
3. *Ibid.*, p. 19.
4. *Ibid.*, p. 90.
5. Armyhistory.org.
6. Dunson, R., *Santa Fe's Belen Cut-off: The Eastern Railway Company of New Mexico* (Coppell, TX: High Plains Historical Foundation, 2024), p. 197.
7. Armyhistory.org.
8. Riskin, p. 93.
9. Quoted in Valle, pp. 254–255.

10 Ball, *Decade of the Trains*, p. 96.
11 Naylor, *Forty Years on the Santa Fe Railroad*, pp. 97–98.
12 Riskin, p. 94.
13 Valle, p. 178.

Chapter 6

1 Julyan, R., The Place Names of New Mexico (Albuquerque, NM: University of New Mexico Press, 1998), p. 290.
2 *Ibid.*, p. 50.
3 Riskin, *The Train Stops Here*, p. 96.

Chapter 7

1 Julyan, *The Place Names of New Mexico*, p. 124.
2 Boyle, D., *Highway 60 & the Belen Cutoff* (Denver, CO: Outskirts Press, 2010), p. 23.
3 Julyan, p. 380.
4 Simmons, Marc, *The WPA Guide to 1930s New Mexico* (Tucson, AZ: University of Arizona Press, 1989), p. 357.
5 Julyan, p. 236.
6 Riskin, *The Train Stops Here*, p. 96.
7 Boyle, *op. cit.*, pp. 11–12.
8 Riskin, p. 89.
9 Julyan, p. 2.
10 Naylor, *Forty Years on the Santa Fe Railroad*, p. 65.
11 Harden, P., *Abo Pass*, in Socorro-history.org./HISTORY/PH_History/2011_abo_pass,pdf.
12 Penner, *Ho! To the Land of Sunshine*, pp. 80, 84.
13 *Ibid.*, p. 91.
14 Julyan, p. 33.
15 Riskin, p. 71.
16 *Ibid.*, p. 72.

Chapter 8

1 Rabinowitz, *Far From Main Street*, p. 26.
2 Butler, M., *Tracking Fred Harvey's Southwest Indian Detours* (Charleston, SC: Fonthill Media, 2024), p. 81.
3 Rabinowitz, *op. cit.*, p.26.
4 Flint, R. and Flint, S., *Overhaul: A Social History of the Albuquerque Locomotive Repair Shops* (Albuquerque, NM; University of New Mexico Press, 2021), p. 127.
5 Cherry E., and See, J., *Atchison, Topeka & Santa Fe Railway Locomotive Shops* (nmarchitectureguide.org/2023/11/11), unpaginated.
6 *Ibid.*
7 *Ibid.*
8 *Ibid.*
9 Flint, *op. cit.*, p. 181.
10 Cherry, *op. cit.*
11 *Ibid.*
12 *Ibid.*
13 Flint, *op. cit.*, p. 156.

14 Riskin, *The Train Stops Here*, p. 26.
15 Walz, R., *Santa Fe's New Mexico Division: Varnish, Coal, Copper and Cattle* (Midwest City, OK: Santa Fe Railway Historical & Modeling Society, 2020), p. 123.
16 *Ibid.*, p. 117.
17 Slaney, D., *Jewel of the Railroad Era: Albuquerque's Alvarado Hotel* (Albuquerque, NM: Albuquerque Museum, 2009), pp. 90–92.
18 Poling-Kempes, L., *The Harvey Girls: Women Who Opened the West* (New York: Paragon House, 1989), p. 199.
19 *Ibid.*, p. 200.
20 *Ibid.*, p. 203
21 *Ibid.*
22 Walz, *op. cit.*, p. 117.
23 *Ibid.*

Chapter 9
1 Butler, *Tracking Fred Harvey's Southwest Indian Detours*, p. 77.
2 Julyan, *The Place Names of New Mexico*, p. 223.
3 Riskin, *The Train Stops Here*, p. 109.
4 Julyan, *op. cit.*, p. 78.
5 *Ibid.*, p. 352.
6 *Ibid.*, p. 144.
7 Simmons, *The WPA Guide to 1930s New Mexico*, p. 324.
8 Riskin, *op. cit.*, p. 108.
9 Julyan, *op. cit.*, p. 219.
10 Reevy, *The Railroad Photography of Jack Delano*, p. x.

BIBLIOGRAPHY

Armyhistory.org

Ball, D. Jr., and Whitaker, R., *Decade of the Trains: The 1940s* (Boston, MA: New York Graphic Society, 1977)

Boyle, D., *Highway 60 & the Belen Cutoff* (Denver, CO: Outskirts Press, 2010)

Bryant, K., *History of the Atchison, Topeka & Santa Fe Railway* (Lincoln, NE: University of Nebraska Press, 1982)

Butler, M., *Tracking Fred Harvey's Southwest Indian Detours* (Charleston, SC: Fonthill Media, 2024)

Cherry, E., and See, J., *Atchison, Topeka & Santa Fe Railway Locomotive Shops* (nmarchitectureguide.org/2023/11/11)

DeNevi, D., *America's Fighting Railroads: A World War II Pictorial History* (Missoula, MT: Pictorial Histories Publishing Company, 1997)

Dunson, R., *Santa Fe's Belen Cut-off: The Eastern Railway Company of New Mexico* (Coppell, TX: High Plains Historical Foundation, 2024).

Flint, R., and Flint, S., *Overhaul: A Social History of the Albuquerque Locomotive Repair Shops* (Albuquerque, NM: University of New Mexico Press, 2021)

Flynn, K., *The New Deal: A 75th Anniversary Celebration* (Layton, UT: Gibbs Smith, 2008)

Harden, P., *Abo Pass* (Socorro-history.org,/HISTORY/PH_History/2011_abo_pass.pdf)

Heimburger, D., and Kelly, J., *Trains to Victory: America's Railroads in World War II* (Forest Park, IL: Heimburger House Publishing Company, 2009)

Hurley, F.J., *Portrait of a Decade: Roy Stryker and the Development of Documentary Photography in the Thirties* (Baton Rouge, LA: Louisiana State University Press, 1972)

Julyan, R., *The Place Names of New Mexico* (Albuquerque, NM: University of New Mexico Press, 1998)

Melzer, R., and Taylor, J., *Images of America: New Mexico in World War II* (Charleston, SC: Arcadia Publishing, 2021)

Myrick, D., *New Mexico's Railroads* (Albuquerque, NM: University of New Mexico Press, 1990)

Naylor, B., *Forty Years on the Santa Fe Railroad: 1921–1961* (Midwest City, OK: Santa Fe Railway Historical and Modeling Society, 2022)

Penner, W., et.al., *Ho! To the Land of Sunshine: A History of the Belen Cutoff* (Albuquerque, NM: P3Planning, 2013)

Poling-Kempes, L., *The Harvey Girls: Women Who Opened the West* (New York: Paragon House, 1989)

Rabinowitz, J., *Far from Main Street: Three Photographers in Depression Era New Mexico* (Santa Fe, NM: Museum of New Mexico Press, 1994)

Reevy, T., *The Railroad Photography of Jack Delano* (Bloomington, IN: Indiana University Press, 2015)

Riskin, M., *The Train Stops Here: New Mexico's Railway Legacy* (Albuquerque, NM: University of New Mexico Press, 2005)

Simmons, M., *The WPA Guide to 1930s New Mexico* (Tucson, AZ: University of Arizona Press, 1989)

Slaney, D., *Jewel of the Railroad Era: Albuquerque's Alvarado Hotel* (Albuquerque, NM: Albuquerque Museum, 2009)

Valle, J., *The Iron Horse At War* (Berkeley, CA: Howell-North Books, 1978)

Walz, R., *Santa Fe's New Mexico Division: Varnish, Coal, Copper and Cattle* (Midwest City, OK: Santa Fe Railway Historical & Modeling Society, 2020)